Information Literacy Assessment in K–12 Settings

Lesley S. J. Farmer
James Henri

THE SCARECROW PRESS, INC.
Lanham, Maryland • Toronto • Plymouth, UK
2008

SCARECROW PRESS, INC.

Published in the United States of America
by Scarecrow Press, Inc.
A wholly owned subsidary of
The Rowman & Littlefield Publishing Group, Inc.
4501 Forbes Boulevard, Suite 200, Lanham, Maryland 20706
www.scarecrowpress.com

Estover Road
Plymouth PL6 7PY
United Kingdom

British Library Cataloguing in Publication Information Available

Library of Congress Cataloging-in-Publication Data

Farmer, Lesley S. J.
  Information literacy assessment in K–12 settings / Lesley S. J. Farmer, James Henri.
      p. cm.
  Includes bibliographical references and index.
  ISBN-13: 978-0-8108-5695-0 (pbk. : alk. paper)
  ISBN-10: 0-8108-5695-6 (pbk. : alk. paper)
  1. Information literacy—Ability testing. 2. Information literacy—Study and
teaching—Evaluation. 3. Library orientation for school children—Evaluation.
4. Library orientation for high school students—Evaluation. 5. School librarian
participation in curriculum planning. I. Henri, James, 1952– II. Title.

ZA3075.F36 2008
028.7—dc22

                                                                        2007028530

Dedicated to our loved ones who supported us at home and abroad.

Contents

Preface: The Back Story

Just as information literacy assessment can be a complex process, so too does the development of this book reflect a complex set of thoughts and actions.

The International Association for School Librarianship (IASL) was the beginning impetus. Knowing of my work in the association and in the school librarianship field, James Henri, who at the time was a vice president in that association, appointed me as IASL Information Literacy SIG chair. Building on that effort, he then invited me to teach at the University of Hong Kong for the 2005 summer session. Simultaneously, he suggested that we coauthor a book on information literacy assessment, a timely topic that intrigued both of us. During that summer, James and I had several insightful discussions about information literacy, each of us drawing upon our respective experiences and knowledge. I brought an American perspective while he drew from Asian and Australian perspectives; both of us also had professional connections in Europe and Africa. In addition, I was able to take advantage of my time in Hong Kong to access materials about information literacy that would have been more difficult to find back in the states.

When the time arrived to write up our findings, James provided a "big picture" perspective, and I was able to fill in the lines. Thus, the first chapter provides an intellectual overview, written largely from James's strength. In the remaining chapters I detail the processes of information literacy. We reviewed and edited each other's work so the final product blends our philosophies, practices, and research. It not only takes a village to raise a child; it takes a world of librarians to assess information literacy.

Lesley S. J. Farmer

Introduction

$\mathcal{I}$nformation literacy is a current hot topic in education as well as in society. But, as with other literacies, it can be difficult to define, let alone assess, the degree to which one is information literate. As teacher librarians try to help the school community to incorporate information literacy into the curriculum and instruct students so they can become information literate, the role of assessment becomes key—and problematic. What should be assessed, how should it be assessed, is there even a valid *and feasible* set of assessment tools? As important, how should the academic community act upon the data? When information literacy is considered from a global perspective, the issues become even more complex—and more critical to address.

THE SOCIETY OF INFORMATION

The twentieth century may well be remembered for its exponential growth of information and technology. Not only has more information been created in the last one hundred years than the rest of recorded history altogether, but the simultaneous global access to that information could not have been imaginable a hundred years ago. Worry about lack of information has been replaced by information anxiety, the result of information overload and the sense that one cannot manage the information available. Recent decades have been termed the "information age," and the early twenty-first century is giving rise to the "knowledge age" with the awareness that information in itself cannot solve problems; it is the effective *use* of information that promises solutions. People need to be information literate.

In light of these realities, it is startling that a few decades ago few people talked about information literacy. And once it became a topic of discussion, it was given little hope of becoming more than a passing fad. Bundy[1] notes that in 1990 futurist Kim Lang heralded information literacy as a faddish, upcoming "new buzzword." Six years after Lang's prediction, Candy observed that "information literacy is the *zeitgeist* of the times . . . an idea whose time has at long last come. It is consonant with the reform agendas in government, in communications technology and in education . . . with employers' demands for an adaptable and responsive workforce. It is increasingly multidisciplinary and must be included across the curriculum at whatever level of education or training we are involved in. And finally it is consistent with the notion of lifelong learning and the fact that the only constant is change."[2]

Now, a decade after Candy's proclamation, the term *information literacy* has reached all walks of life. Even international agencies have rallied to information literacy as a cause célèbre. The 2003 World Summit on the Information Society, endorsed by the United Nations General Assembly, recognized the global challenges "to harness the potential information and communication technology" in a "common desire and commitment to build a people-centred, inclusive and development-oriented Information Society, where everyone can create, access, utilize and share information and knowledge, enabling individuals, communities and peoples to achieve their full potential in promoting their sustainable development and improving their quality of life."[3] The UNESCO Information for All Programme reinforced that principle, claiming that "information literacy and lifelong learning have been described as the beacons of the Information Society, illuminating the sources to development, prosperity and freedom."[4]

If this rhetoric can be believed, it would seem that information literacy has become for the twenty-first century what literacy was for the twentieth century. Of course, it could be argued that literacy is a basic concept and that such concepts as information literacy and media literacy are subsumed by the more fundamental and broader concept. But, in reality, the use of "literacy" has struggled to adopt these broader dimensions. Oberg, for example, observed that "literacy is often defined in terms of reading and writing; it is less often defined in terms of listening and viewing or speaking and image-making."[5] Certainly while literacy is recognized as an important underlying and underpinning base to information literacy,[6] it has become distinct from information literacy. In any case, addressing information literacy—defining it, facilitating it, and assessing it—must be a core set of activities for librarians.

INFORMATION OVERLOAD AND INFORMATION ANXIETY

Information proliferation is at the root of this shift from "mere" literacy to information literacy. In his blockbuster book *Future Shock* (1970), Alvin Toffler coined the phrase "information overload," spawning a generation of discussion about the relative value of information: was information an aid or a hindrance to decision making?[7] Two decades later, Wurman detailed conditions leading to information overload: a process he called "information anxiety." Wurman created a marvelous image with his claim that the weekday edition of the *New York Times* contained more information than the average person in seventeenth-century England would likely have encountered in a lifetime. According to Wurman, "Information anxiety is produced by the ever-widening gap between what we understand and what we think we should understand."[8] Wurman also warned that information anxiety limits people to only seeking information with no time left over for them to reflect on that information. No wonder that Bundy transitioned the discussion from information anxiety to information stress syndrome.[9] If information overload existed in the 1970s, an era that predates the personal computer, the mobile telephone, the Internet, Google, and Amazon.com, then today's population must certainly live in a post-overload society.

While Toffler and Wurman principally comment on the adult world, Akin demonstrates that information overload has become a significant problem for schools.[10] Certainly, the growth of the Internet since 1990 has magnified the information challenge. To a large extent it seems that information is readily accessible on every topic simply by typing a word or two into a search engine. The problem is that so much information is available that only those who are equipped to deal with it are likely to see the distinction between relevant information and pertinent information—or understand that the idea of finding the right answer is usually only theoretically possible, whereas finding good arguments in support of a proposition is achievable.[11]

INTERACTING WITH INFORMATION

Regardless if information is a human construct or a natural phenomenon, humans need to make meaning of information in order to survive. The eighteenth-century essayist Samuel Johnson is reputed to have claimed that there are two kinds of knowledge: "We know a subject ourselves, or we know where we can find information on it."[12] Inherent in this position is the recognition that in order for a person to be informed, that person must have ways of choosing and discarding information as compatible and incompatible with existing knowledge and understanding; it further implies the ability to discard current beliefs and understanding upon the arrival of new information. This action becomes more complex when socially contextualized. The same information may elicit different responses not only because of an individual's prior experiences or current state of mind, but also because each person is influenced to some extent by norms and values that are created and shared by the broader community. On the other hand, an individual's response to information may help forge its common understanding.

More than two decades ago, Irving noted that the information imparted to eleven-year-olds will be obsolete by the time they leave school. The word *imparted* implies that Irving was describing a learning environment where the students were not actively engaged in constructing personal understanding, but rather were taking on others' understanding. In effect, she was describing eleven-year-olds as scribes. In addition, she was pointing to the need for continued engagement because understanding is not a one-time event but rather a journey of discovery. In any case, "old ideas" are being transmitted in a "new" environment, and it is fair to say that youth will not settle for the outdated information if confronted with present-day incompatible realities.[13]

What, then, is the link between information and learning? Henri notes that a "parrot can talk, but doesn't know what it says. A machine can copy, but it has no idea of the value of what it is copying. Electronic text can be copied and pasted into new places, but without the application of the mind it has no new meaning. By definition, copied material lacks originality, and therefore adds no meaning. Scribes and sign-writers copy for a living and the quality of their work is measured against the accuracy of the imitation. For the most part learning is about making something personally understandable from a range of information sources."[14]

Dervin describes learning as a process of construction that deals with uncertainty; in her sense-making approach to understanding learning, she describes information as whatever an individual finds informing. Thus, information literacy could be fairly identified as the mastery of processes of becoming informed.[15, 16]

FROM INFORMATION COPING TO INFORMATION LITERACY

In his report to the U.S. National Commission on Libraries and Information Science titled *The Information Service Environment—Relationships and Priorities,*

Zurkowski advocates the establishment of a national program aimed at achieving information literacy within a ten-year time frame. He describes information literacy in terms of an individual's capacity to use information tools and primary sources to address problems.[17] This approach to information literacy has important implications for education in general and librarians in particular. Nahl describes this process as one where "information triggers changes in the user's perceptions which alter how the information is perceived. The user is seen, not as a passive receptacle, but as an active participant in a constructive process of information processing. Though users are unique individuals, there is a common or universal process through which all users pass in adaptation to a particular information activity. Addressing user-centered services to these commonalities requires scientific knowledge about the actions, thoughts, and feelings that constitute the experience of being a novice user."[18]

What, then, is the current understanding of information literacy, and how can it be integrated into teaching and learning? In his review of the concepts that deal with the question of successful use of information, Bawden identifies a number of alternative terms such as *information competency*, *information skills*, and *mediacy* but determines that information literacy is the most widely used and dominant concept.[19] The more recent adoption of information literacy by UNESCO (United Nations Educational, Scientific, and Cultural Organization) in its *Prague Declaration*[20] and *Alexandria Proclamation*[21] has firmly grounded the concept even though there are problems associated with translating the meaning into other languages.

Thinking in pedagogical terms, Moore and Page position information literacy "at the confluence of resource-based learning practice, constructivist and metacognitive theories, and the practice of developing thinking skills through modelling and scaffolding."[22] The nature of information can be understood and acted upon within a context of curriculum using established sense-making processes.

FACILITATING LEARNING

Libraries should be at the heart of learning within the school community. They provide a cost-effective collection of resources that can be used by each person according to his or her own needs at the time of encounter. Access and use of that collection, though, depends on each person's ability to engage meaningfully with information and to make sense of it. While no instruction is *required*, certainly the teacher librarian has the training and expertise to facilitate this process in partnership with the rest of the school community.

Since the core activities of teacher librarians include gathering, organizing, storing, and facilitating the retrieval and use of information, their collection of resources represents high-quality models of information literacy; teacher librarians model the very essence of the information-literate person. Even the messy, open-ended world of the Internet comes under the scrutiny of the teacher librarian, who creates webliographies and library portals to optimize access to relevant information based on the needs of the school community.

The "real" world outside the library is not so well organized and controlled. In effect, students experience a scaffolded information universe in the library. Sanger notes how education overall offers a mediated experience: "Observing classrooms makes one aware of artificiality. The relations between individuals, the sets and subsets of rules, implicit and explicit, the stuff of the curriculum and the manner of its delivery gradually erode direct experience." Focusing on information literacy, Sanger asserts that "information handling is, largely, the handling of mediated experience, not the handling of persons and things directly. Metacognition, through the channel of critique, is perhaps the only way in which artificiality is exposed and mediational operations become understood."[23]

However, such a selected universe can still stymie young minds. Sanger points out the uncertainty that students must face.

> Information handling may be seen to be a description of those processes we engage in when we wish to resolve uncertainty or develop a clearer knowledge of what we are uncertain about. Indeed, in order to further a quest to understand, we may need to tolerate uncertainty to a late point in an investigation—and that can create tension and conflict. Experience of dealing with uncertainty is part of the necessary qualification of any information user. It is the antithesis of the emotionally uncertain pupil who runs to resources to fill his or her project folder with the certainties of other people's products.[24]

Kuhlthau's key contribution to the uncertainty debate was to demonstrate that the path between uncertainty and satisfaction is not a positive straight line; the information seeker begins the initiation stage of the process in a state of uncertainty.[25] Therefore, to help students experience beginning success as a way to set the stage for continued discovery, teacher librarians provide helpful signage and displays to subtly guide student encounters with information. Then based on students' naturally occurring information needs, teacher librarians can provide one-on-one and group advice and instruction in locating, evaluating, and sharing information. Because teacher librarians know how information is structured, they can share best practices in extracting and making meaning from a variety of resources. Rather like the teacher who carefully constructs math problems to result in "whole" numbers as a way to ease students into the messy world of real-life mathematics, so too does the teacher librarian provide a well-constructed microcosm of the world of information, with carefully designed information literacy instruction, giving students the intellectual tools they need to successfully "muck about" in the world independently and make reasoned decisions based on evaluated information.

Since the main emphasis in education is student achievement of identified academic outcomes, tying information literacy instruction to the rest of the school curriculum optimizes student transfer of learning. In fact, information literacy offers an intellectual "glue" to connect often disparate subject matter; students can relate hypotheses to thesis statements and use numerical analysis to make sense of history as well as science experiments. Moore explains how information literacy can interface with curriculum: "Information literacy standards and rubrics provide behavioural descriptors to guide curriculum design and evaluation of student learning. These activities are further informed by a variety of models used to describe information problem-solving in inquiry, discovery, and problem-based learning activities. These models are perhaps the most familiar face of information literacy in schools and provide educators with a framework within which specific information skills can be targeted and their coordination can be fostered."[26] In short, information literacy instruction helps students learn how to learn.

ASSESSING INFORMATION LITERACY LEARNING

While the ultimate test of information literacy is self-sufficient, efficient use of information, assessment of students' information competency throughout their school years through well-positioned interventions and modified instruction is an essential task of the teacher librarian and other educators in order to optimize learning. As with the earlier example of math problems, identifying valid and reliable assessment instruments to measure information literacy can be challenging. Simple math problems are fine for measuring arithmetic operations skills, but to measure sophisticated mathematical understanding and applications, such as designing an optimal stress-bearing bridge, requires a correspondingly sophisticated and authentic assessment. So while worksheets assess a student's ability to file books in the correct order, they cannot measure a student's ability to transform knowledge effectively. Just as the most authentic measure of mathematical bridge construction is the actual building of a bridge and evaluating its structural integrity, so too do student research-based projects and community-based actions constitute the most valid measures of information literacy. However, the time involved in assessing each aspect of the process as well as the product can be daunting; a well-constructed argument or information application can combine information literacy elements so thoroughly that it is nigh impossible to parse out each factor. Locating or creating worthwhile assessment instruments is challenging in itself. Altogether, designing information literacy instruction and learning tasks, and incorporating relevant assessments, becomes a demanding process for the school community, spearheaded by the teacher librarian. How those assessments are used to improve the curriculum, instructional design, learning environment, and educators themselves is yet another complex task, particularly since information literacy should itself be woven seamlessly with the rest of educational endeavors. Nevertheless, assessment in and of itself is basically wasted time if it is not acted upon.

GLOBAL REALITIES OF INFORMATION LITERACY

Meeting the daily challenges of information literacy can tax the individual teacher librarian. There is always too much to do in too little time; no one person can be responsible for information literacy. It requires the concerted commitment and coordination of the entire school community to make a significant difference in young people's abilities to make sense of the world of information and find their niche within.

Most school communities would say that they too do not have the capacity to address information literacy optimally; too many other competing demands siphon off time and energy. Thus, it takes professionals working together, whole communities working together, whole governmental entities working together to tackle the issue head-on and in coordinated ways.

Information has "gone global," and so too has the need to effectively deal with that information assumed international importance. Information literacy has had to grow in complexity itself in response to the myriad forms of information that now exist—and may potentially take form in the future. Concurrently, instruction in learning those sets of skills and attitudes has to assume complexity and flexibility to mirror increasingly diverse users' needs and interests. Federated international instructional design, delivery, and assessment offer a coordinated way to address the unevenness of information realities around the world.

At the same time, the educational community needs to be sensitive to cultural and individual differences. Collectively examining the issues of information literacy, particularly in terms of assessing it, provides a means to tease out the specific needs and generate ways to address those needs through differentiated instruction and relevant learning resources.

ORGANIZATION OF THE BOOK

Today's teacher librarians certainly live in "interesting" times. They have the potential to impact the future through their concerted efforts in helping youth become informed and reflective learners and doers. This book examines information literacy assessment in light of library, educational, and societal realities.

- Chapter 1 examines definitions of information literacy, noting the university and cultural aspects of this complex set of skills, knowledge, and dispositions.
- Chapter 2 explains the importance of information literacy, from library programs of service to societal implications.
- Chapter 3 explores learning, information literacy, and assessment. It details how students encounter and interact with information with a possible result of learning.
- Chapter 4 outlines the conditions for information literacy assessment.
- Chapter 5 explores the role of assessment.
- Chapter 6 examines the process of assessing information literacy.
- Chapter 7 lists potential problems in assessing information literacy and provides ways to deal with those issues.
- Chapter 8 provides a classified list of user-tested information literacy assessment instruments.

James Henri and Lesley Farmer coauthored this introduction and chapter 1. The remaining chapters were written by Dr. Farmer.

By looking at the larger contexts of information literacy and its assessments, teacher librarians can develop relevant instruction that will optimize student learning so that students can become effective lifelong learners who can understand information and generate their own information as they gain and generate knowledge about their worlds.

NOTES

1. Alan Bundy, "For a Clever Country: Information Literacy Diffusion in the 21st Century" (background and issues paper for the First National Roundtable on Information Literacy, Australian Library and Information Association, Melbourne, February 2001).

2. Philip Candy, "Major Themes and Future Directions," in *Learning for Life: Information Literacy and the Autonomous Learner: Proceedings of the Second National Information Literacy Conference Held in Adelaide, Australia, 30 November–1 December 1995*, ed. D. Booker, 136 (Adelaide: University of South Australia, 1995).

3. United Nations, *Declaration of Principles. Building the Information Society: A Global Challenge in the New Millennium* (The Hague, Begium: UNESCO, 2003), 1.

4. UNESCO, "Information Literacy," Information for All Programme (IFAP), portal.unesco.org/ci/en/ev.php-URL_ID=21293&URL_DO=DO_TOPIC&URL_SECTION=201.html (accessed December 21, 2006).

5. Dianne Oberg, "Perspectives on Information Literacy," *School Libraries Worldwide* 7, no.1 (January 2001): i.

6. Elizabeth Lee, "Reading and the Information Literate Community," in *Leadership Issues in the Information Literate School Community*, ed. James Henri and Marlene Asselin, 65–78 (Westport, CT: Libraries Unlimited, 2005).

7. Alvin Toffler, *Future Shock* (New York: Random House, 1970).

8. Richard Wurman, *Information Anxiety* (New York: Doubleday, 1989), 32.

9. Bundy, "For a Clever Country."

10. Lynn Akin, "Information Overload and Children: A Survey of Texas Elementary School Students," *School Library Media Research* 1 (1998).

11. Carol Kuhlthau, *Seeking Meaning: A Process Approach to Library and Information Services*, 2nd ed. (Westport, CT: Libraries Unlimited, 2004).

12. James Boswell, *The Life of Samuel Johnson* (London: Baldwin, 1791).

13. Ann Irving, *Study and Information Skills across the Curriculum* (London: Heinemann, 1985).

14. James Henri, "Understanding the Information Literate School Community," in Henri and Asselin, *Leadership Issues*, 19.

15. Brenda Dervin, "Useful Theory for Librarianship: Communication, Not Information," *Drexel Library Quarterly* 13 (1977): 16–32.

16. Brenda Dervin, "Information as a User-Construct: The Relevance of Perceived Information Needs to Synthesis and Interpretation," In *Knowledge Structure and Use: Implications for Synthesis and Interpretation*, ed. Spencer A. Ward and Linda J. Reed, 154–83 (Philadelphia: Temple University Press, 1983).

17. Paul Zurkowski, *The Information Service Environment—Relationships and Priorities* (Washington, DC: National Commission on Libraries and Information Science, 1974).

18. Diane Nahl, "The User-Centered Revolution: 1970–1955," in *Encyclopedia of Microcomputers*, ed. Allen Kent and James G. Williams, vol. 19, 153 (New York: Marcel Dekker, 1996).

19. David Bawden, "Progress in Documentation: Information and Digital Literacies: A Review of Concepts," *Journal of Documentation* 57, no. 2 (2001): 218–59.

20. UNESCO, *The Prague Declaration: Towards an Information Literate Society* (Washington, DC: U.S. National Commission on Library and Information Science, 2003), www.nclis.gov/libinter/infolitconf&meet/post-infolitconf&meet/PragueDeclaration .pdf (accessed July 22, 2006).

21. UNESCO, *Beacons of the Information Society: The Alexandria Proclamation on Information Literacy and Lifelong Learning* (report from the High-Level Colloquium on Information Literacy and Lifelong Learning, Alexandria, November 6–9, 2005). www .ifla.org/III/wsis/BeaconInfSoc.html (accessed July 31, 2007).

22. Penny Moore and Nicki Page, "Teaching for Information Literacy: Online Professional Development Challenges," in *School Libraries for a Knowledge Society* (proceedings of the 31st Annual Conference of the International Association of School Librarianship, Seattle, 2002), ed. Diljit Singh et al., 153 (Zillmere, Australia: International Association of School Librarianship, 2002).

23. Jack Sanger, *The Teaching, Handling Information and Learning Project* (London: British Library, 1989), 319–21.

24. Sanger, *Teaching*, 348.

25. Kuhlthau, *Seeking Meaning*.

26. Penny Moore, "An Analysis of Information Literacy Education Worldwide" (white paper prepared for UNESCO, the U.S. National Commission on Libraries and Information Science, and the National Forum on Information Literacy, for use at the Information Literacy Meeting of Experts, Prague, July 2002).

• 1 •

Definitions of Information Literacy

$\mathcal{A}$ beginning definition of information literacy is "the ability to locate, evaluate, manage, use and share information purposefully." However, does this definition have universal acceptance? How do reading, critical thinking, communication skills, and technological expertise overlap information literacy? Until these concepts can be parsed systematically, librarians will have a difficult time working with their academic communities locally—and internationally—to address information literacy. Which principles are culturally defined and which transcend social borders to become core global ideas?

WHAT IS LITERACY?

Librarians and other educators continue to debate the term *literacy*, largely because the intellectual skills needed to survive in society have changed over the ages. The first concepts of literacy focused on the ability to read Latin; writing was not considered part of literacy since surfaces for scribing were so scarce. The typical goal was to read familiar text, rather than to decipher new text. Now, the ability to generate new text and knowledge has become an expected part of functional literacy.[1] Bawden posits three facets for literacy: reading and writing, literacy skills, and the ability to learn. Underlying all three facets is the ability to comprehend and understand.[2]

After reading the morass of definitions of literacy, one might do well to turn the definitions on their ends to this effect: what is *il*literacy? The usual context is the act of reading and writing, which differs slightly from the current arena of literacy discussions. In certain areas of the United States, the words *illiterate person* conjure up an image of a scraggly, ill-spoken, unsophisticated

1

hick. Nevertheless, one would be hard put to say that illiterate individuals cannot find success in life; many businesspeople have hidden their illiteracy behind excuses of poor vision or lack of time. On this basis, one element often listed as a critical feature of literacy—"ability to function independently in society"—seems to be disproven. However, over thirty-five years ago, futurist Alvin Toffler challenged that thinking, asserting that the illiterate of the year 2000 "will not be those who cannot read and write, but those who cannot learn, unlearn, and relearn."[3]

Illiterate in the "folk" sense seems to equate to *uneducated*. However, one might have years of formal educational training and remain illiterate, and many people have experienced little in-class instruction yet have learned to read competently and purposefully. The traditional sense, though, of "the educated man" *does* signal self-sufficiency and broad-based knowledge, and today's literate person needs to have those same attributes. It would be safe to say that today's literate person has the knowledge and skills to deal successfully with novel information and situations.

WHAT IS INFORMATION?

If the term *literacy* causes problems, then the term *information* faces similar ambiguity. Confusion about information literacy is understandable. Is information literacy one aspect of the more specific idea of "literacy," merely a response to information anxiety?

Raber deals with this issue extensively;[4] at one end of the spectrum, information may be considered in terms of products such as texts, documents, recordings, and the packaging and storing of things: information as a thing.[5] Raber argues that it is axiomatic that information appears in a material form. As material object, information can be collected, organized, stored, and retrieved. Raber makes the additional claim that information in its material form rests on the "notion that there are tangible objects and expressions with the quality of being informative. This quality, while characteristic of the formal structure of that object in itself, does not depend on whether the object is perceived to be informative nor on whether it actually informs anyone."[6]

In this construct, it makes sense to consider that information exists independently of human beings. However, the boundaries of this concept could be limitless: is it possible to describe an object or a phenomenon that is not, or could not be, informative? If "potentially meaningful data," or "contextualized data," is defined as information, then cloud patterns could constitute information—as would tire tracks, skirt racks, and turtle backs. Fairthorne was so convinced by the vacuous nature of the concept that he suggested that it carried no useful meaning; information could indeed be a catchword for everything.[7]

At the other end of the spectrum is the claim that information does not exist outside human brains. Bouazza claims that information is a phenomenon, the reality of which is entirely dependent upon human experience and perception.[8] Information is a creation of human consciousness. Raber clarifies the situation thusly:

> Information must be viewed as a form of knowledge which informs by reducing uncertainty, solving problems, or otherwise serving to reveal to us the nature of our reality and contributes to our understanding of our world and ourselves. In this sense, information is a matter of effect and depends on how we use it to attribute meaning to the world and our lives. It is literally the means by which we change our minds by reinforcing and challenging the mental and conceptual categories that form our world views. The development and restructuring of this model as we move through life occurs whenever we send, receive, or employ communicative messages.[9]

CHANGING CONCEPTS OF INFORMATION LITERACY

The concepts behind information literacy and information instruction have existed over a century. The idea of helping people locate information has its roots in antiquity; even the library in Alexandria probably included guidance on the handling of its documents. Higher education in the latter half of the nineteenth century promoted the use of libraries as a repository for scholarly learning, and librarians were known to lecture to classes. Indeed, in 1876 Melvil Dewey asserted that "the time is when a library is a school, and the librarian is in the highest sense a teacher."[10] The first recorded credit course in bibliography was offered in 1880 at the University of Michigan, and by 1919 the idea of integrating library skills instruction into the curriculum was voiced. In 1928, Charles Shaw promoted the idea of a hybrid librarian, knowledgeable in library organization and teaching techniques.[11]

About the same time that the idea of the library as intellectual laboratory was touted by Shores,[12] the first scientifically based research on the need for information literacy skills found that university students lacked expertise in using library resources.[13] Nevertheless, bibliographic instruction, as it was wont to be called, faded into the background until the 1960s. What passed for instruction was chiefly guidance in physically accessing resources; close, critical reading of text was the purview of subject teachers.[14]

The contemporary notions of information literacy beyond "point and cite" library skills were promulgated in the 1960s, primarily within the school library context, in light of emerging information technology. Roe linked "the intimidating growth of knowledge and the age of rapid technological change" with the need to "learn to learn."[15] Shapiro and Hughes even contended that information technology was a new liberal art.[16]

Nevertheless, the usual date associated with the coining of the term *information literacy* is 1974 when Paul Zurkowski employed that term in his report to the U.S. National Commission on Libraries and Information Science titled *The Information Service Environment—Relationships and Priorities*. In this document, Zurkowski advocated the establishment of a national program aimed at achieving information literacy within a ten-year time frame. He described information literacy in terms of an individual's capacity to use information tools and primary sources to address problems.[17]

The statement of the American Library Association Presidential Committee on Information Literacy is regarded as one of the seminal publications that gave information literacy legitimacy: "Ultimately, information literate people are those who have learned how to learn. They know how to learn because they know how knowledge is organized, how to find information, and how to use information in such a way that others can learn from them. They are people prepared for lifelong learning, because they can always find the information needed for any task or decision at hand."[18]

DEFINITIONS OF INFORMATION LITERACY

Most of the definitions of information literacy align with the definition generated by the American Library Association Presidential Committee on Information Literacy: "To be information literate, a person must be able to recognize when information is needed and have the ability to locate, evaluate, and use effectively the needed information."[19] A major paradigm shift in literacy is couched within the basic 1989 statement; the information seeker—rather than an instructor or other expert—controls the process; the emphasis is self-actualization. For this reason, if no other, the concept of information literacy marks a new era in education, for it signals that the learning universe is open-ended, not just a status quo passing on of prior knowledge. Learning is truly lifelong.

However, no universal agreement exists on a single information literacy definition, for several reasons: the impetus for addressing information literacy, the educational context of information literacy, economic and political contexts of information literacy, the cultural values and norms for literacy, and the information universe itself. Even the geographic extent of inquiry, from a single librarian to an entire nation, impacts the course of action.

Moreover, the objective and methodology used in examining information literacy results in different definitions of it. For instance, librarians are looking at

- information-seeking behaviors and skills,
- situated information literacy,
- people's knowledge structures, and
- information curriculum.[20]

Fjällbrant and Malley succinctly summarize the changing landscape of information literacy:

> Those involved in this development [user education for schoolchildren] (not all of the work is new) describe the work as "information skills" (again not new). And although adding new terminology (or reinterpreting old terminology) to a subject already burdened with varying and often confusing descriptors must be viewed circumspectly, the use of the term information skills does usefully illuminate the nature of the new emphasis. It is an "umbrella" term incorporating study skills, learning skills and communication skills, as well as library skills. . . . Of course there is nothing entirely new in all this—various librarians have argued along some of these lines before. What is new is that the personnel involved in this work have emerged from the different backgrounds of teaching, educational research and libraries, bringing with them expertise and specialist knowledge from these different areas.[21]

Even the term *information literacy* is not totally embraced. Other terms used to describe these sets of skills, knowledge, and dispositions include the following:

- Information literacy skills
- Information skills
- Information competence/competency
- Information-related competencies
- Information fluency
- Research skills
- Information inquiry
- Learning standards
- Information technology literacy

- Information and communications technology skill
- Information and communication technology literacy
- Digital literacy
- *Alfabetización informacional*
- *Informatiekunde*: knowledge of information
- *Competences documentaires*
- Functional competence
- Meta-competence[22]

Not surprisingly, frequent discussion focuses on parsing these definitions. For example, Kirschner distinguishes between "competencies" (a combination of complex cognitive skills) and "competence" (ability to flexibly coordinate these different aspects of competent behavior). [23] Still others wish to differentiate among levels of information literacy just as literacy has been defined at differing levels of sophistication.[24]

Likewise, the following representative definitions provide a starting place for consideration.

- "Information literacy and computer literacy [are] . . . the knowledge and skills concerning the use of computers for getting information to solve a given problem or to know more about a certain subject, as well as for the control of processes."[25]
- "Information literacy is a basic individual capacity for subjectively choosing and utilizing information and information media."[26]
- "Information literacy, which encompasses knowledge of one's information needs and the ability to identify, locate, evaluate, organize and effectively use information to address issues or problems at hand, is a prerequisite for participating effectively in the information society, and is part of the basic human right of life long learning."[27]
- "Information literacy is knowing when and why you need information, where to find it, and how to evaluate, sue and communicate it in an ethical manner."[28]

Sometimes information literacy is defined in terms of a person's attributes or couched in terms of operational definitions. Australia and New Zealand's information literacy framework principles describe the information literate person.[29] Doyle developed a set of rubrics to assess the information literate person.[30] Bruce took a phenomenological approach, describing information literacy tasks.[31] In her analysis of information literacy definitions, Webber generated a set of characteristics describing an information literate person:

- Effective information seeking
- Informed choice of information sources
- Information evaluation and selection
- Comfort in using a range of media to best advantage
- Awareness of issues to do with bias and reliability of information
- Effectiveness in transmitting information to others[32]

Recent literature has added the component of *managing* information, largely in response to issues of information overload.[33]

Often information literacy is confused with research skills. Several models of information literacy are essentially steps or elements for a particular set of strategies for a purposeful intellectual information task.[34, 35, 36, 37, 38, 39] However, information literacy transcends any one set of research processes. Information literacy also applies to ways that individuals *encounter* information, such as by way of advertisements or a telephone call. They still have to make sense of the stimulus and decide how and whether to act upon the information.

While Bundy and others rightly contend that a universally accepted definition and assessment of information literacy would advance international efforts and sustainability, librarians need to act now. Rather than waiting for the perfect definition of an ever-changing set of competencies and attitudes, perhaps the best solution that librarians can settle for is a locally agreed-upon sense of information literacy. As long as the legal educational entity and its stakeholders can define and operationalize information literacy, and use those agreed-upon ideas to advance student learning, then a positive outcome is more likely to occur.

OVERLAPPING LITERACIES

Shapiro and Hughes posit several facts of information literacy:

- *Tool literacy*: understanding information technology tools
- *Resource literacy*: understanding the access methods and formats of information resources
- *Social-structural literacy*: understanding how information is socially situated and produced
- *Research literacy*: using relevant information technology tools
- *Publishing literacy*: formatting and publishing research and ideas in multimedia formats
- *Emergent technology literacy*: using emerging information technology

- *Critical literacy*: critically evaluating the capabilities and limits of information technology[40]

Likewise, the California Library Association listed four subliteracies of information literacy: (1) reading and writing, (2) computing literacy, (3) media literacy, and (4) network literacy.[41]

Their lists highlight the nuances of information literacy and also raise the question about other literacies that might support or overlap the intent of information literacy. Indeed, the question has been posed: if other literacies or competencies together cover all the aspects of information literacy, does information literacy, per se, need to exist?

Several countries, particularly in Europe, combine information and technology literacy in some form, be it information and communication technology (the most common term) or digital competency. The International Society for Technology in Education 2000 technology standards largely reflect information literacy: researching, problem solving, communicating, developing products, acting ethically; the main difference is the mechanical operation of technologies separate from information.[42] One simple counterexample distinguishes information literacy from technological literacy: oral interviewing skills; one can gather and make meaning information by talking with another individual without any use of technology.

The University of California, Los Angeles, posits four twenty-first-century literacies—information, cultural, visual, and media—which it contends have discrete disciplines. Media literacy focuses on individuals as consumers of mass media messages. Cultural literacy deals with languages and culturally developed norms. Visual literacy assumes that images have their own "language." Information literacy in this construct resembles traditional research and sense-making processes.[43]

Some elements of information literacy overlap media literacy, which focuses on the intentional messages of the mass media. Mass media itself depends on technology to broadcast its message, with the communication channel as the core element. At the National Leadership Conference on Media Literacy, participants agreed to define media literacy as the ability to "access, analyze, and produce information *for specific outcomes*."[44] The emphasis is on the audience as critical consumer; the usual first encounter is one of receiving rather than self-initiation. Nevertheless, research processes can be used in interacting with media.

For a while, visual literacy was confused with media literacy. The former far precedes the latter. Since the basic premise of visual literacy is the ability to understand, create, and use visual images, the source of information might date back to cave drawings—with the underlying assumption that the images are human made. Images can be constructed for one's own amusement as well as for public display or persuasion. Visualization can consist of signs (one-to-one correlations between image and object) and symbols (abstraction of an idea or object); it can be used to represent processes.[45] Graphic organizers, thus, constitute a visual tool, that is, "a symbol graphically linked by mental associations to create information and a form of knowledge about an idea."[46] To differentiate itself from media literacy, visual literacy as an academic field has focused more on visual aspects of instruction and design.

Critical thinking and problem solving are two other concepts that vie for information literacy attention. Critical thinkers know why to learn, what to learn, and how to learn. The main competencies include analysis, interpretation, inference, evaluation, and self-regulation, all of which constitute elements of information literacy.[47] Information literacy goes beyond those skills and includes the identification and effective access to needed information.

Generic problem-solving steps include (1) identifying a problem and understanding it; (2) devising a plan to solve the problem, including generating possible solutions; (3) deciding on a solution and implementing it; and (4) analyzing the solution.[48] Pure and applied scientists often use design briefs as a tool to structure problem solving. The main emphasis is purposeful inquiry, with a sense of closure. In that respect, information literacy is much more open-ended, from the start onward.

In summary, what distinguishes information literacy from other literacies is the combination of competencies and dispositions that enable one to deal meaningfully with a variety of unforeseen types of information: to access it, critically examine it, make meaning of it, relate it to other information, share it, and use it to make decisions and generate new knowledge.

INFORMATION LITERACY AND TEACHER LIBRARIANS

Information literacy, then, might be said to encompass those capabilities to identify information needs and to deal with recorded information. However, even if information is limited to *recorded* ideas, one could theoretically become information literate without ever entering a library; mass media provide mountains of information that may be easily accessed. What is the role of the library and the teacher librarian in this social context?

Basically, librarians collect, store, organize, and ease the retrieval of information. The library is one physical entity that heretofore provided a cost-effective means of storage and access. Being unaware of libraries as information centers and how they operate limits a person's options for accessing and using information sources. Furthermore, the librarian's expertise transcends any physical setting, particularly in the twenty-first century. The world of information constitutes the parameters of librarianship—and information literacy. And as educators, teacher librarians provide the core expertise to help young people build those information literacy competencies.

NOTES

1. Brett Blake and Robert Blake, *Literacy and Learning: A Reference Handbook* (Santa Barbara, CA: ABC-CLIO, 2002).

2. David Bawden, "Progress in Documentation: Information and Digital Literacy: A Review of Concepts," *Journal of Documentation* 57, no. 2 (March 2001): 218–59.

3. Alvin Toffler, *Future Shock* (New York: Random House, 1970), 414.

4. Douglas Raber, *The Problem of Information* (Lanham, MD: Scarecrow Press, 2003).

5. Michael Buckland, "Information as Thing," *Journal of the American Society of Information Science* 42, no. 5 (1991): 351–60.

6. Raber, *Problem of Information*, 55.

7. Robert Fairthorne, "Information: One Label, Several Bottles," in *Perspectives in Information Science*, ed. Anthony Debons and William Cameron, 144–64 (Norwell, MA: Kulwer Academic Publishers, 1975).

8. Abdelmajid Bouazza, "Information User Studies," in *Encyclopedia of Library and Information Science*, vol. 44, suppl. 9, ed. Allen Kent, 144–64 (New York: Dekker, 1989).

9. Raber, *Problem of Information*, 95.

10. Melvil Dewey, "The Profession," *American Library Journal* 1 (September 1987): 5.

11. Michael Lorenzen, "A Brief History of Library Information in the United States of America," *Illinois Libraries* 83, no. 2 (2001): 8–18.

12. Louis Shores, "The Liberal Arts College: A Possibility in 1964?" *School and Society* 41 (January 26, 1935): 110–14.

13. Chauncey Louttit and James Patrick, "Study of Students' Knowledge in the Use of the Library," *Journal of Applied Psychology* 16 (October 1932): 475–84.

14. Blake and Blake, *Literacy and Learning*.

15. Ernest Roe, "$27 Million Dollars Worth of Better Education," *Australian Library Journal* 18, no. 6 (1969): 196.

16. Jeremy Shapiro and Shelley Hughes, "Information Technology as a Liberal Art," *Educom Review* (March 1996): 31–35.

17. Paul Zurkowski, *The Information Service Environment—Relationships and Priorities* (Washington, DC: National Commission on Libraries and Information Science, 1974).

18. American Library Association. *Presidential Committee on Information Literacy: Final Report* (Chicago: American Library Association, 1989), 1.

19. American Library Association, *Final Report*, 1.

20. Christine Bruce, "Information Literacy Research: Dimensions of the Emerging Collective Consciousness," *Australian Academic and Research Libraries* 31, no. 2 (2000): 91–109.

21. Nancy Fjällbrant and Ian Malley, *User Education in Libraries*, 2nd ed. (London: Clive Bingley, 1984), 123.

22. Sirge Virkus, "Information Literacy in Europe: A Literature Review," *Information Research* 8, no. 4 (July 2003): 1–64.

23. Paul Kirschner, "Using Integrated Electronic Environments for Collaborative Teaching/Learning" (keynote speech, 8th Annual Conference of the European Association for Research on Learning and Instruction, Gothenburg, Sweden, August 26, 1999).

24. OECD and Statistics Canada, *Literacy in the Information Age: Final Report of the International Adult Literacy Survey* (Paris: OECD and Statistics Canada, 2000).

25. Bram Van Weering and Tjeerd Plomp, "Information Literacy in Secondary Education in the Netherlands: The New Curriculum," *Computers and Education* 16, no. 1 (1991): 17.

26. Hitoshi Inoue, Eisuke Naito, and Mika Koshizuka, "Mediacy: What Is It? Where to Go?" *International Information & Library Review* 29, nos. 3–4 (1997): 413.

27. UNESCO, *The Prague Declaration: Towards an Information Literate Society* (Washington, DC: U.S. National Commission on Library and Information Science, 2003), 1, www.nclis.gov/libinter/infolitconf&meet/post-infolitconf&meet/PragueDeclaration .pdf (accessed July 22, 2006).

28. Chartered Institute of Library and Information Professionals, "Information Literacy: Definition," 1, www.cilip.org.uk/professionalguidance/informationliteracy/ definition/ (accessed December 22, 2006).

29. Alan Bundy, "Growing the Community of the Informed: Information Literacy— A Global Issue" (paper presented at the Standing Conference of East, Central and South Africa Library Associations, Johannesburg, South Africa, April 2002).

30. Christina Doyle, *Information Literacy in an Information Society: A Concept for the Information Age* (Syracuse, NY: ERIC Clearinghouse on Information and Technology, 1994).

31. Christine Bruce, "Information Literacy: A Framework for Higher Education," *Australian Library Journal* 44 (August 1995): 158–69.

32. Sheila Webber, "Getting the Knowledge," *Library and Information Update* 1, no. 7 (2002): 52–53.

33. Seeds University Elementary School, *Managing Information in a Digital Age* (Los Angeles: University of California, 2002).

34. Michael Marland, *Information Skills in the Secondary Curriculum* (New York: Metheun, 1981).

35. Michael Eisenberg and Robert Berkowitz, *Information Problem-Solving: The Big Six Approach to Literacy and Information Skills Instruction* (Norwood, NJ: Ablex, 1990).

36. Marjorie Pappas and Ann Tepe, "Preparing the Information Educator for the Future," *School Library Media Annual* (1995): 37–44.

37. John Herring, *Teaching Information Skills in Schools* (London: Library Association Publishing, 1996).

38. Standing Conference of National and University Libraries, *Information Skills in Higher Education: A SCONUL Position Paper* (London: Standing Conference of National and University Libraries, 1999).

39. Council of Australian University Librarians, *Information Literacy Standards* (Canberra: Council of Australian University Librarians, 2001).

40. Shapiro and Hughes, "Information Technology as a Liberal Art," 31–35.

41. California Library Association, "Competencies for California Librarians in the 21st Century," www.cla-net.org/resources/articles/r_competencies.php (accessed July 31, 2007).

42. International Society for Technology in Education, *National Educational Technology Standards for Students* (Eugene, OR: International Society for Technology in Education, 2000).

43. Seeds University Elementary School, *Managing Information.*

44. Patricia Aufderheide, ed., *Media Literacy: A Report of the National Leadership Conference on Media Literacy* (Aspen, CO: Aspen Institute, 1993), 6.

45. Susan Chipman, Judith Siegal, and Robert Glaser, eds., *Thinking and Learning Skills: Current Research and Open Questions* (Hillsdale, NJ: Erlbaum, 1984), 5.

46. John Clarke, "Using Visual Organizers to Focus on Thinking," *Journal of Reading* 34, no. 7 (1991): 527.

47. Peter Facione, Noreen Facione, and Carol Giancarlo, "The Disposition Toward Critical Thinking: Its Character, Measurement, and Relationship to Critical Thinking Skill," *Informal Logic* 20, no. 1 (2000): 61–84.

48. George Polya, *How to Solve It* (Princeton, NJ: Princeton University Press, 1988).

• *2* •

The Importance of Information Literacy

*I*s information literacy a library "thing" or should it be considered as a cross-curricular outcome? Since the standards associated with information literacy—being able to locate, evaluate, manipulate, organize, and communicate information effectively and ethically—are used in a variety of academic and personal settings, it would make sense that those related standards would impact student learning overall. Who values information literacy—and who should? How information literacy is learned and practiced across societies reflects social attitudes—and can influence the political-economic scene.

CHANGING VIEWS OF LIBRARY EDUCATION

Increasingly, teacher librarians consider information literacy to be a central component of a library program of resources and services. The American Association of School Librarians asserts that the mission of the school library program is to "ensure that students and staff are effective users of ideas and information."[1] This mission reflects current educational philosophies in the United States, and has a slightly consumerism connotation.

Traditionally, most librarians concentrated on providing a highly selective, well-organized collection of resources that the community could easily access *in a physical sense*. This philosophy remains a core value, particularly in public libraries. School library programs and, to some extent, academic library programs added an explicit library user education function because they were part of educational institutions. Library user education focused on locating information and used a tool-based approach (e.g., how to use a dictionary, how to read a map, how to find an encyclopedia article). This program model fit the traditional, static mode of education in which the basic goal was to transmit existing knowledge: students were given—or had to find—facts, which they collected, organized, and then reproduced to demonstrate "knowledge" to the teacher. Literacy was defined in terms of being able to read and comprehend an existing text.

However, in today's global economy, change has become the constant, and education has the role of not only passing on existing knowledge but also preparing students to create new knowledge—to survive in a future world that has not yet been defined. Education now emphasizes lifelong learning and process-based knowledge. Likewise, literacy now encompasses reading and writing in order to survive in society.[2] Indeed, the term *literacy* has sometimes been replaced by *multi-literacies*, and has been both parsed and broadened to explicitly call attention to technology literacy, media literacy, visual literacy, aural literacy, numeracy, and even social literacy. School library programs have responded to the notion of process-based literacies in their promotion of—and instruction in—information literacy, which involves a number of interdependent competencies.

The impact of technology has also changed the face of education. Students have the potential to use many more tools to access, manipulate, and communicate knowledge. Even in schools where little digital technology is evident, education is impacted because students see the disconnect between outdated school practices and the realities of the outside world. Any more, the issue is seldom the ability to find *any* information; rather, the challenge is to discern and select relevant and useful information. Libraries are no longer closed universes of preselected, appropriate educational resources; they are, instead, portals to the world of information. In this open environment, teacher librarians have to teach students how to be critical consumers of information. On the other hand, students are increasingly assuming the role of expert as they teach adults how to use technological tools. This dynamic of shared learning and expertise highlights the need to reexamine how formal educational experiences are planned and implemented. In this environment, technology literacy largely overlaps information literacy in that technology tools may be used to locate, evaluate, use, and communicate information. Nevertheless, technology literacy also deals with mechanical skills of operating machinery, which might not be strictly construed as information-centric.

THE VALUE PLACED ON INFORMATION
LITERACY BY TEACHERS

Despite the efforts of librarians, information literacy per se has not been embraced by the educational community as a whole, largely because the term itself has not existed for a generation yet, and partly because academic preparation of most educators did not explicitly include information literacy—and still does not in many cases throughout the world because the collegiate faculty also did not get exposure to that term.

Sometimes the solution is just a matter of "translating" information literacy into related terms that teachers are more likely to use and value: research skills, critical thinking, problem solving, design briefs, scientific process. Several educational philosophies align with information literacy.

- *Cognitivism* has as its intent the construction of knowledge through interaction and experimentation. Students are taught thinking skills so they can become self-directed learners. Teaching practices focus on processes.
- *Existentialism* assumes a subjective reality, with students creating personal meaning in their examination with information.
- *Experimentalism* assumes that the world changes constantly and that education's role is to discover current reality and find ways to improve society. Pedagogically, experimentalism favors problem-based and inquiry-based learning.
- *Pragmatism* focuses on practical skills and knowledge. It emphasizes active learning and hands-on applications. Group work is favored.[3]

Teachers who support such engaged learning have an easier time understanding the role and impact of information literacy and are typically more open to collaborative instructional design that integrates information literacy into their pedagogical aim and approach.

School and academic librarians are faced with teaching information literacy not only to primary and secondary students but also to faculty themselves. If teachers have the outdated attitude that they should "know it all" rather than the more realistic attitude that they are expert learners (in some areas), then training them becomes a challenge for librarians. Teachers also tend to focus on content while teacher librarians tend to focus on process. On the other hand, teachers who embrace lifelong learning and who strive to provide students with authentic learning environments are likely to appreciate and support information literacy in a collaborative manner.

IMPACT OF INFORMATION LITERACY ON STUDENT LEARNING

Traditional library skills are usually understood—and considered to be the school library's curriculum. However, the impact of information literacy will not be felt if constrained to library lessons. Particularly in today's climate of accountability, the school community often has to be "convinced" of information literacy's values as it pertains to education as a whole. Dozens of research studies exist that link information literacy and student learning overall.[4, 5] Some key findings follow.

- Information literacy improves reading comprehension.
- Students in schools with teacher librarians are more likely to enjoy reading and meet reading standards.[6]
- When information literacy is integrated into academic domains, students internalize skills better.
- Collaboratively designed integrated information literacy instruction improves learning and research products.
- Students who are taught information literacy in secondary schools are more successful in higher education than students without that instruction.
- Information literacy is a way of thinking, which impacts lifelong learning.

Nevertheless, classroom teachers are more likely to believe their peers and ask for concrete local evidence rather than rely on librarian-originated reports that may seem self-serving. Here are some ways to provide such documentation.

- Student demonstrations of information literacy in action can be videotaped.
- Samples of information-rich student work can be shared.
- Credible teachers who have experienced success in incorporating information literacy can serve as spokespersons for the library program.
- Online and print-based lesson ideas that incorporate information literacy *and* address content standards can be located and shared.
- Teacher librarians can research and share articles in subject-specific journals of educational organizations (e.g., *English Teacher, Science, Teaching Children Mathematics*) that discuss information literacy's positive impact on student learning.

SOCIETAL VALUE OF INFORMATION LITERACY

At the World Summit on the Information Society, international stakeholders stated their shared values of information literacy: "Information Literacy lies at the core of lifelong learning. It empowers people in all walks of life to seek, evaluate, use and create information effectively to achieve their personal, social, occupational and educational goals. It is a basic human right in a digital world and promotes social inclusion of all nations."[7]

Although it sometimes seems as if teacher librarians created information literacy and its need, current key decision makers recognize the importance of information literacy. As early as the 1991 SCANS (Secretary's Commission on Achieving Necessary Skills) report, governmental agencies have noted the need for employees who can locate, interpret, and organize information; communicate information; create documents; solve problems; work with a variety of technology; and know how to acquire new knowledge.[8]

In the knowledge age, companies realize the importance of their intellectual capital or assets, and they are couching enterprises within a framework of a learning organization. Senge has identified five principles within this framework: personal mastery, mental models, shared vision, team learning, and systems thinking.[9] As with the ensuing SCANS report, these characteristics map well onto information literacy.

Partnership for 21st-Century Skills includes U.S. businesses, educational organizations, and government entities. This advocacy group focuses on ways to incorporate digital-age competencies, including information and media literacy, into education. They contend that "there is a profound gap between the knowledge and skills most students learn in school and the knowledge and skills they need in typical twenty-first-century communities and workplaces. To successfully face rigorous higher education coursework, career challenges and a globally competitive workforce, U.S. schools must align classroom environments with real world environments by infusing twenty-first-century skills into their teaching and learning."[10]

In a landmark study of CEOs from twenty-eight countries, Rosen documented four global literacies need in today's business world: personal literacy (self-knowledge and self-esteem), social literacy, business literacy, and cultural literacy.[11] As businesses increasingly realize the importance of intellectual capital, knowledge management has become a key ingredient for success. In 1995, G-7 leadership agreed that a global information society needed to be built, providing infrastructure and applications as they impact societies and cultures.[12] Particularly since one of the main reasons for education is to prepare its students to contribute to society's economic well-being, it makes sense to incorporate information literacy into the curriculum.

UNESCO (United Nations Educational, Scientific, and Cultural Organization) Bangkok has identified communication and information as a major program, with information literacy constituting a major thread within that initiative. This international organization asserts, "Information literacy enhances the pursuit of knowledge by equipping individuals with the skills and abilities for critical reception, assessment and use of information in their professional and personal lives. For the society to have information literate adults, information literacy education needs to start as early as possible."[13]

UNESCO as a whole has embraced information and communication technology and is facilitating global discussion and efforts. "Everyone should be offered the opportunity to acquire the necessary skills in order to understand, participate actively in, and benefit fully from, the Information Society and the knowledge economy. Given the wide range of ICT [information and communication technology] specialists required at all levels, building the institutional capacities to collect, organize, store and share information and knowledge deserves special attention. Governments should develop comprehensive and forward-looking strategies to respond to the new human capacity needs, including the creation of an environment that supports information literacy, ICT literacy and life-long learning for the general public."[14] Even beyond economics, information literacy is needed in order to fully realize one's self-potential and to be a responsible and participatory citizen. On a more profound level, information literacy is imperative for a democratic, open society.

The intersection of technology and globalization has led to more intense and pluralistic interactions across societies. Because information's meaning and impact is contextualized, shared knowledge and understanding can be harder to achieve. In a world scarred with political turmoil and terrorism, information literacy has never been so important.[15] School librarians, as well as other information professionals, should be discussing strategies to promote the value of information literacy—and ways to optimize its attainment by global citizens—through initiatives facilitated via international professional associations.

INFORMATION LITERACY VALUES IN POLICIES

What institutions value, they plan for and write policies about. As asserted in a review of Hong Kong information policy, "if information is the oxygen of learning then the development and articulation of information policies are likely to be a core issue for these schools."[16] At the 2005 World Summit on the Information Society, the participants called "upon international and intergovernmental organizations to develop, within approved resources, their policy analysis and capacity-building programmes, based on practical and replicable experiences of ICT matters, policies and actions that have led to economic growth and poverty alleviation, including through the improved competitiveness of enterprises."[17]

In some countries, information literacy is a national initiative either grounded in governmental or economic realities or proposed as part of a national educational framework.[18] Representative examples follow.

- Australia's Department of Education, Science, and Training requires that postsecondary students attain information literacy through integrated curriculum and practices. In 2003, the Australian Library and Information Association developed a national policy statement on information literacy for all Australians (www.alia.org.au/policies/information .literacy.html).
- The Hong Kong SAR government's five-year strategy "Empowering Learning and Teaching with Information Technology" provides for information technology (IT) infrastructure and focuses on integrating IT into learning and teaching, including a broad framework for information literacy, so that students can become lifelong learners.[19]
- Botswana government's "Long Term Vision 2016" includes "the desire to produce citizens who are informed and are able to use information effectively."[20]
- France's national educational system requires that information literacy be embedded in secondary- and higher-education curriculum.
- The Norwegian national curriculum includes as a basic skill "the ability to use information and communication technology." Additionally, a national plan titled "Make Room for Reading!" focuses on reading ability and appreciation.[21]
- The European Observatory for Information Literacy Policies and Research (www.ceris.cnr.it/Basili/EnIL/gateway/gatewayhome.htm) serves as a web portal to country documents in this arena, focusing on higher education initiatives. As of July 2006, Austria, Denmark, Finland, Germany, and Poland have submitted policies. In some cases (e.g., Austria), the policies are generated by an educational ministry, but in other cases (e.g., Germany), the source is economic. In Finland, an Information Society Council was established to connect all relevant public and private stakeholders.

International and national professional organizations, usually of librarians, also develop policy statements about information literacy, but these documents have no legal status and so are not enforceable.

Information literacy plans and policies may exist as well on regional, local, and site levels. Again, government- and education-specific entities can create these legal documents. Librarian professional associations can often influence these bodies because they have established individual working relationships with their representatives. These policies can vary widely, depending on the context, personalities, and situation at hand.

FROM INFORMATION LITERACY GOALS TO STANDARDS

What should students be able to know and do? In the world of education, values can be translated into goals that are then particularized into standards that students are expected to meet. Typically, standards identify the acceptable or desired level of competency in general terms. Standard indicators specify the intended performance: what competent behavior looks like. If curricular areas list standards or student learning outcomes, teacher librarians can "map" information literacy onto existing competencies and then determine to what extent teachers value those skills.

A number of national and organizational standards for information literacy have been developed or are being discussed seriously. As with policies, these may have legal status in terms of granting degrees or allocating funding. In other cases, information literacy standards reflect a strictly professional or cultural belief in and commitment to a set of lifelong competencies. The International Federation of Library Associations has strongly recommended an international set of information literacy standards as a "means of controlling the quality of information preparedness of a person. Secondly, there is a causative and effective connection between information society establishing and cardinal changes in education."[22] While several countries are developing national information literacy standards, only a few have published their final forms. Representative standards follow.

- American Association of School Librarians: www.ala.org/ala/aasl/ aaslproftools/informationpower/InformationLiteracyStandards_final.pdf
- Association of College of Research Libraries (United States): www.ala .org/ala/acrl/acrlissues/acrlinfolit/infolitstandards/standardstoolkit.htm
- Council of Australian University Librarians: www.caul.edu.au/caul-doc/ InfoLitStandards2001.doc
- Australian and New Zealand Institute for Information Literacy: www .anziil.org/resources/Info%20lit%202nd%20edition.pdf
- French Information Literacy Framework of Competencies: www .ac-poitiers.fr/tpi/formanet/formatio/referenc/sommaire.htm

- United Kingdom Joint Information Steering Committee: www.library
  .mmu.ac.uk/bigblue/finalreport.html

In several countries, the umbrella "literacy" is labeled information and communication technology (ICT) competency, reflecting the leap directly into the twenty-first century rather than reaching back to older information literacy definitions. Occasionally, these competencies coexist with information literacy standards but are developed by different governmental agencies. Sample ICT standards are included here.

- International Society for Technology in Education: www.iste.org/
  inhouse/nets/cnets/students/s_stands.html
- Belgium Education Department of Flanders: www.elearningeuropa
  .info/index.php?page=doc&doc_id=5092&doclng=6&menuzone=1
- United Kingdom Qualifications and Curriculum Authority: www
  .ncaction.org.uk/subjects/ict/levels.htm

Reflecting an educational philosophy that is more content or curriculum centered, several educational entities focus on information literacy teaching objectives. A few cases are presented here.

- Australian Computer Society: www.acs.org.au/icdl/
- Namibia National Institute for Educational Development: www.nied
  .edu.na/publications/other%20resources/Published%20ICT%20Policy
  %202005%20-%2015%20March%202005.pdf
- New Zealand Ministry of Education: www.tki.org.nz/r/nzcurriculum/
- Norwegian Ministry of Church, Education, and Research: www
  .regjeringen.no/en/dep/kd/Documents/Brochures-and-hand
  books/2003/The-Committee-for-Quality-in-Primary-and
  .html?id=87998
- United Kingdom Department of Education and Skills: www.standards
  .dfes.gov.uk/schemes2/it/?view=get

Still another approach to information literacy and ICT standards is teacher centered: identifying their competencies to teach information literacy and ICT.

- International Society for Technology in Education: www.iste.org/
  inhouse/nets/cnets/teachers/t_stands.html
- Australian Council for Computers in Education: www.acce.edu.au
  /tltc/default.asp

- Australian School Library Association and Australian Library and Information Association: www.alia.org.au/policies/teacher-librarian .standards.html
- Canadian Association for School Librarians: www.cla.ca/casl/ literacyneeds.html
- French Ministry of National Education: www2.educnet.education.fr/ sections/formation/programme/competences
- United Kingdom Teacher Training Agency: ecs.lewisham.gov.uk/talent/ pricor/ictcomps.html

Increasingly, educational and professional entities appear to be locating existing standards, particularly versions created in the United States, and adopting them rather than creating their own from whole cloth. Teacher librarians realize that their work is already cut out for them: raising the awareness level of stakeholders as to the value of information literacy and then implementing interventions to help students meet information literacy standards.

NOTES

1. American Association of School Librarians and Association for Educational Communications and Technology, *Information Power: Building Partnerships for Learning* (Chicago: American Library Association, 1998), 1.

2. Brett Blake and Robert Blake, *Literacy and Learning: A Reference Handbook* (Santa Barbara, CA: ABC-CLIO, 2002), 11.

3. Robert McNergney and Joanne Herbert, *Foundations of Education: The Challenge of Professional Practice,* 3rd ed. (Boston: Allyn and Bacon, 2000), 136.

4. Lesley Farmer, *Student Success and Library Media Programs: A Systems Approach to Research and Best Practice* (Westport, CT: Libraries Unlimited, 2003).

5. International Association of School Librarianship, "School Libraries Make a Difference to Student Achievement," School Libraries Online, www.iasl-online.org/ advocacy/make-a-difference.html (accessed July 31, 2007).

6. Don Klinger, *School Libraries and Student Achievement in Ontario* (Ontario, Canada: Ontario Library Association, 2006).

7. Sarah Garner, *High-Level Colloquium on Information Literacy and Lifelong Learning.* (Alexandria, Egypt: International Federal of Library Associations, 2005), 3.

8. Secretary's Commission on Achieving Necessary Skills, *What Work Requires of Schools: A SCANS Report of America 2000* (Washington, DC: Government Printing Office, 1991), iii.

9. Peter Senge, *The Fifth Discipline: The Art and Practice of the Learning Organization* (New York: Doubleday, 1990).

10. Partnership for 21 Century Skills, "Our Mission," www.21stcenturyskills.org/index.php?option=com_content&task=view&id=188&Itemid=110 (accessed July 22, 2006).

11. Robert Rosen et al., *Global Literacies* (New York: Simon & Schuster, 2000).

12. International Federation of Library Associations, "Cooperation on Applications and Test-Beds," January 12, 1995 (document created in preparation for the G-7 Ministerial Conference on the Information Society, Brussels, February 25–26, 1995), www.ifla.org/documents/infopol/intl/g7/g7-113qa.txt (accessed July 22, 2006).

13. UNESCO Bangkok, "Communication and Information," 1, www.unescobkk.org/index.php?id=1897 (accessed July 22, 2006).

14. United Nations, *Declaration of Principles. Building the Information Society: A Global Challenge in the New Millennium* (The Hague, Belgium: UNESCO, 2003), 6.

15. David Johnson and Gunther Kress, "Globalisation, Literacy and Society: Redesigning Pedagogy and Assessment," *Assessment in Education* 10, no. 1 (March 2003): 5–14.

16. Sandra Lee, James Henri, and Eva Kandelaars, "Information Policy in Hong Kong and Beyond: A Review of the Literature with Implications for School Libraries," *New Review of Children's Literature and Librarianship* 11, no. 1 (2005): 64.

17. International Telecommunication Union, *Tunis Agenda for the Information Society* (Tunis: World Summit on the Information Society, November 18, 2005), 16.

18. Jesus Lau, "Information Literacy: An International State-of-the-Art Report," www.uv.mx/usbi_ver/unesco (accessed July 11, 2006).

19. Hong Kong Education and Manpower Bureau, "Empowering Learning and Teaching with Information Technology," www.emb.gov.hk/index.aspx?langno=1&nodeid=2497 (accessed July 11, 2006).

20. Angelina Totolo, "Information Technology Adoption in Botswana Secondary Schools and Its Implications on Leadership and School Libraries in the Digital Era," in *Information Leadership in a Culture of Change: IASL Reports, 2005,* ed. Sandra Lee et al., chap. 39, pp. 1–16 (Erie, PA: International Association of School Librarianship, 2005).

21. Elisabeth Rafste, Tove Saetre, and Ellen Sundt, "Norwegian Policy: Empowering School Libraries," *School Libraries Worldwide* 12, no. 1 (January 2006): 50–59.

22. Natalila Gendina, "Information Literacy for Information Culture" (paper presented at the annual conference of the International Federation of Library Associations, Buenos Aires, August 2004), 2.

· 3 ·

Learning, Information Literacy, and Assessment

*I*n examining information literacy, it is necessary to think about the nature of learning. Too often teacher librarians think in terms of information literacy concepts and processes rather than in terms of students' interaction with information. On the other hand, being informed about the nature of learning helps teacher librarians provide effective and timely guidance as well as determine what appropriate assessment instruments to use—and how to use them.

THE NATURE OF LEARNING: THE CONTEXT OF INFORMATION LITERACY

At its most basic philosophical level, learning involves change—of personal behaviors or dispositions. If incoming information repeats existing information, it may *reinforce* or *affirm* learning, but that does not constitute *new* learning. Nor does a student *have* to learn; teachers can teach, but in the final analysis, students must take responsibility for their own learning. Rather like a gift, if the student does not accept the information, then he or she does not learn. Thus, learning truly is a self-monitoring activity, which changes in nature over time.

To a large extent, learning is developmental, both in terms of changing mind-sets as new ideas meet head-on with prior experience and impressions, as well as in being shaped by personal human development (e.g., brain growth and refinement). Thus, babies tend to not be cognitively aware that they are learning, although they are certainly modifying their behavior in response to their surroundings. Likewise, teens may be able to manipulate audio files, but they may lack the moral imperative to realize the ethical implications of pirating such files. Intellectually, children cannot distinguish between valid and invalid inferences or distinguish between explicit and inferred information until fourth grade, although by third grade children can differentiate between inductive and deductive inferences; only adults can differentiate between inductive inferences and guesses.[1, 2] Additionally, because different aspects of humans develop at diverse points in life—emotional maturity lagging behind physical growth spurts, for instance—no simple path to learning exists. Still, learning is usually considered a cumulative activity as one builds a repertoire of learning tools and memories of pieces of information.

At the cranial level, learning involves connecting neurons. As learners perceive patterns in information—be they intellectual or psychological—those patterns can become organized into mental models. Internally, learners connect the known and the unknown.[3] On the physiological level, individuals connect with their environment through their senses; how they perceive that environment—be it natural or manmade—influences the possible related learning. Interestingly, as children become more self-aware, they also become more "other" aware, noting how their own limited knowledge gives rise to their needing to gain information from others.[4]

Indeed, learning is typically a social activity, connecting humans in potentially meaningful relationships. Even if a person reads a book and tells no one, the ideas originate with another person so a meeting of the minds still occurs, although the acquired knowledge would be considered *implicit* knowledge, that is, information that has not been expressed. On the other hand, when readers explicitly share their experience and knowledge, they make their knowledge external; they also usually increase their involvement and understanding through immediate feedback that results in negotiated learning.[5] Collaborative learning offers the opportunity to learn something that could not be accomplished alone: a situation where the whole is greater than its parts. A community of learners offers a way to initiate people into group-generated knowledge and value sets; neophytes can accelerate their learning in this setting. On the other hand, an oppressive environment that tries to stifle learning or has few learning assets also impacts one's learning, in a deleterious manner.[6]

As learners mature and become more information literate, they develop a self-identity that recognizes their uniqueness, and then they act upon that self-knowledge.[7] For, ultimately, learning is more than receiving, consuming information; the flip side of learning is doing. Indeed, as literate learners relate to the environment, they can find their niche within society and contribute to it. They add to the body of knowledge and facilitate learning.

Note that schooling is practically nonexistent in this discussion. Learning is a natural process that can potentially occur anytime, anywhere for the conscious individual. Formal education tries to determine the content and conditions for learning that optimize purposeful learning that is useful within society. Information literacy constitutes a distillated set of internalized processes that help people engage with information and act upon it.

INTERACTING WITH INFORMATION

Educators need to examine how individuals interact with information in order to assess their interdependent cognitive, affective, and kinesthetic learning. It should be noted, however, that the conditions for interaction may occur long before the individual enters the picture.

Learning Preconditions

Education has as its goals, among others, to prepare students to become effective lifelong learners, responsible citizens, and positive contributors to society. Educational standards help define what students should be able to know and do independently of the teacher. Indicators operationalize those standards into concrete and measurable behaviors and dispositions. Information is a bulwark of that educational goal. While some educators may assert they are teaching children, not content, information must be part of the equation for learning to occur. If the goal is self-sufficient learning, then students must be given opportunities to deal with information critically and successfully. Educators then must decide what kinds of learning activities and what conditions for learning will provide the most effective impact on self-knowledge.

Within that context, the resources for learning need to be considered ahead of time in order to be present in a timely manner.

- Where will learning occur: in the classroom, in the library, in the lab, in the community, at home?
- What will be the time frame?
- Who will instruct: the classroom teacher, the teacher librarian, other school staff, students, community experts?
- What information sources will be used: print, nonprint, electronic materials owned or accessed in the school? What should be their quantity and quality?
- What learning aids will be used: graphic organizers, templates, guide sheets, multimedia presentations?

Nevertheless, when educators in general, and teacher librarians specifically, think about learning activities to help one become more information literate, they sometimes forget to think about the prior knowledge base and mind-set that the person already has. Prerequisite skills may be identified, with the aim of moving from the known to the unknown, but the tacit implication exists that students are deficient or lacking. Taking an attitude that all students can bring gifts to the table offers a more positive foundation for learning. Some of those attributes are genetic (e.g., gender, ethnicity, some physical attributes), some are culturally or situationally set (e.g., language, values, experiences), and some are the result of the child's own responses to the world at large (e.g., learning to swim, playing house, taking care of siblings).

Those preexisting conditions impact current learning for several reasons: students can build on their prior knowledge; they may have no prior knowledge in that domain so *may* make connections or not; or they may confront conflicting information, in which case they have to either choose to reject or choose to accept, which may entail unlearning or rejecting the prior information. In addition, the immediate situation also affects interaction with information: mental state because of inner or outer conflicts, physical health, other people's behaviors—even the temperature of the room can impact behavior.

The ramifications for assessment are many. Some of the factors to assess—and means to so assess—include

- *Ranked preferred student outcomes and standards*: Delphi method by stakeholders, focus group discussion of stakeholders, questionnaires of graduates, institutes of higher education, and employers;
- *Learning activities*: diagnostic pretests, collection/resource mapping, time management, discussion of instruction strategies, content analysis of available learning aids and assessment instruments;
- *Conditions for learning*: observation of learning community, student quick writes, time management analysis, analysis of access to information;
- *Student background*: content analysis of student and community records, student and family journals and interviews, focus group discussions with school community members, IQ and personality tests.

Awareness

For learners to deal with information, they must first become aware of it. Life is full of information and informational needs: from stop signs to epistemologies, from finding a pencil sharpener to finding ways of dealing with illness.

Learners constantly filter outside stimuli based on their immediate condition. Or, some event may trigger a person's attention and response. To become aware, the person must be conscious and receptive; if too many distractions exist, the person may not be able to focus on the information. It is possible that a person does not want to move from the status quo and does not want any stimulation; attention-getting may then prove more difficult.

In school settings, it is usually the teacher who tries to call a student's attention to information—or the need for information. Indeed, the existence of the need is, in itself, a piece of information that requires a sense of awareness for it to be acted upon (beyond primal actions of breathing and other survival instincts). When educators can draw attention to a learner's *own* informational needs, be it as a positive experience or as a response out of fear of the consequences if they ignore the information (such as getting burned), then the information is more likely to be given the attention needed to become engaged with it.

It should be noted that sometimes learners are not aware of the information because their senses cannot access it (such as an audiobook to the deaf) or they do not have the resources to access it (such as Internet connectivity). When awareness is out of the learner's control, then the individual who wants the learner's attention must set up the conditions for awareness.

How is awareness assessed? By observation, generally. Simple clues such as degree of focused attentiveness and verbal responsiveness are relevant indicators. The environment also needs to be examined to be sure that learners have the opportunity to become aware; for instance, are resources, including the equipment to access them, readily available? Does scheduling allow time for learners to use the materials needed? If people are not aware of those supporting conditions, they cannot engage with the information. By finding out whether people are aware or not, educators can then develop ways to cause that awareness to happen, usually on an individual basis.

Engagement

Learners have to engage with information in order to make sense of it. The Board on Children, Youth, and Families asserts that teachers need to help all students engage in their learning both cognitively and emotionally so they can understand new information in terms of their own contexts.[8] The American Association of Higher Education emphasizes the positive impact of engagement between students and teachers, and between students.[9] Students need to *want* to succeed intellectually and think that they can, and teachers need to make sure that the learning environment enables students to feel a welcome part of the class.

While educators tend to focus on initial engagement, drawing upon motivational theories, they should keep in mind that the decision to *keep* engaged is an ongoing, conscious one. At any point, learners can disengage; the benefits of continuing the interaction have to outweigh possible negative experiences, such as frustration in locating or comprehending the information.

In the minds of students, several consequences of disengagement exist:

- Learners lose self-concept and self-esteem, which may spiral down in future situations of engagement.
- Learners like school and schoolwork less and may experience increased anxiety.
- Learners feel more peer pressure to either leave an achieving group or reject engagement if their peers are also disengaged.
- Learners lessen their relationships with teachers, although they may want to be able to talk to a teacher about their disengagement.
- Learners become more anxious about their futures.[10]

In short, students may well be aware of the implications of "giving up," but other pressures or priorities may override their initial feeling of "going along" with the process of dealing with information.

Motivation plays a key role in engagement. While the ultimate goal is to get learners to become self-motivated, educators often have to spark that internal desire—or provide an external motivation at some point. Glasser[11] and Tomlinson[12] posit five needs of learners that can be leveraged to motivate them to become engaged in information-related activities; these needs resemble Maslow's hierarchy of needs,[13] it should be mentioned.

- *Basic affirmation and survival*: Student is accepted within the learning environment.
- *Belonging and contributing*: Student can contribute to knowledge building.
- *Freedom and purpose*: Student can explore and problem-solve.
- *Power*: Student can make choices and decisions.
- *Satisfaction and enjoyment*: Student can pursue information of personal interest; student's mind is challenged within proximal development zone.

While learners are engaged with information, they are accessing it physically and intellectually. Before they can comprehend the information, they need to decode its "language," be it verbal, visual, or audio. Only then can they begin to understand the content in terms of associated vocabulary, semiotics, and concepts. If learners do not have the prerequisite skills (linguistic, technical, experiential), they will not be able to connect; in these cases, educators need to scaffold the learning so students can bridge the intellectual gap.

With its cognitive and affective factors, engagement can be complex to assess. As before, observation can serve as an initial way to tell if individuals are engaged with information. Verbally, learners may sound out words or ask questions about the information. They may consult other sources to help them understand the material: dictionaries, encyclopedias, websites. Writing or drawing can also indicate engagement: highlighting passages, marking quotes, taking notes, creating concept maps, or drawing diagrams. When learners show their disengagement—through yawns, random flipping through pages, off-task socializing, and so on—the cause for disengagement should be identified. If it is an affective issue, then educators need to motivate learners to refocus or, perhaps, give them a mental break so they can be more productive later. If the issue is cognitive frustration, then educators need to help fill in the gaps through alternative resources or required skills. If several students express mental disengagement, then it may be time to regroup, rediagnose the learners' current knowledge and skill level, and modify the learning activity to provide a smaller transfer of learning.

Evaluation

Just because one understands information, does not mean that one will use it. The first consideration is usually the task at hand: what relationship does the information have with the identified task? If, for instance, one comes upon a fact that does not apply to the immediate problem to be solved, chances are good that the fact will be ignored. It should be noted that sometimes one may see a serendipitous connection between that information and the original problem and then incorporate it into the process, which can enrich the final results. In other cases, if the individual has a personal interest in that area, he or she might pursue that information or jot it down for future reference. This "bird walking" activity might distract from the current task, such as occasions when students start clicking from one hyperlink to the next until they have forgotten the original reason that they were looking for information. Depending on one's perspective, these sidebar connections do add to the personal body of knowledge; however, they may result in a disorganized mental framework that hampers deep learning.

If the information does relate to the task at hand, other considerations arise. If the new data affirm present knowledge, the learner's present status is confirmed and, most likely, no real learning occurs. If the data *build* on the learner's current mental scheme, then that information can be easily incorporated. If the information contradicts present knowledge, the learner has to decide which data to keep and which to ignore or unlearn. Again, cognitive and affective factors come into play.[14, 15]

The more important the information (both mentally and psychologically), the greater impact the decision will have. For instance, if evolution theory contradicts a strongly held personal and familial belief, then it may be hard to accept it. Contradictory new information considered to be trivial to one individual (e.g., the ingredients in suntan lotion) might be easier to accept because it does not negatively impact one's personal identity or way of life; of course, that new information might also be easily ignored or rejected *because* it makes no difference. To add complexity to the matter, one person's trivial information might be critical to another person (such as several allergic reactions to some types of suntan lotion, to continue the example).

Evaluation can transcend the individual examination of the information itself to consider a set of information points or the interaction strategy in toto. In some cases, the new, contradictory information may force one to decide whether the task direction or definition needs to be changed. Sometimes learners will continue using one strategy to solve a problem even if the information indicates that such a pursuit is meaningless or detrimental to the final results. The decision maker has to weigh the benefits and costs of such a change: Will the new information and corollary new strategy result in better results and learning? Is the added time involved in this change worth the effort? This kind of mental process reflects metacognition and raises the level of information interaction to a higher plane.

Assessment of evaluation seems straightforward: How efficiently and effectively does one evaluate information? What is the basis for his or her decision? How does one deal with new, contradictory information? Typically, the learner provides evidence orally or through writing. To get beyond the obvious responses (e.g., "I used this source of information because it was authoritative and related to my topic"), one needs to provide specific evidence as the basis for decision making, such as significant quotes and background information about the author. Getting at the affective domain, which may be valid, can be difficult if the learning environment discourages such "emotionalism." Peer review may be inadequate for this stage in assessment if it does not draw from experts. However, even teacher librarians often disagree on a definitive list "the best sources" of information for a given topic and student population—and may well hold opinions that differ from other educators. Even the process by which people evaluate relevant sources, which could be "captured" in a rubric, is open to discussion. Ultimately, the most valid assessment consists of examining the use of the information in deriving the final solution.

Nevertheless, when evaluation processes are clearly off base, such as always choosing the first source found or going to a nineteenth-century medical dictionary to study stem-cell research, educators can surmise that the learner lacks evaluation skills, at which point they can teach explicit guidelines for evaluating the quality of information and its relevance.

Manipulation of Information

The central question at this point is, what shall I do with the information? Theoretically, if all a person has to do is parrot back information, then information manipulation really is not necessary. But such an approach trivializes information and reflects low expectations of learners. Nevertheless, information literacy skills, especially when termed *library skills*, too often stop before reaching this stage.

Instead, one should consider all the potential ways that information can be transformed into knowledge: through interpretation, organization, synthesis, reformatting, changing, relating, or combining it with other information. The basis, then, for answering the question of what to do with information is determining the reason for using the information in the first place: the intended task or goal.

One way to understand this concept of information manipulation is to think of information as a data set. Examples might be reading scores, demographic data, historical events, economic data, people's opinions, lists of formulas, topological maps, art reproductions from a museum. Assuming that the data are accurate and useful for the defined task, then one has to decide how to represent and interpret that set of data meaningfully for oneself and the target audience. Would a timeline be an effective way to organize events, for instance, or would that purpose be better suited through a marked political map or graphic organizer? The answer depends on the stated goal. If the task is to determine the impact of the cold war, all of these organizing mechanisms might provide important clues so the information literate person would probably look at the data from various angles in order to discover underlying principles of influence that might intersect and give a more nuanced picture.

In any case, information manipulation consists of four major processing skills: (1) extracting the information, (2) deciding how to represent the information, (3) determining the method of manipulating the information, and then (4) knowing how to do the manipulation itself. Usually, students first learn how to extract information that is represented in some fashion: locating key words, highlighting important phrases, taking notes on the main ideas. This skill reflects an information "consumer" attitude. The "producer" side of this process is the ability to represent a given set of data: graphically, numerically, as a diagram, as a lab report. Next, they would learn how to manipulate those representations; for example, learners might draw conclusions from a data table in an almanac by graphing the numbers to reveal logical patterns. Alternatively, they might learn how to read a physical-political map legend in order to make hypotheses about why cities grew where they did. As learners become proficient in different manipulation strategies, they can begin to ascertain when a method would be appropriate given the nature of the data and the intended use of them.

As mentioned earlier, when several data sets exist, particularly when they are represented in different ways, the learner has to figure out how to compare them. Similar to the task of finding the lowest common denominator in mathematics, the learner has to seek common intellectual ground for possibly contradictory information. By finding common elements or patterns across data sets, learners can organize the data in order to facilitate comparisons and cross-data decisions. In the process, they may transform those separate data sets into a complex model that can explain underlying ideas and principles. Furthermore, by triangulating the data, learners are more apt to develop a valid and reliable picture of the phenomena under investigation.

It should be noted that part of manipulation consists of managing the information itself: keeping track of it and recording salient parts of it. Learners may have brilliant insights, but if they cannot back up their ideas with evidence because it has been lost or mislaid, their credibility drops. One of the best ways to assess the quality of manipulation is to replicate the process, so if documentation about the process is missing, then it may be, in effect, an irreproducible event. Certainly when assessors see messy papers and incomplete information, they find those elements a distraction from the effort at best, and a symptom of disorganized thinking at worst.

Assessing such manipulations can be daunting. Since the assessment method should reflect the nature of the process, discrete operations such as reading a map can be more easily and accurately assessed than the development of a biome simulation over time. Typically, younger students are given more explicit structures and smaller manipulation tasks that can be assessed step-by-step to check the accuracy of each element. As learners mature and become more sophisticated in their approach to information, the assessment can be approached as a holistic rubric where the whole is greater than its parts. Having outside experts provides an authentic way to assess these learners' manipulation strategies.

Still, if one so desired, even those complicated manipulations can be parsed into their composite parts for the sake of fine-grained analysis. Usually, such an approach is done only when the project somehow falls below the standard, and the educator and learner are trying to figure out where the manipulation went awry. For this reason, assessing large projects along the way at designated benchmarks can help the learner make adjustments and change directions proactively. It should be noted, however, that some global learners may have difficulty with a benchmark approach, appearing to be disorganized in the middle of their work, so educators need to be considerate of different individuals' manipulation styles.[16] Additionally, some data may be manipulated in a number of ways to reach the final goal, so flexibility in assessment is also recommended as long as it is equitable and fair.

Application

How does one *act* on the information? That is often the ultimate real-life goal. Perhaps by analyzing available information, one decides how to vote in an election. After looking at a number of cars according to predetermined criteria, one might decide to buy a certain model. By examining local water quality, one might give testimony in a public hearing and recommend ways to improve the water's condition. On the other hand, one may decide to do nothing, or to act purely on whim, after looking at all the facts. Additionally, the process of examining issues can be enjoyable in itself: the mental journey becomes an end in itself.

Nevertheless, education should foster the application of gained knowledge. Not only does it provide concrete evidence of learning, but it also demonstrates the value of interacting with information. It can improve oneself and one's surroundings. It offers a sense of control and power.

It can be very disheartening for a student to spend countless hours writing a report or white paper, hand it in to the teacher, get a mark for it, and then be told to open the textbook to the next chapter. Communication is virtually one way from the student to the teacher, with no apparent impact made on anyone; no authentic audience exists, no venue for implementation exists, not even an opportunity to share with classmates exists. Much more fulfilling is creating that white paper for the local government and presenting it at a town hall meeting so others can hear the findings and recommendations; if that student then joins a local group to implement those recommendations, then that learning can impact others. Additionally, the fact that the recommendations are being carried out is a publicly validated assessment of the ability of the student to interact meaningfully with information.

By now it should be clear that action can occur on several levels. The learner might be applying information to a familiar situation or transferring it to an entirely new environment. The learner might be answering a simple question or solving an immediate problem. On the other hand, the person might be working on a long-term strategy or contributing significantly to a subject knowledge base. If the application is one practiced by the individual already, there might be a small transfer of learning. When the use is novel to the individual, it might be uncomfortable but a deeper learning experience. In some cases, the use and application of information can not only transform the environment but also change a person's own self-concept.

Assessing the application or use of information may be accomplished on a theoretical, logical basis or in situ. Is the application explained clearly? Does the application follow from the information logically? Is the application feasible? These assessment questions can be posed in the form of a criterion-based rubric and measured by experts who know the topic or educators who can communicate and reason well. However, providing a venue for in-the-field critiquing and implementation can be one of the most powerful ways to assess the effective application of information.

LEARNING LEVELS AND INFORMATION LITERACY

When educators discuss levels of learning, they are often speaking about the attitudinal degree of relationship between the learner and information. Often learning is divided into surface and deep learning, where the former reflects little meaningful engagement with information: "photocopying" activity. Deep learning implies mental and psychological grappling with different information to transform information into an internalized body of knowledge. Popper contrasts learning for a task and learning for generalizations.[17] Apple compares "finding stuff" and "finding out stuff."[18]

Ng and Bereiter posit three levels of learning goals, which map well onto information literacy:

- *Completion*: Learners "do" the answers (unmotivated).
- *Instructional*: Learners do what the teacher wants them to do (other-motivated).
- *Knowledge building*: Learners have a personal stake in the activity (self-motivated).[19]

In this construct, Ng and Bereiter also note the correlation between (1) the time horizon and goal level, knowledge building having the longest time frame; and (2) the degree of abstraction and goal level, knowledge building leading to the most abstract.

Sugrue examined the three dimensions of cognitive components of problem solving, which is a subset of information literacy. The first dimension, knowledge structure, is subdivided into concepts (declarative knowledge), principles (procedural knowledge), and "links from concepts and principles to conditions and procedures for applications."[20] Metacognitive functions include planning and monitoring. Motivation constitutes the third dimension, subdivided into perceived self-efficacy, perceived demands of the task, and perceived attraction of the task.

Limberg examined information-seeking behavior, and noted students' psychological responses to information.[21] Her research resembles Ng's and Bereiter's:

- *Find facts*: Toss out whatever does not fit or is inconvenient to find.
- *Find the right answer*: Find a balance between pros and cons; subjective information is hard to deal with.
- *Scrutinize and analyze*: Get at underlying values.

Wells takes a social-historic approach to learning and knowledge building that parallels learning development:

- *Instrumental*: individuals in action with primary artifacts (dating from 2 million years ago)
- *Procedural*: miming between individuals in action with tools (dating from 1 million years ago)
- *Substantive*: group members speaking and reflecting on action (dating from 50,000 years ago)
- *Esthetic*: group members creating artistic representations (dating from 50,000 years ago)
- *Theoretical*: specialist community members explaining the world using decontextualized representations (dating from 2,500 years ago)
- *Meta*: groups and individuals trying to control their own mental activity using mental and semiotic process representations (now)[22]

Other ways to differentiate levels of learning include the following:

- Instrumental >> communicative or practical >> emancipatory[23]
- Direct experience >> generalize from experience >> contextualize learning and extract rules >> existentialism[24]
- Knowledge about/facts >> know-how >> enlarging understanding/ bringing ideas to birth[25]
- Rote >> procedural >> knowledge building[26]
- Descriptive >> analytic >> evaluative[27]
- Present meaning scheme >> new meaning scheme >> transformation of meaning scheme >> perspective transformation[28]

- Instant/reflex >> rapid/intuitive >> deliberative/analytic[29]
- Learning to learn/basic research >> learning to construct/evaluation >> learning to create/knowledge creation[30]
- Fast surfing >> broad scanning >> deep diving[31]
- Using existing knowledge >> constructing knowledge >> creating knowledge new to a discipline[32]

One researcher's highest level of learning can be another researcher's mid level, so these descriptors as a whole reflect a wide range of competencies. It is also important to note that levels can fluctuate during the learning process, depending on the overall task and its components. Moreover, a simple skill may underlay a profound insight.

The level of learning also depends on the locus of control of the learning. For instance, if the teacher controls the learning task, it is likely that younger learners will meet that level but will rarely surpass that level. So if the teacher asks students to memorize a poem, rote learning will likely be the result; few students will read about the poet's life or link the poem to other concepts or experiences. If the teacher designs a learning task that involves sophisticated literacy skills, a greater depth of learning is possible, although a student still has the option to learn at a surface level. On the other hand, when students "own" the task or have choices when interacting with information, they are more likely to engage in deeper learning. Such a shift in control usually requires an inquiry-based or constructivist approach to teaching and learning.[33]

Reflecting the concept of learning levels, learning effectiveness can be assessed on several levels. On an individual level, student learning can be assessed in pre- and posttests or other evidences of knowledge (e.g., concept-mapping, journaling, short-answer test). Educators can measure the differences in knowledge and skill based on instructional goals, new concepts learned outside of the intended content, retention of knowledge from pre- to posttest, and mental models or schema changes. The same differences can be measured on a group level through group-generated concept maps, vocabulary lists, and K/W/L charts (what I know, what I want to know, what I learned), to name a few.

Learning effectiveness can also be measured in terms of interactions between individual and group achievement, which can take several forms:

- *Individual-to-individual*: what peers pass on to peers on an individual basis
- *Individual-to-group*: what one student transfers to the group as a whole
- *Group-to-individual*: what the group as a whole transfers to one student (usually implies retention of learning from pre- to posttest)

- *Rejection at group level*: pretest concepts not transferred to the group
- *Rejection at individual level*: pretest concepts not transferred to the individual
- *Overlapping*: where concepts were both rejected and transferred within the group[34]

THE AFFECTIVE SIDE OF LEARNING AND INFORMATION LITERACY

Looking at learning levels also requires examining the role that emotions play. If one feels distant, he will learn little; if one is actively engaged emotionally, she is more likely to learn to the extent that the information and context make for deep learning. If one feels confused or frustrated, he or she may not be ready to learn. On the other hand, emotional "ahas" signal deeper learning.[35] Senge suggests that individuals sense the world, reflect on it, and then act on it, with the depth of reflection indicating their depth of learning.[36] Farmer's study on socio-emotional maturity and information literacy concluded that students' self-esteem, communication style, attitude toward authority, and resilience impacted their ability to do research projects, for instance.[37] Nabi asserts that emotions can "frame" information-processing, both as a topic is introduced with a specific emotional "spin" and as learners come to the information with an emotional bias (e.g., fear or anger).[38] Heinstrom documented correlations between different approaches to information-seeking behavior and emotional factors:

- Informational fast surfers had a surface study approach and emotionality; they were less open to experience and low conscientiousness.
- Informational broad scanners were more likely to be extraverted, open, and competitive.
- Informational deep divers tended to be analytical and strategic.[39]

Several of the above mentioned learning constructs recall three affective-domain models of human development: Maslow's hierarchy of needs, Kohlberg's stages of moral development, and Bloom's affective domain.

Maslow's five original stages can be linked with information literacy as follows:

- *Survival*: basic instincts
- *Safety/security*: "street smarts"

- *Belonging*: compliance with school and society (other-motivated)
- *Self-esteem (need to know and esthetic components)*: "classic" definition of information literacy
- *Self-realization*: lifelong learning[40]

Likewise, Kohlberg's stages of moral development can be aligned with information literacy dispositions:

- *Egocentric*: immediate need or instinct of little children
- *Punishment/obedience*: engaging in information literacy activities in order to avoid punishment rather than for the sake of the activity itself
- *Instrumental relativist or reciprocity*: engaging in information literacy activities for a grade or other extrinsic motivation
- *Interpersonal concordance*: engaging in information literacy to "get along" with the group or to please the teacher (i.e., conform to social expectations)
- *Law and order*: information literacy "by the rules"
- *Social contract*: utilitarian information literacy
- *Universal ethical principle*: joy of learning[41]

Bloom's five levels of affective learning can apply to information literacy dispositions:

- *Willingness to receive and pay attention*: passive information literacy
- *Responding and involved in a subject or activity*: compliant information literacy (other-motivated)
- *Committed to the underlying value guiding the behavior*: information literacy "by the rules"
- *Organization of values*: "classic" definition of information literacy
- *Value complex*: lifelong learning[42]

Powell's levels of communication provide another lens for looking at the affective side of information literacy:

- *Phatic (conventional messages)*: information off the top of one's head
- *Factual*: fact-based information literacy (e.g., trivia facts, scavenger hunts)
- *Evaluative*: information literacy "by the rules"
- *Gut-level*: "classic" definition of information literacy (scrutinizing and analyzing)
- *Peak*: joy of learning[43]

Of course, emotional states are dynamic throughout the learning process, as documented in Kuhlthau's classic study of students' feelings as they progressed through a research project. As students interact with information they may start with fear or optimism, and then experience confusion and frustration before they gain self-confidence.[44] Butler and Cartier examined how emotional stages reflect students' inquiry learning success; for instance, low self-esteem or low interest can result in poor achievement, and high stress during the inquiry process can also negatively impact results.[45] Villegas, Rapp, and Saven linked Kolb's experiential learning model with stages in experimenting with a simulation model, and noted the learner's emotional "aha" moments.[46] Reilly, Kort, and Picard have been studying affective computing and have developed a model relating phases of learning to emotions.[47] The two dimensions are constructive learning/unlearning and negative/positive affect. As one adds and subtracts knowledge, he or she experiences different emotions. For example, the negative affect of frustration leads to unlearning or subtraction of information. To add to the complexity, each individual's personality and learning style will also result in different emotional responses to learning, and situationally provoked emotions can also impact learning (e.g., a sudden call from the principal, a fire drill, a surprise birthday balloon).

Several methods may be used to assess affective learning, the chief ones being observation and self-disclosure. It should be noted, however, that younger children may have trouble defining their own emotional state accurately, and older students may hide or deny their true feelings for a number of reasons (e.g., need for social acceptance, fear of punishment, self-identity conflict). Picard and Daily offer several body-based measures of affect:

- *Facial activity*: Can differ from true inner feelings (thermal video provides a way to measure stress).
- *Posture activity*: Shows degree of interest.
- *Hand tension and activity*: Reveals degree of frustration (pressure is higher during a frustrating task).
- *Gestures*: Shows expression.
- *Vocal expression*: Demonstrates degree of arousal.
- *Language and choice of words*: May align with or disguise emotions.[48]

IMPLICATIONS FOR TEACHER LIBRARIANS

As educators, teacher librarians have an obligation to help students and staff become "effective users of ideas and information."[49] In the past, teacher librarians typically used the following conceptual framework to advance this agenda: type of reference tool, systematic literature searching, form of publication, primary/secondary sources, publication sequence, citation patterns, and index structure.[50] Instruction emphasized tools rather than meaningful interaction and application of information. Nowadays, teacher librarians see themselves as effective partners for lifelong learning, providing a rich learning environment that can be efficiently accessed physically, and they have the skills to help students learn how to efficiently access information intellectually and interact with it purposefully.[51]

This responsibility for teaching information literacy does not lie solely on the shoulders of teacher librarians. As part of lifelong learning, information literacy instruction and learning should be integrated throughout the curriculum and supported by the entire school community. Other school staff have content expertise or other process expertise such as reading or technology. In combination, these content and processing competencies can accelerate and deepen learning. Thus, to facilitate *student* interaction with information, the education community needs to interact with each other and strategically plan and assess interactive learning opportunities.

NOTES

1. Carole Beal, "Development of Knowledge about the Role of Inference in Text Comprehension," *Child Development* 61 (1990): 1011–23.

2. Bradford Pillow, "Children's and Adults' Evaluation of the Certainty of Deductive Inferences, Inductive Inferences, and Guesses," *Child Development* 73, no. 3 (2002): 779–92.

3. Karl Popper, *World of Propensities* (Bristol, England: Thoemmes, 1990).

4. Charles Helwig and Susan Kim, "Children's Evaluations of Decision-Making Procedures in Peer, Family, and School Contexts," *Child Development* 70, no. 2 (1999): 502–12.

5. Ikujiro Nonaka and Hirotaka Takeuchi, *The Knowledge-Creating Company* (New York: Oxford University Press, 1995).

6. Ross Todd, "Information Literacy in Electronic Environments: Fantasies, Facts, and Futures" (paper presented at the Virtual Libraries: Virtual Communities IATUL Conference, Queensland University of Technology, Brisbane, Australia, 2000).

7. Diane Ruble and Gordon Flett, "Conflicting Goals in Self-Evaluative Information Seeking: Developmental and Ability Level Analyses," *Child Development* 59 (1988): 97–106.

8. Board on Children, Youth, and Families. *Engaging Schools: Fostering High School Students' Motivation to Learn* (Washington, DC: National Academies Press, 2003).

9. Arthur Chickering and Zelda Gamson, "Development and Adaptation of the Seven Principles for Good Practice in Undergraduate Education," *New Directions for Teaching and Learning* 80 (1987): 75–81.

10. Jean Rudduck, Roland Chaplain, and Gwen Wallace, eds., *School Improvement: What Can Pupils Tell Us?* (London: David Fulton, 1995).

11. William Glasser, *Choice Theory in the Classroom* (New York: Harper, 1988).

12. Carol Tomlinson, *The Parallel Curriculum: A Design to Develop High Potential and Challenge High-Ability Learners* (Thousand Oaks, CA: Corwin Press, 2002).

13. Abraham Maslow, *Motivation and Personality* (New York: Harper, 1954).

14. Bonnie Cheuk, "Modelling the Information Seeking and Use Process in the Workplace," *Information Research* 4, no. 2 (1998), informationr.net/ir/4-2/isic/cheuk.html (accessed July 31, 2007).

15. Joseph Rosse and Herman Miller, "Toward a Comprehensive Model of the Employee Adaptation Decision Process" (paper presented at the annual meeting of the Western Decision Sciences Institute, Portland, ME, April 18, 2000).

16. Mona McCormick, "Critical Thinking and Library Instruction," *Reference Quarterly* 22, no. 34 (1983): 339.

17. Popper, *World of Propensities.*

18. Microsoft Monitor Research Services, "Find Stuff, Start Something," *Microsoft Monitor Weblog* (May 15, 2005): 1, www.microsoftmonitor.com/archives/2005/05/find_stuff_star.html (accessed July 31, 2007).

19. Evelyn Ng and Carl Bereiter, "Three Levels of Goal Orientation in Learning," *Journal of the Learning Sciences* 1, nos. 3–4 (1991): 243–71.

20. Brenda Sugrue, "A Theory-Based Framework for Assessing Domain-Specific Problem Solving Ability," *Educational Measurement: Issues and Practice* 14, no. 3 (1995): 31.

21. Louise Limberg, "Information Seeking and Learning Outcomes: A Study of the Interaction between Two Phenomena," *Scandinavian Public Library Quarterly* 31, no. 3 (1998): 28–31.

22. Gordon Wells, "Dialogue about Knowledge Building," in *Liberal Education in a Knowledge Society*, ed. Barry Smith, 111–38 (Chicago: Open Court, 2002).

23. Jurgen Haberma, *Knowledge and Human Interests* (Boston: Beacon Press, 1971).

24. Gregory Bateson, *Steps to an Ecology of Mind* (London: Paladin, 1973).

25. Mortimer Adler, *The Paideia Proposal: An Educational Manifesto* (New York: Macmillan, 1982).

26. Carl Bereiter and Marlene Scardamalia, "Rethinking Learning," in *The Handbook of Education and Human Development*, ed. David Olson and Nancy Torrance, 485–513 (Cambridge, MA: Basic Blackwell, 1996).

27. Leon James, "Creating an Online Learning Environment that Fosters Information Literacy, Autonomous Learning and Leadership: The Hawaii Online Generational Community-Classroom," *Trends and Issues in Online Instruction* (Spring 1997), www.soc.hawaii.edu/leonj/leonj/leonpsy/instructor/kcc/kcc97.html (accessed July 31, 2007).

28. Jack Mezirow, et al., *Learning as Transformation: Critical Perspectives on a Theory in Progress* (San Francisco: Jossey-Bass, 2000).

29. Michael Eraut, "Informal Learning in the Workplace," *Studies in Continuing Education* 26, no. 2 (2004): 247–73.

30. Chee Yip, Pui Cheung, and Cheng Sze, *Towards a Knowledge-Creating School* (Hong Kong: Pui Ching Middle School, 2004).

31. Jannica Heinstrom, "Fast Surfing, Broad Scanning and Deep Diving: The Influence of Personality and Study Approach on Students' Information-Seeking Behavior," *Journal of Documentation* 61, no. 2 (2005): 228–47.

32. Ecology Society of America, "Inquiry Framework: Levels of Student Ownership," tiee.ecoed.net/teach/framework.jpg (accessed July 3, 2007).

33. Ecology Society of America. "Inquiry Framework."

34. Robert Gagne, *The Conditions of Learning and Theory of Instruction*, 4th ed. (New York: Holt, Rinehart and Winston, 1985).

35. Sue Owen, "It Takes More Than Breadcrumbs to Learn Generic Skills: Collaborating to Improve Information Literacy" (paper presented at the HERDSA Annual Conference, Christchurch, New Zealand, July 7–9, 2003).

36. Peter Senge, *Presence* (Waltham, MA: Pegasus, 2004).

37. Lesley Farmer, "Developmental Socio-Emotional Behavior and Information Literacy" in *Information and Emotion: The Emergent Affective Paradigm in Information Behavior Research and Theory*, ed. Diane Nahl and Dania Bilal, 99–120 (Medford, NJ: Information Today, 2007).

38. Robin Nabi, "Exploring the Framing Effects of Emotion: Do Discrete Emotions Differentially Influence Information Accessibility, Information Seeking, and Policy Preference?" *Communication Research* 30, no. 2 (2003): 224–47.

39. Heilstrom, "Fast Surfing."

40. Maslow, *Motivation and Personality*.

41. Lawrence Kohlberg, *The Philosophy of Moral Development* (San Francisco: Harper & Row, 1981).

42. Benjamin Bloom, ed., *Taxonomy of Educational Objectives; the Classification of Educational Goals, by a Committee of College and University Examiners* (New York: Longmans, Green, 1956).

43. John Powell, *Why Am I Afraid to Tell You Who I Am?* (Niles, IL: Argus Communications, 1969).

44. Carol Kuhlthau, *Seeking Meaning: A Process Approach to Library and Information Services*, 2nd ed. (Westport, CT: Libraries Unlimited, 2004).

45. Deborah Butler and Sylvie Cartier, "Multiple Complementary Methods for Understanding Self-Regulated Learning as Situated in Context" (paper presented at the American Educational Research Association conference, Montreal, April 2005).

46. Jaime Villegas, Birger Rapp, and Bengt Saven, *Simulation Supported Industrial Training* (Linkoping, Sweden: Linkoping University, 2005).

47. Rob Reilly, Barry Kort, and Rosalind Picard, "External Representation of Learning Process and Domain Knowledge: Affective State as a Determinate of Its Structure and Function" (paper presented at the conference of the IEEE Artificial Intelligence in Education, San Antonio, TX, May 2001).

48. Rosalind Picard and Shaundra Daily, "Evaluating Affective Interactions: Alternatives to Asking What Users Feel" (paper presented at the CHI workshop on Evaluation Affective Interfaces, Portland, OR, April 2005).

49. American Association of School Librarians and Association for Educational Communication and Technology, *Information Power: Building Partnerships for Learning* (Chicago: American Library Association, 1998), 6.

50. Pamela Kobelski and Mary Reichel, "Conceptual Frameworks for Bibliographic Instruction," *Journal of Academic Librarianship* 7 (May 1981): 73–77.

51. Harold Tuckett and Carla Stoffle, "Learning Theory and the Self-Reliant Library User," *Reference Quarterly* 24 (Fall 1984): 58–66.

· 4 ·

The Conditions for Information Literacy Assessment

*I*nformation literacy as a set of skills or a mind-set can be seen as valuable from the individual's point of view, to a programmatic scale, to a site or system level, to a governmental scale, all the way to an international perspective. The true test of its value, however, is in its implementation and assessment. At each level, the conditions for learning and practicing information literacy must be explicitly identified and assessed in order to optimize the factors for student success. Both internal assurances and external accountability need to be in place in order to ensure that all students are given equitable and ongoing opportunities to learn these skills and apply them to a variety of academic and personal contexts. Only then will students themselves value information literacy and strive to become information literate.

THE BIG PICTURE: THE CULTURAL CONTEXT

Regardless of the scale, when people form together into stable groups with sustained shared value/belief systems and normative expectations/behaviors, they comprise a culture. UNESCO (United Nations Educational, Scientific, and Cultural Organization) defines culture as "the set of distinctive spiritual, material, intellectual and emotional features of society or a social group, and that it encompasses, in addition to art and literature, lifestyles, ways of living together, value systems, traditions and beliefs."[1] An individual may belong to several cultures: family, worksite, neighborhood, race, profession, social club, political party, country. Likewise, a group may belong to several cultures; teacher librarians may be members of a site library staff, a union, a district, a state organization, a national organization, and an international organization.

Some of these cultures may overlap or even contradict, in which case, the individual or group must either live with the disequilibrium or resolve the conflict (i.e., reject one or the other, reject both, or incorporate parts of each). A culture may also be measured in terms of how cohesive it is in terms of inside and outside pressures; if conflict arises from outside its borders, do members stay within the culture or switch allegiance to the other culture?

Culture plays a significant role in community attitudes toward education, which informs information literacy instruction and practice. Seufert identifies a number of learning system dimensions that can be culturally profiled.[2]

- *Educational epistemology:* to pass on knowledge, to preserve the status quo, to socialize, to prepare workers, to help students self-actualize
- *Pedagogical epistemology:* instructivism to constructivist
- *Underlying psychology:* behavioral to cognitive
- *Goal orientation:* sharply focused to unfocused, short-term versus long-term, individualistic versus society
- *Experimental value:* abstract to concrete
- *Role of instructor:* master lecturer to egalitarian facilitator, interpreter to questioner
- *Value of errors:* errorless learning to learning from experience
- *Motivation:* extrinsic to intrinsic
- *Structure:* high to low
- *Accommodation of individual differences:* none to multifaceted
- *Learning control:* none to unrestricted
- *User activity:* rote to generative
- *Cooperative learning:* none to integral

For instance, if a cultural norm about the role of the instructor is to tell students what is right and true, then independent critical evaluation of information might be discouraged. If a culture values independent thinking and competitiveness, then collaborative research might be considered cheating. If the culture believes in a highly structure educational experience, then students may feel lost in loosely defined or student-defined projects.

Just as the meaning of information is cultural contextualized, so too are the conditions for information literacy. As teacher librarians seek support for information literacy, they need to examine the cultural landscape in order to discern—and align with—shared values and expectations. Ignorance or denial of cultural norms will spell disaster for information literacy initiatives. If the most influential culture shares the goals and strategies of information literacy, then the teacher librarian has a natural "in." If the culture is strong, then the path to success is even better paved. On the other hand, a strong culture that discounts information literacy and has a closed attitude can pose challenges. A culture that undervalues information literacy may be won over if they have a more accepting nature—and can be persuaded by an overlapping stronger culture to join in the overarching goal.

THE BASIS: ACCESS TO INFORMATION

While it may seem self-evident, for students to become information literate requires that they encounter information and engage in it. Textbooks and other materials given to students provide preselected, appropriate information that can serve as a controlled environment in which students can comprehend and use information. Classroom teachers are usually comfortable in this closed universe because they know the material themselves and can resolve student problems predictably. Teaching students how to discern such prescribed information does develop critical-thinking skills. However, it does not address a vital part of information literacy: selection.

On the other hand, if students are left to their own devices to find information, they are likely to seek the path of least resistance (as do many adults): asking friends and family, using resources found at home. Young students are often unaware of the variety of possible resources and centers of information, and may even classify some resources as purely entertainment (e.g., television and radio) rather than recognize their informational role, per se.[3]

The school library provides an effective bridge between classroom materials and the vast world of information. The physical collection includes a variety of selected educational resources at different reading levels so students can choose relevant and developmentally appropriate materials for their task at hand. This informational universe is still controlled, but it offers opportunities for students to self-regulate their information interaction, and teacher librarians can help them develop those skills.

If the library has Internet connectivity, students can access subscription databases and digital reference sources as well as filtered websites. This information universe is almost limitless, but, again, the teacher librarian can guide students in navigating the sea of information and in learning how to select, evaluate, and use appropriate sources efficiently.

The extent to which the library can provide information resources—and access to them—creates the parameters for school-controlled conditions for information literacy. The accessibility and quality of those resources depends on the school community: staff presence and expertise, facilities, financial and management decisions, and policies.

A KNOWLEDGE MANAGEMENT MODEL
OF INFORMATION LITERACY FACTORS

Resources in themselves are not enough to guarantee information literacy; students still need an environment that is conducive to learning the processes by which they can locate, evaluate, use, and share information. Such an environment requires the effective allocation and management of material and human resources.

Knowledge management has become a buzzword in today's business world. Increasingly, enterprises realize the importance of intellectual capital. Companies hire individuals with tacit (internal) knowledge and socialize them within the company so that such knowledge will be made explicit and shared with their employees so that new combinations of ideas can emerge and then be internalized; dynamic organizations encourage dialogue between tactic and explicit knowledge. This SECI (Socialization/Externalization/ Combination/Internalization) model, developed by Nonaka and Takeuchi,[4] exemplifies the use of information literacy to advance a common good. Knowledge management consists of the systematic management of such collective information: gathering, organizing, sharing, and analyzing it. By providing on-demand access to managed knowledge, entities can deal effectively with situations that emerge by drawing upon cumulated experience.[5] Organizational systems expert Bellinger contends that individual information literacy can lead to informed group decision making. It has become evident that information literacy impacts the societal whole—and that the society's status impacts educational attempts to prepare information literate citizens.

Nonaka further refined the SECI model by positing two organizational approaches to amplify organizational knowledge by individual contributions: a middle up-down model, where a team leader helps synthesize the group's ideas and facilitates their impact on others, and a hypertext model, where formal and informal links among individuals and groups optimize relationships between ideas.[6] Teacher librarians can foster information literacy well in both organizational models with their connection across the school community.

Osborn, Thomas, and Hartnack have applied a knowledge management model to educational settings and particularized it for information literacy efforts.[7] The following factors need to be considered in the broader educational sphere as well as within each school setting.

- *General knowledge:* reading and writing skills; critical-thinking skills; ability to learn independently using a wide variety of sources

- *Subject knowledge:* in-depth, domain-specific knowledge gained from academic preparation and experience (e.g., how does a mathematician think)
- *Information literacy:* knowledge and use of information literacy and associated skills; belief in the value, promotion, and support of information literacy in teaching and learning
- *Cultural knowledge:* inherited and learned knowledge and values about the dominant culture and other cultures; attitudes and norms surrounding information literacy
- *Languages:* attitude about, knowledge of, and use of dominant language and other languages used by the community; understanding of language learning processes; relationship of language to information literacy
- *Intellectual capital:* knowledgeable individuals who have the potential to impact information literacy efforts; attitudes and values of intellectual capital
- *Educational professionalism:* values and practices of teaching and learning related to information literacy; ethical code of conduct; active participation within the educational community; ongoing professional development
- *Educational collaboration:* communication and joint efforts among stakeholders that impact information literacy
- *Leadership and management policies:* structure of decision-making processes; development of student outcomes relative to information literacy; resource allocation practices relative to information literacy
- *Educational policies:* board-approved policies and mandates relative to information literacy; monitoring of resources and services; accountability efforts
- *Legal and religious policies:* societally derived regulations and value systems that impact information literacy (e.g., privacy, access to information)
- *Knowledge of communities:* cultural values and practices, sociopolitical issues, and economic issues as they relate to information literacy
- *Partnerships:* mutually supportive relationships (e.g., suppliers, donors) between the school community and the community at large that impact information literacy

These factors do not necessarily advance information literacy. For example, if policies provide no money for joint planning time or library collections, information literacy will be impeded. Ignorance about information literacy or inaction in its support also negatively impacts information literacy. In short, each of these factors—or stakeholders—needs to become aware of (1) information literacy's importance and (2) the positive role that it can play in information literacy's endeavor.

CURRICULUM AS A CONDITION
FOR INFORMATION LITERACY

Information literacy needs to be realized through its presence in the curriculum, which is in turn impacted by the model's factors. It needs to be explicitly addressed through direct instruction and meaningful learning activities, and it needs to be integrated throughout the school program rather than isolated in some sort of parallel universe of learning. Its assessment should be an essential aspect of whole-school planning and implementation.

While curricular presence is important, it is not enough. As early as 1989, the American Library Association's Presidential Committee on Information Literacy asserted, "What is called for is not a new information studies curriculum but, rather, a restructuring of the learning process. Textbooks, workbooks, and lectures must yield to a learning process based on information resources available for learning and problem solving throughout people's lifetimes."[8]

In short, to support information literacy, curriculum throughout the educational community, needs to look different. Basic information literacy skills cross disciplines and grades: identifying an information task, determining key words, reading information, evaluating resources, communicating information. However, information literacy needs to be contextualized in order to make meaning.

- *General knowledge:* lifelong learning skills are integrated throughout the curriculum
- *Subject knowledge:* domain-specific resources and opportunities for contextualized interaction with them are provided
- *Information literacy:* teacher librarians provide a full range of resources and services that support the curriculum
- *Cultural knowledge:* curriculum gains meaning through cultural context
- *Languages:* reading and writing form the basis for accessing, understanding, sharing, and generating information
- *Intellectual capital:* administrators hire, train, and promote knowledgeable staff who incorporate information literacy into the curriculum

- *Educational professionalism:* instructional design and implementation reflect information literacy values and practices effectively and ethically; a learning community exists in support of information literacy–infused curriculum
- *Educational collaboration:* communication and joint efforts among stakeholders support information literacy incorporation into the curriculum
- *Leadership and management policies:* scheduling facilitates educational collaboration; information literacy resources are allocated
- *Educational policies:* boards approve and oversee policies requiring information literacy student outcomes and curriculum that address those outcomes; boards hold stakeholders accountable for information literacy efforts
- *Legal and religious policies:* societally derived regulations and value systems support information literacy (e.g., privacy is respected, access to information is insured)
- *Knowledge of communities:* the educational system is aware of community-based information literacy values and practices, and facilities their involvement in the curriculum
- *Partnerships:* stakeholders seek opportunities for ways to partner in support of curriculum that incorporated information literacy (e.g., Internet connectivity discounts, joint library programs and internships)

Stakeholders can be clustered in order to examine the conditions needed for information literacy to be advanced.

INTELLECTUAL CAPITAL AS A CONDITION FOR INFORMATION LITERACY

The heart of education is its people. Education exists because of the students and is only as effective as the personnel who facilitate student learning. The entire school community has the potential to contribute to information literacy efforts both individually and collectively:

- *Principals* model and inspire the community to a shared vision of information literacy, supervise teachers and hold them accountable to information literacy goals, seek support and funding, and advocate for the library media program.[9]
- *Classroom teachers* provide content and developmental context, design and implement instruction and learning activities, and assess results relative to information literacy.

- *Teacher librarians* work with all students and teachers across the curriculum in terms of information literacy processes, teach information literacy, promote reading, and manage information resources and facilities.
- *Technology specialists* manage technology resources, help train personnel, and deal with technology plans and policies that impact information literacy.
- *Reading specialists* diagnose and suggest interventions for struggling readers, share bibliographies of leveled reading, and assess facilities in order to optimize reading environments.
- *Special education specialists* diagnose and suggest interventions for students with special needs, suggest assistive technologies and other appropriate resources, and suggest facility accommodations to facilitate information literacy for students with special needs.
- *Counselors and psychologists* address students' academic and personal difficulties, coordinate postsecondary learning activities, and connect the school and the community, all of which can impact information literacy efforts.
- *Health personnel* can make sure the library is a safe environment and suggest appropriate accommodations for students with health challenges so they can become information literate.
- *Cocurricular personnel* (e.g., activities personnel) link information literacy to personal interests through content and original expression.
- *School board members* make policies about the school program and resource allocations to support the program.[10]

As mentioned in the previous chapter, for students to become information literate, the rest of the school community needs to be information literate. Too often it is assumed that since adults have graduated from secondary and possibly postsecondary institutions, they are information literate themselves. While educators survive in society and may have learned to think like a historian or other domain-specific expert, they might not have explicitly addressed information literacy processes or know how to design learning activities that integrate such direct training. On the other hand, teacher librarians do not possess in-depth knowledge about all curricula. Rather, the goal is to identify and complement each other's areas of expertise with the intent of "filling in the information literacy gaps" so that needed structures and processes are in place for the stakeholders to collaboratively provide the conditions for information literacy to be achieved by all students.

Underlying assumptions about information literacy lead to decisions about information literacy *instruction*. Historically, librarians used phrases such as "library instruction," "user education," and "bibliographic instruction," each of which reflects a specific philosophy about the relationship among librarian, user, and resources. The first, for instance, focuses on a sense of place or learning environment: the universe for information use. The second term focuses on the recipient of information, with an implication that the person is somehow deficient. The third term focuses on the *content* of instruction, with an emphasis on technical skills.

Probably the most important factor in using intellectual capital is instructional design and implementation:

- Identifying the desired student outcomes
- Identifying the content/information literacy standards and concrete indicators
- Identifying relevant and available material resources
- Designing instruction: content, delivery
- Designing learning activities
- Assessing processes and products throughout (i.e., prerequisite skills, current student knowledge and needs, behaviors and attitudes throughout the experience, results)

Each step is critical, and problems at any step can negatively impact the final result. Fortunately, when each step is well executed, the results demonstrate how the whole is greater than the parts.

Likewise, instructional design transcends any one instructor since it is possible that a group might develop an interactive online tutorial independent of any specific course or designated instructor. Particularly as just-in-time and situated learning are gaining educational credence, instructional design constitutes a thoughtful process in itself. Additionally, the incorporation of self-standing learning objects into instruction also speaks to the potential modularity of instructional design.

Clearly, instructional design not only refers to a one-time effort, but also needs to be implemented as a schoolwide endeavor so that all stakeholders can contribute—and can depend on each other to provide the prerequisite skills that articulate the curriculum and optimize learning.

LEADERSHIP AS A CONDITION FOR INFORMATION LITERACY

For intellectual capital to be wisely "invested" and used, it needs to be supported through resources and expectations that good leadership can facilitate.

In 2004, the Australian government established a national research project, "Leadership and Learning with Information and Communication Technologies," to investigate school-based leadership models that support teacher development and student learning through the incorporation of ICT (information and communication technology). Principals were identified as leaders for

- spearheading a shared vision of what is valued in teaching and learning,
- developing a school culture,
- setting the instructional direction, and
- developing leadership in others.[11]

Focusing on the principal's role in mainstreaming information literacy instruction, Campbell found similar roles:

- vision building
- evolutionary planning and restructuring
- resource mobilization
- monitoring and problem solving
- empowerment[12]

Relative to information literacy, the principal and other administrators can play a pivotal role,

- creating a school culture of collaboration and learning;
- scheduling time for collaborative planning and assessment;
- recognizing teacher librarians as professional partners in the school's program;
- appointing teacher librarians to curriculum and other decision-making committees;
- encouraging teacher librarians to present at staff development sessions;
- delegating responsibility to teacher librarians, such as budgeting and program management;
- seeking outside support and funding to facilitate information literacy;
- recognizing and rewarding information literacy efforts; and
- advocating for information literacy within the school and larger community.[13]

Teacher librarians must collaborate closely with administrators to facilitate active advocacy and support, aligning the library program's information literacy agenda to the school's vision and strategic plan. The library program can model best practices relative to information literacy. Teacher librarians can also support administrators' efforts that incorporate information literacy.

As important as the principal and other administrators are as leaders, an even more powerful model of leadership is that of collaborative leadership. This model is based on an inclusive environment where information and expertise is shared, and the community is empowered to act upon a collective vision. Both the cognitive and affective domains are acknowledged, which can facilitate more sensitivity to cultural realities.[14] Nissen, Merrigan, and Kraft identify four tasks needed to implement collaborative leadership:

1. Plan for collaboration
2. Identify current formal and informal leaders
3. Identify collaborative leadership tasks
4. Balance short- and long-term outcomes[15]

This collaborative model also facilitates the typical teacher librarian leadership style: leading from the middle. In her study of situating information literacy, Asselin asserts that "teacher librarians need to reposition themselves as leaders in the new literacies required for learning and solving problems with the Internet and ICT. There is a clear need for instructional leadership in existing critical-level new literacy learning outcomes and in assessment and evaluation of all aspects of the new literacies of the Information Age."[16]

In terms of information literacy advocacy, teacher librarians can lead in several arenas:

- Developing curriculum that incorporates information literacy
- Collecting and analyzing student work to assess student information literacy levels
- Conducting literacy reviews and action research projects to provide evidence-based best practice about information literacy
- Developing and implementing staff development about information literacy
- Serving on decision-making boards that allocate resources for information literacy
- Creating policies that value and support information literacy
- Collaborating with community members who are involved in information literacy efforts

COMMUNITY AS A CONDITION FOR
INFORMATION LITERACY

Education is ultimately a community-based endeavor. Even with national curriculum and standards, how information literacy is played out depends on the community's resources and expectations. This impact may seem short-termed as societies become more transient, but it may be equally argued that the information literacy education of local youth may influence the future of people across the sea—and the nature of information itself.

On a broader scale, the public sector plays several significant roles in support of information literacy.

- *Facilitation:* providing financial and political backing on information literacy initiatives; providing venues for discussing information literacy priorities; advancing information communication infrastructure
- *Regulation:* providing and enforcing ICT laws and regulations; accrediting educational institutions; establishing ICT standards and guidelines
- *Use:* bridging educational and economic information literacy applications; identifying and meeting information needs; producing and disseminating information; keeping current in information literacy trends; promoting ICT development and education[17]

School personnel, and teacher librarians, need to assess the community's material and human resources as a means to enrich students' engagement with information.

- *Who produces information?* Businesses, government, education, agencies, organizations, groups, individuals
- *How is information disseminated?* Newspapers, radio, television, telephone, signs, posters, company memos, church bulletins, Internet, loud speakers, street talk
- *What centers of information exist?* Libraries, other schools and institutes of higher learning, museums, historical sites, community agencies, community centers, religious centers
- *Who has information literacy expertise?* Librarians, educators, technology specialists, information producers and disseminators

Together with community members, school personnel can determine the potential role of community resources with regard to student information literacy: suppliers of information, instructors, clients of student information projects (e.g., reading to toddlers, tutoring children, creating community informational web portals), disseminators of student informational products. In this respect, service-learning provides authentic experiences where students can apply their information literacy skills and can contribute to their community in meaningful ways.

It should be noted that when educational information literacy practices veer too far from community values and norms, then disconnects occur: between teachers and families, between children and families, between administrators and community leaders. On the other hand, education and community can inform each other about novel views regarding information literacy and the evolving world, so that both parties can adjust to an unforeseeable future. Otherwise, either will be stuck in the past, unable to survive or compete successfully.

School personnel must be aware of these cultural values in order to validate current beliefs and bridge to new understandings. When schools serve a variety of cultures, which may clash, then administrators and teacher librarians need to focus on identifying overriding common information literacy values and goals that all community members can agree to. Otherwise, students may get mixed messages about information and its use, and instruction may be undermined by family values. Little positive learning will occur. Therefore, school personnel may find that they need to educate the community about information literacy so that they feel less threatened by change and more empowered to help young people. To this end, teacher librarians should find other educational colleagues such as academic librarians with whom to strategize.

COLLABORATION AS A CONDITION FOR INFORMATION LITERACY

Even if all the ingredients for information literacy are in place, little student learning will occur if those ingredients are not effectively combined and implemented. Too often, educational stakeholders exist in a mental silo, carrying out their own agenda with little regard to its impact on others—or realization that others' efforts might benefit them. Particularly in today's educational environment where schools are asked to assume so many responsibilities, ongoing communication and collaboration are key for optimal results.

Collaboration can be considered along a couple of dimensions: the parties involved, and the quality of the collaboration itself. The former can range from two individuals to the entire school and beyond. Since any two entities can form a potential collaborative relationship, when several entities collaborate group dynamics can emerge. Figure 4.1 shows two possible scenarios. The

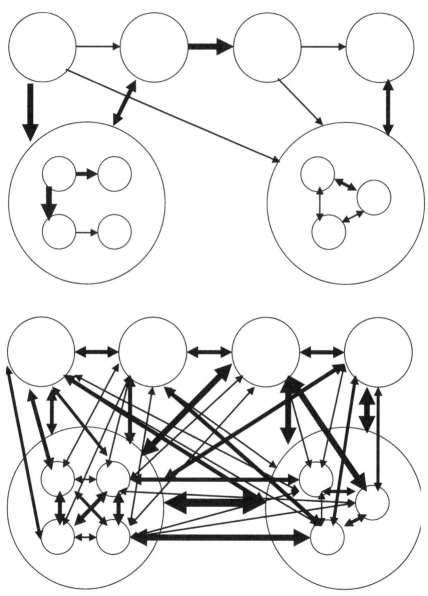

Figure 4.1.   Sets of Circles

smaller circles represent individuals, and the larger circles represent groups. The arrow direction represents the direction of communication. The arrow's thickness represents the strength of the relationship. The top image reflects a traditional top-down communications situation with little interaction. The bottom image, on the other hand, reflects a rich interdependent collaborative environment.

Groups automatically form in school settings because people have similar tasks: by position (e.g., teachers), by target audience (e.g., grade levels), by content expertise (e.g., mathematics), by seniority (e.g., first-year staff). Each person within the group assumes at least one psychological role, such as expert, enthusiast, processor, problem solver, scapegoat, and so forth. Over time, as members negotiate roles and behaviors, they develop norms that help them sustain their existence and facilitate their efforts. As goals are reached or members change, the group reforms.[18] When a group with common values and goals strives together to improve, it can become a community of practice. The members build a joint body of knowledge, and help new members become contributing participants.[19]

In the field of collaborative learning, several key elements comprise best practice. These elements apply equally well to schoolwide collaboration.

- *Heterogeneous groups* facilitate cross-fertilization of different ideas.
- *Academic tasks* provide meaningful direction.
- *Social tasks* facilitate trust and interdependence.
- *Distributed leadership* offers multiple opportunities for broad-based decision making and optimizes implementation.
- *Group autonomy* gives people more authority to control their behavior.
- *Group accountability* reinforces interdependence.
- *Individual accountability* makes each person responsible for his or her contribution to the overall goal.

As might be guessed, both individuals and groups can act as entities in collaborative efforts.

In any case, though, for those elements to be effective, tasks and roles need to be clearly delineated, and efforts need to be monitored and assessed.[20] In investigating possible inhibitors and enablers of information literacy efforts within the school community, Kuhlthau found three primary inhibitors: lack of time, confusion of roles, and poorly designed assignments. Four basic enablers he found were team-teaching approach, sharing understanding of learning as a constructivist process, shared commitment to lifelong learning, and competence in developing learning activities and strategies.[21] Teacher librarians need to assess their environments to determine what inhibitors and enhancers exist so they can plan strategically in their pursuit of an information literacy agenda.

PLANS AND POLICIES AS A CONDITION FOR INFORMATION LITERACY

For information literacy to be supported, plans and policies must be in place and monitored. Policies may also set up the conditions for information literacy planning and implementation. The California Department of Education has identified representative focus area policies that can impact information literacy.

- *Staffing:* established staffing levels for library programs, both professional and paraprofessional; volunteer staff policy; hiring and evaluation criteria; district or system leadership and coordination responsibilities; established lines of authority; staff development policy
- *Collaboration:* teaching staff evaluation criteria on collaboration; scheduling facilitating collaboration; required representation by library on committees
- *Access:* facility hours and services; circulation policies; resource sharing policies
- *Resources:* selection policy; challenged materials policy; acceptable use policy; disposal policy; funding policy
- *Student achievement:* graduation requirements; expected student outcomes; assessment processes and analysis[22]

While plans and policies are necessary for information literacy efforts, they are not sufficient in themselves. Policies should stem from identified needs and values. For policies to be effective, they should be created by all of the stakeholders who are influenced by them. Thus, a policy on information literacy student outcomes should include input from library staff, students, faculty, administrators, and possibly community members. Otherwise, the school community will not have a sense of ownership for the policy and may be unwilling to enforce it; the policy will likely be ineffective. Generally speaking, the smaller the distance between the decision maker and the person who implements those decisions, the more likely that such decisions will be implemented. National plans and policies can be extremely difficult to monitor unless a thorough infrastructure is in place to audit local efforts and a strong incentive program (or punitive action) motivates stakeholders.

AN INPUT-OUTPUT MODEL OF INFORMATION LITERACY

To insure that students become information literacy requires that the *conditions* for achieving information literacy be met. All the stakeholders must align information literacy with their goals and objectives, curriculum, teaching and learning (for the entire community), assessment, and governance. Another way to approach this task is to think of the entire school as a system of inputs and outputs.

- *Input products* are resources that contribute to the goal of information literacy: people (e.g., staff, students, families, community members), facilities (e.g., rooms, furniture, connectivity), material resources (e.g., print, equipment, supplies), curriculum, policies, budget, time, expertise.
- *Input processes* are actions using input resources that are intended to facilitate information literacy: designing and delivering instruction (e.g., teacher librarians, classroom teachers, technology specialists), collaborating and networking, creating documents to support information literacy (e.g., bibliographies, reference guides, web tutorials), doing staff development, allocating resources (e.g., line item budgets, hiring staff), acquiring resources (e.g., collection development, professional reading).
- *Output processes* are actions that demonstrate information literacy: student activity (e.g., reading, communicating, carrying out scientific experiments, enrolling in information literacy–rich courses), staff activity (e.g., using technology when teaching, interpreting data, revising curriculum, discussing reading), governance activity (e.g., revising policies, informing the community, seeking grants).
- *Output products* are new resources created as a result of information literacy: student work (e.g., reports, presentations, grades/marks/graduation), staff work (e.g., curriculum documents, reports, revised curriculum), governance work (e.g., policies that support information literacy, increased budgets to support information literacy, revised hiring criteria that require information literacy).
- *Impact* is the ultimate, long-term influence of information literacy: lifelong and self-sustained learning, prepared employees, improved teaching, a community culture that supports and demonstrates information literacy.

Table 4.1 offers a visual way to map out the indicators that demonstrate the conditions for meeting one aspect of information literacy: *evaluate information effectively*.

Table 4.1. Indicators That Demonstrate the Conditions for Evaluating Information Effectively

	Teacher Librarians	Classroom Teachers	Support Staff	Administrators/ Board	Students	Community
Input Products	Library facility; collection, web portal; tech resources; info lit curriculum; expertise	Classes; tech; texts; class collections; curriculum; expertise	Offices; tech, specialized collections; expertise	Budget, schedule, tech, expertise; plans	Personal and family resources and expertise	Public/private libraries/ agencies; resources; expertise
Input Processes	Research skill; identify skill standards and indicators; assess need; identify relevant curricular areas; design and teach skills to school community; select and manage resources and other library services (e.g., reader's advisory)	Identify skill standards and indicators; assess need; identify relevant curricular areas; design and teach skills; select and manage resources	Identify skill standards and indicators; assess need; identify relevant services; teach or promote skills; select and manage resources	Develop/ implement policies for skill standards and indicators; gather and analyze assessment need data; allocate resources; supervise staff; manage resources; set and manage schedule; network with community	Demonstrate current skill; identify need	Identify skills needed within community; create information; manage resources

Output Processes	Assess skill; modify teaching and learning activities; manage resources and services; increase expertise	Assess skill; modify teaching and learning activities; manage resources; increase expertise	Assess skill; modify teaching and learning activities; manage resources; increase expertise	Gather and assess data; revise resource allocation; monitor staff; revise schedule; increase expertise; communicate impact; revise practices and documents	Read critically; choose resources; compare information; communicate evaluation	Modify information; modify services; gain expertise
Output Products	Improved collection	Improved curriculum	Improved resources	Improved curriculum; improved staff; revised policies	Evaluation documents; marks/grades	Improved documents and resources
Impact	Improved services and resources; greater expertise	Improved teaching and resources; greater expertise	Improved services and resources; greater expertise	Improved governance; more expert school community	Critical information user; effective decision maker	Improved services and resources

It should be noted that this model focuses on student outcomes, which reflects a student-centered educational philosophy; students are the "ends" and inputs are the "means." Many school systems still operate on a content-based philosophy in which students have to "plug in" to the curriculum, the latter serving as the "end" goal. Interestingly, even that traditional model can incorporate information literacy. For instance, teaching the scientific method, which could be one content area, implicitly involves information literacy processes; teacher librarians can make that implicit knowledge explicit. The limitation of the traditional model, though, is that it does not stress lifelong learning habits nor does it tend to address individual learning differences. Thus, the power of information literacy may be missed in the process.

To optimize information literacy efforts, the entire enterprise must value and work collaboratively to enable students to evaluate skills effectively. Broad-based planning also offers a stronger argument for appropriate resource allocation. The responsibilities are shared—as are the benefits and successes. Such cross-site validation requires ongoing communication and monitoring in order to optimize instruction and learning. For instance, if history teachers know that students learn how to evaluate websites in language arts classes, then they can focus on teaching students how to evaluate print-based primary sources. Likewise, science and math teachers can collaborate when teaching numerical data analysis so that students can apply that skill when conducting science experiments. By mapping the entire curriculum, folding in information literacy skills, the school community has a value-added basis for systematic planning, implementation, and assessment. The result? A total learning community that values information literacy.

THE CHANGING LANDSCAPE

As laudatory as these efforts appear, they require a flexible mind-set and organizational structure. Because information and information literacy changes constantly, because the world at large changes constantly, the school community must respond to these dynamics if they hope to have any chance of facilitating student information literacy achievement. Simultaneously, schools serve as institutions of the dominant culture. Therefore, tensions exist between established power and purposeful improvement. Some of the current trends in education include

- *School purpose*: from selecting the best to ensuring that all students learn;

- *Nature of knowledge*: from absolute truths to making meaning;
- *Nature of learning*: from passive reception to active engagement;
- *Nature of teaching*: from sage on the stage to guide on the side;
- *Curriculum*: from a highly structured sequence set of fixed knowledge to a cyclical set of contextualized perspectives;
- *Leadership*: from hierarchical authority to transformative empowerment;
- *Assessment*: from standardized input points to integrated and outcomes-centered cycles of inquiry.[23]

These patterns are not absolutes that teacher librarians can count on. Rather, they point out options that can be called upon when discussing education options.

All the conditions for information literacy—resources, intellectual capital, leadership, community, plans and policies, collaboration—need to be continuously audited, assessed, and negotiated in order to provide the most efficient educational experiences to support information literacy. Teacher librarians must be aware of these changing dynamics, and serve as change agents, providing appropriate leadership via professional development, communities of practice, and school reform efforts.

Teacher librarians cannot force change on the rest of the school community, however. Even "islands" of innovation are not as successful as systemwide approaches to change because the former may not be scalable. These islands usually involve close-knit relationships among a small group of educators: a closed culture. Even though outside funding can help these islands achieve long-term status, the goals and expectations are usually very narrow and specific. Schoolwide initiatives, on the other hand, enlist the principal's support, leverage larger-scale resources, generate supporting policies, and encourage the establishment of support mechanisms.[24] Therefore, teacher librarians should strive to leverage the use of collaboration and distributed leadership to facilitate the conditions for information literacy success.

NOTES

1. UNESCO, "Universal Declaration on Cultural Diversity," www.unesco.org/education/imld_2002/unversal_decla.shtml (accessed July 22, 2006).

2. Sabine Seufert, "Cultural Perspectives," in *Handbook on Information Technology for Education and Training*, ed. Heimo Adelsberger, Betty Collis, and Jan Pawlowski, 418 (Munich: Springer-Verlag, 2002).

3. Andrew Shenton and Pat Dixon, "The Development of Young People's Information-Seeking Behaviour," *Library & Information Research* 28, no. 90 (2004): 31–39.

4. Ikujiro Nonaka and Hirotaka Takeuchi, *The Knowledge-Creating Company* (New York: Oxford University Press, 1995).

5. Gene Bellinger, "Knowledge Management—Emerging Perspectives," Systems Thinking, www.systems-thinking.org/kmgmt/kmgmt.htm (accessed July 22, 2006).

6. Ikujiro Nonaka, "A Dynamic Theory of Organizational Knowledge Creation," *Organization Science* 5, no. 1 (1994): 14–37.

7. Marilyn Osborn, Ethel Thomas, and Dorthea Hartnack, "An Evolving Model of Knowledge Management in Education and the South African Reality: How Knowledge Management, Information Literacy and Reading Skills Are Information Learning at a High School and a Primary School in Gauteng, South Africa," in *Information Leadership in a Culture of Change: IASL Reports, 2005*, ed. Sandra Lee et al., chap. 32, pp. 1–15 (Erie, PA: International Association of School Librarianship, 2005).

8. American Library Association, *Presidential Committee on Information Literacy: Final Report* (Chicago: American Library Association, 1989), 7.

9. Diane Oberg, "Principal Support: What Does It Mean to Teacher-Librarians?" (paper presented at the annual conference of the International Association of School Librarianship, Worcester, UK, August 1995).

10. Lesley Farmer, *Collaborating with Administrators and Educational Support Staff* (New York: Neal-Schuman, 2007).

11. Kathryn Moyle, "Leadership and Learning with ICT: Voices from the Profession" (paper presented at the Ed-Media conference, Orlando, FL, June 2006), 89–96.

12. Barbara Campbell, "High School Principal Roles and Implementation Themes for Mainstreaming Information Literacy Instruction" (PhD diss., University of Connecticut, 1994).

13. James Henri, *The School Curriculum: A Collaborative Approach to Learning*, 2nd ed. (Wagga Wagga, Australia: New South Wales Center for Library Studies, 1988), 42–44.

14. David Chrislip, *The Collaborative Leadership Fieldbook* (San Francisco: Jossey-Bass, 2002).

15. Laura Nissen, Daniel Merrigan, and M. Katherine Kraft, "Moving Mountains Together: Strategic Community Leadership and Systems Change," *Child Welfare* 84, no. 2 (2005): 12–140.

16. Marlene Asselin, "Teaching Information Skills in the Information Age," *School Libraries Worldwide* 11, no. 1 (2005): 33.

17. Raymond Khoury, "National ICT Priorities" (paper presented at ICT Lebanon 2004: The Arab Technology for Development Conference, Beirut, September 23, 2004), www.pca.org.lb/docs/dr.%20raymond%20khoury.ppt (accessed July 21, 2006).

18. David Johnson, *Cooperative Learning in the Classroom* (Alexandria, VA: Association for Supervision and Curriculum Development, 1994).

19. Etienne Wenger, *Communities of Practice: Learning, Meaning, and Identity* (Cambridge: Cambridge University Press, 1998).

20. Lesley Farmer, *Cooperative Learning Activities in the Library Media Center*, 2nd ed. (Westport, CT: Libraries Unlimited, 1999), 2–5.

21. Carol Kuhlthau, *Seeking Meaning: A Process Approach to Library and Information Services*, 2nd ed. (Westport, CT: Libraries Unlimited, 2004).

22. California Department of Education, Elementary Teaching and Learning Division and the High School Teaching and Learning Division, *Check It Out!* (Sacramento: California Department of Education, 1998).

23. James Thompson, "Resource-Based Learning Can Be the Backbone of Reform Improvement," *Information Library. NASSP Bulletin* (May 1991).

24. Alona Forkosh-Baruch, David Mioduser, and Rafi Nashmias, "Diffusion Patterns of ICT-Based Pedagogical Innovations" (paper presented at the Ed-Media conference, Orlando, FL, June 2006), 64.

The Role of Assessment

$\mathcal{A}$ssessment is a key factor in information literacy because it determines what needs to be known and performed under what conditions (e.g., time frame, location, method of demonstration). Assessment can measure the status quo of information literacy and the conditions supporting information literacy learning. Once an educational system or library system can agree on assessment tools and procedures, they can use them to diagnose gaps in learning, and use the results to plan interventions in an effective manner. Assessments can also facilitate communication within and across educational communities in order to develop best practices. It is also important to determine which assessment elements are culturally or societally bound and which elements have international implications.

THE CORE ROLE OF ASSESSMENT:
STUDENT ACHIEVEMENT

What is the bottom line in assessing information literacy? Determining student information competence. The educational community needs to consider this point as the lynchpin for all its information literacy assessment endeavors. Moreover, its vision and raison-d'etre should be information competence for *all* students. In the final analysis, it doesn't matter how many books or teacher librarians a school has, but how those resources are used to ensure that all students become information literate.

Of course, the school community needs to define what is desirable through the establishment of information literacy standards. Then it needs to develop valid and reliable indicators to assess student information literacy: what is "good enough" under what specific conditions. Based on assessment data analysis, the school community can then conduct a needs assessment of its program to determine what resources and actions must be in place and implemented in order to advance and support student information literacy.

Once those conditions for supporting information literacy endeavors are defined, they can then be used as outcomes in themselves and can be assessed in light of their quality and their impact on student learning. That is, student information literacy can be assessed within the context of the value-added efforts of the school's program.

What assessment questions are asked—and how the assessment is administered—obviously shapes the answers. Thus, if the role of assessment is to preserve and reinforce current practice, then those in power will likely ask individuals who support them (out of conviction or fear) questions that underscore present efforts: Does the principal encourage teacher librarians to incorporate information literacy into their instruction? Are budget line items for information literacy resources clearly articulated? The questions may be valid and reliable, but they are unlikely to draw a complete and accurate picture.

In short, assessment of student information literacy is not just a summative exercise; it is a complex and ongoing systematic process of gathering data about the variables underlying student achievement, analyzing that data, and acting upon the findings. The process is symbiotic in that the school program and outside influences drive assessment, and assessment can drive school improvement. At the least, assessment can provide the "glue" for productive educational communication and decision making by clarifying and driving the ends and the means, based on educational and social values.

ASSESSMENT AS A VALUES-BASED MIND-SET

Teacher librarians constantly assess information literacy factors: Are students paying attention? Are students finding what they need? Are the books being used? If the teacher librarian is instructing several groups of students, the first group is often the "practice case"; the teacher librarian observes "what works" and what doesn't, and then makes adjustments accordingly for the rest of the groups. In some situations, the teacher librarian may realize that students don't have the prerequisite skills to be successful with the intended learning activity. For instance, the lesson might focus on note taking, but the teacher librarian realizes that students don't know how to identify the main idea and supporting facts. Effective teacher librarians try to back up and address that information skill first. Such assessment practices demonstrate a professional reflective attitude and provide a good starting point for systematic assessment.

However, to be truly effective, assessment needs explicit and systematic use; an episodic, hit-or-miss attitude will not result in significant, sustainable improvement. For instance, if the teacher librarian assesses *every* third-grade class's ability to locate a book and notes that one class excels, then it is possible to delve into the reasons for that difference. Does the third-grade teacher's instruction or assignment differ? Is the class composed of high achievers or better readers? Did those students get more time in the library or experience different library instruction? By asking possibly relevant questions, generating possible reasons (variables) for the difference in performance, forming hypotheses, and then testing those independent variables, the teacher librarian can create possible interventions that will positively impact student performance in the other classes. Of course, for such assessment and intervention effort to make a difference, the teacher librarian needs the cooperation of the third-grade teachers. By being able to use empirical assessment data, the teacher librarian strengthens the basis for defending and advocating for the library programs. Additionally, the collaborative effort also provides the teacher librarian with an ally to further *their* case.

Frankly, teacher librarians who operate isolated from the rest of the school community find that they have limited impact on student learning. There are too many variables that are not under the library program's control: scheduling, curriculum, staffing, home reading habits, to name a few. However, when teacher librarians work with other people to address overriding issues such as information literacy, then each person can identify those variables over which he or she *does* have control—or is impacted by others' control—and together they can assess student progress and the conditions for learning. Assessment data analysis can then be parsed into its component parts in order to understand the possible impact of each variable. Using that information, targeted interventions can be developed and tested, with the knowledge and cooperation of all stakeholders. Even though the school community cannot control outside conditions (e.g., local crime, economic status, family problems), it has a better chance of improving those variables that exist *within* the school program. In short, assessment can be used as a means to build shared meaning, vision, and action.

USING ASSESSMET TO DESCRIBE

The most obvious reason to assess is to "inventory" and describe the status quo. What do students know? What is the average copyright date of the library's book collection? What degrees do teachers have? How much homework is given each day? What is the teacher-to-student ratio? How many computers does the school have, and how many are in the library? Are parents happy with their children's education? Are graduating students prepared for jobs? Most schools have to send annual reports to some legal body as evidence of accountability. The data points that are asked of schools are supposedly chosen because they reflect valued aspects of education. They help to predict student success. The underlying reason for such accountability is to make sure the school is doing its job.

In order for assessment data to have meaning, to ascertain whether the school *is* effective in carrying out its mission, the assessment data have to be compared to something: usually a desired standard. These targeted data points may be determined based on criterion-based standards, such as the ability to solve quadratic equations (with an indicator providing the conditions and the base level of acceptable performance), or norm-referenced standards, such as reading scores. Even with criterion-based standards, most schools compare their assessment data with their peer institutions (with similar populations and programs) in order to assess their relative success.

Teacher librarians value information literacy, so they assess it. Thinking about information literacy assessment helps the school community to clarify its expectations, which also helps students succeed. The bottom line is, how information literate are students?—which, in turn, begs the question, what are the indicators that a student is information literate? Too often, the assessment instrument is defined *before* it is determined if that measure is a valid predictor of the intended result. The other bad habit is to locate or develop an assessment instrument after all instruction and activities occur, thus limiting its usefulness. The next chapter will detail how to select and administer valid and reliable assessment instruments.

Notwithstanding the quality of the assessment, teacher librarians tend to measure what they can control: student information literacy performance within the library *and* the controllable conditions of the library program that might impact such student performance. These variables include, among others,

- the quantity and quality of the library collection,
- the quantity and quality of the library staff,
- the quality of the facilities,

- the quantity and quantity of technology,
- the quality of the instructional program, and
- the nature and quality of library services.

Even these variables are not strictly under the control of teacher librarians since site decisions about budgets, hiring, curriculum, and allocation of time will impact the library program. In short, it behooves teacher librarians to work with the rest of the school when assessing the status quo of information literacy.

Thus, convincing the rest of the school to assess information literacy translates into helping the school community *value* it. Next, the school community needs to understand that the entire enterprise is responsible for students' information literacy, not just the library. One way to instill that sense of responsibility is to measure the students' information literacy performance and then identify and assess those conditions that might influence student achievement. An easy first step is to list all the existing assessments done within the school, which should generate a rich data set. The next step is to analyze the data in terms of information literacy: what variables might be predictors of student success? In some cases, the correlation might be obvious, such as reading scores. Since selection and evaluation of textual information requires reading skills, reading might be considered a prerequisite information literacy skill. Other data points might not be as obvious, such as years of teaching experience at the site. That variable might have to be "unpacked" into smaller pieces of data, such as curricular knowledge (of one's own and of other teachers') curriculum, knowledge of school personnel, knowledge of students, knowledge of the library. Theoretically, the more knowledgeable one is in one's settings, the easier it is to identify sources of support and interact with them. The systematic process of analyzing existing assessment data with an information literacy "lens" can, in itself, uncover surprising patterns. Comparing the data sets with recognized information literacy standards can lead to effective effort for student improvement.

USING ASSESSMENT TO IDENTIFY NEEDS

At this point, information literacy might be regarded as a pleasant set of skills and processes to be addressed by teacher librarians. For information literacy to impact the rest of the school community, some kind of need on that community's part must emerge; the status quo cannot remain comfortable. At this point, a needs assessment, even if it consists of faculty discussion, should be conducted. Since a main goal of education is to prepare students to meet specified standards of learning outcomes, a needs assessment can examine the school's conditions for learning. A couple of good research-based models look at the school's infrastructure and culture.[1, 2]

Instructional Program:

- Are educators highly qualified and competent?
- Is the curriculum characterized as rich and challenging?
- Is there a shared belief in high academic standards and expectations for students?
- Are classes and the school as a whole well organized and managed?
- Is the curriculum coordinated and supported by strong leadership?

Student Motivation and Engagement:

- Are students actively involved in concrete, authentic learning experiences?
- Do enrichment activities outside school hours and beyond the campus enhance learning?
- Do educators draw upon a wide repertoire of teaching strategies in response to identified needs?

Student and Family Needs:

- Does the school address the physical and emotional health needs of students?
- Are appropriate interventions and special assistance given to students and families with special needs?
- Does the school provide a safe, supportive, and respectful climate?

Collaboration among School, Home, and Community:

- Do professional teaching and learning teams further school efforts?
- Does the school model a learning community?
- Are school efforts monitored, assessed, and acted upon to optimize impact?
- Are families actively engaged in their children's education?
- Does the school provide opportunities for students to connect to the broader learning community?

By thoughtfully considering these elements, the school community should be able to identify issues that can benefit from the use of information literacy. At this point, teacher librarians can present information literacy best practices that model ways to meet those needs: through readings, presentations, workshops, and interactive WebQuests. Some examples follow:

- Information literacy can be used as a means to coordinate curriculum.
- Information literacy provides a concrete means for students to engage in personally meaningful learning activities.
- Information literacy facilitates learning that crosses school-community lines.
- Information literacy helps students find information that can help their personal needs.
- Information literacy is most effective when taught collaboratively.
- Families can reinforce and use information literacy skills at home.

To facilitate change, action research groups can explore possible solutions to meet the identified needs, most likely one group per need. This approach supports those "early adopters" who like to take intellectual risks and publicly rewards their efforts. For teacher librarians, the most difficult problem with this approach is a feeling of conflict, trying to decide which group to join; having already established good working relationships with other school-community members can help because another person can speak knowledgeably about a specific aspect of information literacy within another action research initiative. Furthermore, teacher librarians can serve as consultants upon need.

ASSESSMENT AND ACTION

It's one thing to describe what exists; it's another to assess in order to act upon the assessment data. A popular American saying asserts that "weighing the pig doesn't make it gain weight." That is, assessment in itself doesn't make a difference. The significance of assessment is its analysis as a basis for making decisions and acting upon them. Typically, assessment is used for the following reasons:

- To *diagnose* present performance and conditions, such as those related to information literacy, with the intent of creating appropriate interventions

- To provide *formative* information to measure progress toward information literacy
- To generate *normative* information to compare variables correlated with information literacy performance
- To get *summative* information to ascertain the degree to which students are information literate

To make sure that information literacy assessment is valued and acted upon, some kind of consequential accountability system needs to be established, containing the following elements:

- High information literacy standards
- Consequences based on student information literacy performance
- Mechanisms for improving student information literacy, such as staff development
- School-community norms and expectations about information literacy
- Site and district decision-making control
- Student graduation and postexit plans linked with information literacy
- Governmental mandates and resource allocation relative to information literacy
- Public reporting leading to public reputation relative to information literacy
- Accreditation oversight[3]

ASSESSMENT AS A CYCLE OF INQUIRY

Schools say that they are in the business of preparing students. Schools like to think that student achievement reflects the value-added program of resources and services that the school provides. Schools also admit that their efforts and their end "products" are not perfect, but they will assert that they are "trying their best" and are seeking ways to improve their practice and impact. Little improvement will occur, though, if assessment is not "front and center" in the minds of the school community.

Schools try different tactics to address shortcomings. They may "feel" that something isn't right and grab onto the latest fad in a desperate effort to do *anything* to make a difference: grade retention, longer school hours, prescribed reading program software, Internet filters. Perhaps the principal hears about a great turnaround reform model that worked elsewhere and uses the school budget to pay for its whole-cloth adoption at his school. Such panacea solutions usually do not solve the problem or address the underlying reasons for the crisis.

Instead, a cycle of inquiry offers an effective way to use assessment systematically to improve student information literacy. Basically, a cycle of inquiry is a process by which stakeholders

- *Examine the current status of the system and its component parts*: for example, what conditions make up information literacy—curriculum, instruction, resources, performance, and so on;
- *Identify discrepancies within the system, such as differences between input and output*: for example, rich print collection but poor ability to locate relevant information;
- *Determine the reason for discrepancies*: for example, lack of knowledge about library catalogs, inability to develop a research strategy;
- *Review the literature (research and best practice) about possible interventions*: for example, direct instruction and learning activities integrated into the curriculum;
- *Develop and implement an intervention to address the discrepancy*: for example, collaborative instructional design and implementation;
- *Assess the impact of the intervention*: for example, evaluate bibliographies of students' reports.[4]

Starting with assessment data about the status quo of student information literacy, the school community can determine the gap between the present and the ideal. The first inquiry stage asks why such a gap occurs. Available assessment data can jump-start the school community's process of determining possible obstacles to information literacy achievement. Only when the data sets have been exhaustively parsed and examined for underlying conditions should gaps in assessment itself be identified. For example, one of the possible predictors of information literacy performance might be opportunities to practice those skills; one of the conditions impacting practice might be the presence and use of a home computer with Internet connectivity. It is likely that the school has not surveyed households about this and other home conditions that might impact information literacy (e.g., home print collections, existence of a study area, family reading habits, parental education levels). Even though the school community cannot control some of those home variables, if it is found that a correlation does exist between home variables and information literacy, school efforts can influence those variables by conducting parent workshops on family reading activities and study support, and they can loan software-ready computers. After those interventions are applied, the school community can assess students' information literacy performance to determine the impact of those interventions.

THE INTERNATIONAL ROLE OF ASSESSING
INFORMATION LITERACY

In a global society, assessment is often used to compare the impact of education across national borders. The TIMSS (Trends in International Mathematics and Science Study) reports, which assess students' mathematics ability, exemplify the weight that such comparable data generates.[5] Based on the results, professional organizations and government agencies have explored alternative ways to package and deliver content. Because general definitions of information literacy have global validity, some common assessments may be used to compare information literacy and its underlying conditions, such as library staffing or access to information resources. The Program for International Student Assessment (PISA) measures how students interact with simulated tasks in science, mathematics, reading, and general learning.[6] These latter two skills may be considered part of information literacy. In fact, PISA 2003 focused solely on problem-solving tasks.

Such simulations, which try to capture detailed information literacy skills, may have cultural implications. The sample scenarios may have different connotations in different regions of the world. Tests taken on computer automatically disadvantage students without technical experience and might not assess a students' true ability in reading, for example. On a more human note, one of the information literacy skills listed by the American Association of School Librarians is the ability to work collaboratively. In some cultures, students may be accused of cheating if they ask peers for her while other cultures may value such behavior. Even definitions of plagiarism may differ among cultures.

The conditions for attaining information literacy may also differ from region to region. In one example above, if the school and community have little technology, their students cannot hope to compete in some information literacy arenas. How education is established and governed, how curriculum is developed and delivered, how classroom teachers and teacher librarians are prepared all impact student information literacy. Even the difference between a national and a local curriculum can impact information literacy efforts.

Indeed, even identifying universal conditions for information literacy efforts can be problematic. For instance, while it is tempting to state that collaborative teaching is a necessary universal condition for information literacy, evidence across all cultures is uneven. Relative to this point, cross-cultural research on mathematics teaching discovered that no perfect mathematical teaching style exists. No universal single teaching strategy could guarantee students' mathematical competence; rather, effective instruction is culturally defined and contextualized. Teaching quality *within* a culture *could* be compared relative to student achievement, but it could *not* be universally generalized.[7] Thus, teacher librarians would do well to start assessment efforts relative to the cultural expectations in their own region as a basis for cross-cultural research.

The impact on student learning with this culturally sensitive approach to information literacy assessment can be significant, particularly in pluralistic societies. Since one of the missions of education is to acculturate students, the dominant culture is likely to prevail. Particularly if students have been educated in a different culture, and have to transition to a new setting, they need to negotiate the sometimes conflicting cultural expectations. Insensitivity to this reality and lack of relevant accommodation within the school's program can lead to diminished education and limited understanding.[8] As mentioned before, information literacy has some agreed-upon universal elements, but how they are taught, practiced, and assessed may well be culturally defined. At the least, teacher librarians and their colleagues need to check their cultural assumptions about information literacy and choose assessment instruments that are sensitive to cultural implications so that students can demonstrate information competency in several ways—and so that *conditions* for information literacy can take into account cultural differences. The role of this assessment approach may well be to provide a viable mechanism to approach a universally shared meaning of information literacy.

In the final analysis, the role of assessment is to collect data and analyze it systematically; make decisions and act upon them. The potential roles of assessing information literacy have universal commonalities:

- Measuring the status quo
- Reflecting expectations
- Comparing means and ends
- Determining use for strategic planning
- Identifying use for communications

How those assessments are developed, administered, analyzed, and acted upon is typically a local endeavor.

Nevertheless, teacher librarians should seek opportunities to collaborate nationally and internationally to determine the extent that assessment can be used to develop international, cross-cultural implications. Even being able to parse those information literacy performances and conditions that are culturally defined and those that have international validity would advance information literacy appreciably. The significance of such research would be very exciting—and a real help to students in today's multicultural world.

NOTES

1. Coalition for Community Schools, *The Five Conditions for Learning* (Washington, DC: Coalition for Community Schools, 2003).

2. Carmel Crevola and Peter Hill, *Children's Literacy Success Strategy: An Overview* (Melbourne, Australia: Catholic Education Office, 1998).

3. Larry Lashway, *Educational Indicators* (Eugene, OR: ERIC, 2001).

4. Kathleen Cushman, "The Cycle of Inquiry and Action: Essential Learning Communities," *Horace* 15, no. 4 (1999), www.essentialschools.org/cs/resources/view/ces_res/74 (accessed July 31, 2007).

5. Patrick Gonzales et al., *Highlights from the Trends in International Mathematics and Science Study (TIMSS) 2003* (Washington, DC: National Center for Education Statistics, 2004).

6. National Center for Education Statistics, "Trends in International Mathematics and Science Study," nces.ed.gov/timss/ (accessed July 22, 2006).

7. James Stigler and James Hiebert, *The Teaching Gap: Best Ideas from the World's Teachers for Improving Education in the Classroom* (New York: Free Press, 1999).

8. Dolly MacKinnon and Catherine Manathunga, "Going Global with Assessment: What to Do When the Dominant Culture's Literacy Drives Assessment," *Higher Education Research & Development* 22, no. 2 (2003): 131–44.

· 6 ·

Assessment Processes

$\mathcal{T}$he basic processes of assessment are universal in nature. How they are implemented, on the other hand, may depend on cultural or social norms. First, information literacy goals and objectives need to be identified; who makes those decisions? Locating or developing a valid and reliable assessment instrument (or set of tools) requires answering a number of questions: What is assessed? Who is assessed? Who does the assessing? When and how frequently is the assessment done? How is it done? How are the data analyzed? Who analyzes the data? How are the findings acted upon? Who acts upon them? What accountability is present? These decisions may be made and supported (or not supported) at several levels: within the library, within a grade or department, across the site, across an educational system, across a region, across a nation, internationally.

PRINCIPLES OF ASSESSMENT

Assessing information literacy and its support mechanisms takes time and effort: from deciding what to assess through choosing an appropriate instrument, gathering the data, and analyzing the results. Any slip along the way can lessen its effect and benefits, so the process needs to be planned and implemented carefully.

To this end, the American Association of Higher Education Assessment Forum identified nine principles to guide assessment of student learning, which apply well to assessing information literacy.

1. Start with educational values: what should students be able to know and do? Assessment should strive to improve student achievement.

Information literacy needs to be not only valued by the library staff but also considered a core educational value if assessment of it is to make a difference in students' lives.

2. Assessment should recognize that learning is complex and demonstrated over time. One-shot multiple-choice assessments do not capture the richness of learning or the nuanced conditions for success. Teacher librarians appreciate the complexity of information literacy, so it is no surprise that the related process of assessing information literacy also needs to reflect a variety of perspectives and measurements over the course of a student's academic journey.

3. Effective assessment should be driven by clear educational goals and processes. A shared understanding and vision of information literacy is imperative for assessment to be used to improve educational practice and optimize student performance.

4. Assessment should measure both processes and products: the means and the ends. Students can put in much effort with little success; isolating the specific obstacles helps educators create effective interventions that will lead to student achievement.

5. Assessment should be ongoing and cumulative. Neither pre-/posttests nor entrance/exit exams provide enough data to ensure student success. What happens to students throughout the learning experience is key to effective information literacy practice. Each incremental change impacts successive efforts, with continual scaffolding and modifications resulting in significant impact.

6. Assessment should involve broad-based participation. Learning is the responsibility of the entire school community and community at large. Information literacy should not be the teacher librarian's burden but rather a schoolwide commitment to lifelong learning.

7. Assessment should be used to address important, valued issues. Information literacy issues that stand out include plagiarism, Internet abuse, and lack of intellectual discernment.

8. Assessment should be part of the larger picture of conditions for educational improvement. Normally, when analysis of information literacy assessment data leads to interventions, such as scheduling changes, other teaching and learning experiences improve as well.

9. Educators are accountable to their public constituents. Therefore, assessment and actions derived from assessment should be shared with the community at large. Particularly since employers want prepared employees upon entry, communicating improvements in student information literacy demonstrates how schoolwide efforts contribute to the community's economic well-being.[1]

On the practical side, the major questions to ask when determining the most effective assessment process include the following:

- *Why assess?* To gather baseline information, to diagnose strengths and weaknesses, to evaluate, to facilitate planning, to redirect efforts, to change content or instruction, to allocate resources, to motivate, to reward or punish (e.g., acceptance, graduation), to maintain accreditation or licensure[2]
- *What is being assessed?* Needs (of learners, instructors, community, etc.), learning environment and support, content, instruction, outcomes
- *Who is being assessed?* Students, classroom teachers, teacher librarians, administrators, other school staff members, district personnel, preservice teachers, families, community at large; the entire population or a sample (representative or targeted)
- *Who is assessing—and analyzing—data results?* Students, classroom teachers, teacher librarians, administrators, other school staff members, district personnel, preservice teachers, families, community at large, university librarians, university faculty, outside consultants
- *When does assessment occur?* Before, during, or after instruction/input; upon acceptance into a school, at the end of a semester or year, upon exiting a school; time of day or week
- *Where does assessment occur?* In classrooms, in libraries, at institutions of higher education, at home, online
- *How is assessment conducted?* By survey, observation, work analysis, test, rubric, interview, focus group, self-assessment, circulation statistics, usage analysis, systems analysis

DEFINING THE PROCESS

Several terms are used in the assessment world, which should be defined so all parties have a common understanding.

- *Standard:* a statement indicating what students should know and do. Curriculum standards state what should occur in the learning environment.
- *Outcome:* the desired and measurable goal, specifying what schools want students to accomplish.
- *Descriptor:* concrete description of an outcome (e.g., uses technology responsibly, legally, and ethically).

- *Indicator:* specific criteria that demonstrate that one has met a standard or satisfied an outcome (e.g., cites all sources of information accurately).
- *Authentic assessment:* asking for the behavior that the learner is expected to exhibit if the intended learning outcome is met. Usually a realistic task is called for that closely approximates the real-world application of the identified competency. Because the simulation task is complex and often "fuzzy" (ill defined), to measure complex behavior, authentic assessment requires careful delineation of critical criteria, close observation, and holistic grading. An example of an authentic assessment is critiquing student-produced antismoking advertisements.
- *Performance-based assessment:* direct observation of learner behavior that usually involves creating products. Students' actions thus reflect their information literacy knowledge and skills within a real-world context. Usually descriptive rubrics are used to assess the relative quality of the learner's performance.
- *Rubric:* a scoring guide with differentiated rating descriptions. Usually rubrics entail a number of indicators or criteria.
- *Benchmark:* learning performance standards at predetermined points in time, such as the end of the year, or key points in a project, such as a first draft of a report. Benchmarks enable all parties to reflect on their performance or progress formatively so that they can redirect their efforts to optimally meet the ultimate standard.

Before information literacy assessment can occur, the stakeholders have to define *information literacy*. They may choose to adopt existing definitions drawn up by national educational entities, by professional organizations, or by local education. They may build on existing content or curriculum standards. The discussion about terminology, indicators, and benchmarks can be time-consuming and sometimes frustrating, but it is imperative to gain consensus from the start in order to assess learners effectively. Translation of terms into content-specific contexts can be facilitated by teacher librarians since they work across the curriculum. Negotiation and compromise may be needed; if the rest of the school is comfortable with the term *research skills* and not with *information literacy*, teacher librarians should think long and hard before walking away from the discussion, especially if the competencies required *look* like information literacy.

Sometimes it is easier to list the tasks that indicate information literacy. What tasks should learners be able to do? What cognitive skills should be demonstrated? What technical skills need to be performed? How will information literacy be integrated in learning activities? How can information literacy be applied to solve problems and build knowledge? What attitudes should learners display? Whether the tasks lead to definition or vice versa, the goal is to come to agreement about what information literacy means and what it looks like. The ultimate list of tasks should represent the desired domain of information literacy.

The characteristics of those tasks can then be deconstructed into their information literacy components. What variables can be identified, such as generating relevant key words or ascertaining an author's perspective? What skills make a difference in the quality of the final product? What distinguishes unacceptable, acceptable, and target performance? Once these questions have been answered satisfactorily, these variables can be operationalized, that is, transformed into concrete, measurable requirements.[3, 4]

Learning activities must then be designed to address those variables, instructing students how to meet the requirement and giving them opportunities to demonstrate their knowledge. The entire school community should be involved in coordinating those learning activities so that they occur across the curriculum and articulate between levels. In that way, learners can apply these competencies in numerous content areas with different contexts, resulting in deeper knowledge.

SYSTEMS THINKING ABOUT INFORMATION LITERACY

It should be noted that assessment of information literacy should not be limited to student performance. It is equally important to assess the conditions for becoming information literate, that is, the entire school community's systemwide effort. Thus, in determining tasks, the actual design and implementation of learning activities needs to be deconstructed into its composite elements to determine which actions lead to positive conditions for gaining competency. Does collaboration between teacher librarian and classroom teacher, for instance, impact student learning? Does the presence of a rich collection of current and attractive reading material correlate with appreciation of literature? In short, the entire school's processes and products need to be examined in light of information literacy progress.

An effective approach to assessment is a systems approach where each input and output factor is identified. The following critical questions can guide school community members as they assess their environment and review relevant research literature relative to information literacy initiatives.

Input

- What *competencies and dispositions* do staff bring to the school environment? Are they credentialed in their area? Are they new to the field, or do they bring valuable experience from other settings—or other fields?
- What *curriculum* are teachers following? How closely does classroom practice align to district and state content frameworks? Does the curriculum reflect the latest trends in information literacy thinking and pedagogy?
- What *resources* are used to deliver the curriculum? Who determines the textbook and other print resources to use? Are high-quality electronic resources, videos, and manipulatives readily available in sufficient amounts for teacher and student use? Do teachers develop their own learning aids; do they have the materials and skills in order to produce and use them?
- What *instructional strategies* are used? What kinds of learning activities are used to provide students with opportunities to practice and demonstrate content competence? How does the learning environment facilitate information literacy? Not only should teacher librarians examine assignments, but they should also visit classrooms to see classes in action.
- How do teachers *work together*? Do they plan curriculum and learning strategies collaboratively? Do they consult one another when obstacles arise? Do they use teacher aides or tutors to reinforce instruction and learning? What kind of training do they provide these support staff?
- How is *time* allocated: within a class period, in terms of block scheduling, relative to staff development, and opportunities for tutoring?
- What *governance and school community structures* are in place to facilitate pedagogy: staff development opportunities, databases or other mechanisms to share lessons and best practice, telecommunications to facilitate collaboration, funding for conference/continuing education participation?
- What background, experiences, skills, and dispositions do *students* bring to the classroom? Teacher librarians should assess students' information literacy skills as they enter the school in order to optimize learning experiences throughout their academic life. What prerequisite skills are lacking? Without addressing those prior skills, teachers and students will be frustrated in their work.

- What information do *feeder schools* provide about prior teaching and learning? Teacher librarians should meet regularly with library staff from lower grades and higher grades, including postdiploma institutions, in order to facilitate seamless education. Even knowledge about preschool reading readiness can help the elementary teacher librarian provide learning experiences that build on a child's prior understanding and exposure.
- How do *parents/guardians* and *community members* interface with students and the rest of the school? What resources do they provide? What competing priorities do they reflect?

Output

- Does *student work* reflect content knowledge and application as well as information literacy competency? Teacher librarians should routinely examine current student products in order to assess the impact of teaching.
- How do students perform on *standardized tests*? Do they "test" consistently across tests, or does the type of test (e.g., essay versus multiple-choice) impact performance? Whenever possible, test scores should be disaggregated by demographic data, teacher, and feeder school. Test items should also be analyzed to uncover learning/teaching gaps and successes.
- What class *grades* are students receiving? How consistent is grading between teachers, especially those teaching the same content? Is there a connection between grades and library usage?
- What *classes* are students taking? What is the basis for course enrollment? What courses do students drop?
- In what kinds of community *activities* do students participate outside of school? What hobbies do they have? How do they spend their time at home? Do students have opportunities to apply information skills in their personal lives?
- What happens to students when they *exit the school*? On what basis do they leave? Bringing students back to school after they graduate provides valuable insights into their sense of being prepared for future efforts.
- Other output measures provide *indirect data* about academic success: attendance, behavior referrals, parent conferences, teacher turnover rate.

THE ROLE OF TECHNOLOGY IN ASSESSMENT PROCESSES

With the incorporation of technology, the assessment process can increase its effectiveness significantly for several reasons:

- *Speed:* Data can be collected and analyzed quickly.
- *Record keeping:* Online and video interviewing and other electronic communications are instantly archived; digitized data can be exported for efficient analysis.
- *Synchronicity and asynchronicity:* Communication can be conducted and transmitted at times that are convenient for both assessor and assessee.
- *Variety of dissemination options:* Assessment instruments can be broadcast for wide-range access and also directed to individual, targeted audiences.
- *Public and private options:* Data can be collected in a public venue or kept private to insure participant confidentiality.
- *Standardized and individualized assessments:* Assessments can be systemized so that data can be easily merged and compared; just as easily, instruments can be customized to gather very specialized information.
- *Statistical features:* Data analysis software programs such as SPSS and SAS facilitate a broad range of sophisticated processes that can be conducted in hours instead of days; even standard spreadsheet programs provide quick formula calculations and graphic representations.
- *Equitable access and participation:* Assessment processes optimize participation through electronic language translation services, flexibility of response methods and timing, choice of communication formats (text, sound, image, motion), and accommodations for populations with special needs.
- *Increased writing and reflective practice:* Technology increases opportunities and means to express facts and perspectives, and facilitates metacognitive processes; participants can transcend reactive activity and become more engaged and productive.

Two major technology developments in library education advance contemporary assessment: telecommunications-enhanced course delivery and electronic portfolios. In addition, an older technology that has regained assessment respect because of more sophisticated editing and dissemination is video. The features of each technology aid in data collection and analysis. The rest of this chapter will focus on courseware's role in assessment.

DETERMINING THE ASSESSMENT INSTRUMENT

As information literacy tasks, variables, and learning activities are defined, the assessment instrument should also be considered so that all aspects of teaching and learning are aligned and leveraged for maximum effect: outcome, teaching and learning assumptions, content transmission, along with assessment.[5] Ideally, an educational entity, be it a school or district, should develop a set of interconnected information literacy assessment tools across the curriculum and stakeholders. These tools, then, support the entire entity's mission and are used to provide baseline data about information literacy, diagnose gaps in and obstacles to information literacy achievement, as well as measure progress and ultimate success.

Information literacy comprises a complex set of cognitive knowledge, affective dispositions, and psychomotor behaviors that can be very hard to "unpack" into their contributing variables. For instance, how does one measure "appreciation of literature"? Is it the number of books owned or borrowed? No, since one might not read them. Is it the number of books read? Not necessarily, since reading experiences vary widely among individuals. Does comprehension equal appreciation? No, since a reader might understand someone's writing but hate the style or the author's opinion. Choosing to read frequently and independently, rereading a section just for pleasure, or copying down quotes and memorizing them "for fun" might be valid indicators of literature appreciation. However, it is easier to keep circulation records than to ascertain some of these other voluntary or visceral behaviors. Too often educators assess what is easy rather than what is important. The designated assessment instrument must measure the most significant variables accurately and reliably time after time. It is probably more effective to accurately measure a few really important information literacy variables than to assess many simple, low-level information skills.

Typically, the level of assessment aligns with the level of information literacy. For instance, a multiple-choice test can measure use of the library catalog or dictionary. A concept map can measure knowledge of terms and their interrelationships. A questionnaire can measure simple perceptions about information literacy. Authentic assessment can work for a range of competencies, from locating a book on the shelf to conducting a sophisticated research project to addressing a local social issue.

The assessment not only measures students' performance but it can be used to validate the variable itself. For example, if students know how to outline, does that lead to better reports? If not, then the true contributing variable must be found. As with learning activities, determining and designing assessments should be a schoolwide effort in order to leverage measurements so that students do not need to be tested constantly and so interventions can impact student learning in several courses simultaneously.

Some typical assessment instruments follow, noting their strengths and weaknesses:

- *Observation:* provides open-ended, direct evidence in a natural setting (e.g., watching students looking up magazine articles, observing students working collaboratively). Individuals bring their own biases and may see different things, so training and consistent results are needed; observation captures data only for that instant.
- *Individual interview:* provides open-ended, interactive, in-depth data (e.g., having a student think out loud as she searches for a book using an online library catalog, discussing with a teacher about how he develops research projects). Labor-intensive and time-consuming, these interviews produce data that are only as accurate as the questions being asked and the answers being given, so this approach requires training; language barriers may exist as well.
- *Focus group:* provides open-ended, interactive, in-depth data and group dynamics (e.g., asking students about their reading habits, talking with teachers about plagiarism). Data may be skewed or missing because of group norming; this approach requires training; language barriers may exist as well.
- *Telephone or online interview:* provides open-ended, interactive, in-depth data that is space dependent and less intimidating (e.g., contacting parents about their role in their child's education, doing an online survey about perceptions of the library). Interviewers need training, and data may be biased because of access (nonownership or unlisted) and language barriers.
- *Content analysis:* provides unobtrusive data that can be repurposed (e.g., critiquing learning activity handouts, examining sample student work). Confidentiality may limit access or application; data may need to be contextualized.

The most common commercial assessment tools are standardized tests. High-quality ones have been validated with many populations and provide longitudinal reliability. Government licensure and accreditation processes frequently rely on these tests because they provide cross-site comparisons. They may be norm referenced (i.e., test results are compared) or criterion referenced (i.e., results are compared to the correct answer), the latter usually being preferred. In those areas where experts can agree on measurable criteria, representative prompts, and correct answers, then those tests offer a way to assess many learners efficiently. However, for higher level information competencies, such agreements are difficult to achieve. Oftentimes, there is not just one best key word or resource to answer a question or solve a problem. Thus, standardized tests are most appropriate for assessing declarative knowledge such as the use of indexes or the application of map keys. Tool-based standardized tests, then, tend to be the norm. The Educational Testing Service has created a sophisticated scenario-based standardized test to measure entering college freshmen's information and communication technology competency; the software programming enables the test to branch to different questions depending on the testee's responses, the aim of which is to diagnose specific knowledge gaps (www.ets.org/ictliteracy/index.html).

Some factors need to be considered when determining which assessment instrument to use, regardless of its format:

- *Cost*: for instrument itself, recording forms, labor involved in development, administration, data entry and analysis
- *Time*: for development, administration, coding, analysis
- *Availability*: of instrument, associated technology, human resources for development, administration and analysis
- *Skills*: for development, administration, data-collection training, data entry and coding, analysis
- *Legalities*: of confidentiality and privacy, use of instrument, parental permission
- *Culture*: attitudes toward the instrument, language issues, fear of high stakes or repercussions

DEVELOPING ASSESSMENT TOOLS

Developing assessment tools "from scratch" can be time-consuming and unproductive. Since the main considerations are validity (measuring the intended competence) and reliability (obtaining consistent results), evaluating the assessment instrument itself is key. If a credible entity has already designed and validated an assessment tool that measures a desired outcome with the same kind of population, then one should seriously consider using it if it is feasible to so do (i.e., affordable and manageable.).

Nevertheless, sometimes an assessment instrument needs to be developed "from whole cloth" because the objectives are site specific or the target audience has unique needs. Fortunately, technology has facilitated this task. The assessor can now repurpose documents as assessment instruments more easily and can disseminate them more efficiently. Files can also be imported into spreadsheet and statistical software programs without rekeying.

Products

One obvious way to find out if someone is information literate is to ask him or her to create a product that reflects competency. Traditionally, book reports have been used to demonstrate that a student has read the source, and research papers have been used to demonstrate that a student can conduct research independently. Ideally, the products should demonstrate conceptual and procedural knowledge applied to real-world contexts. With the advent of digital technology, the repertoire of products has grown exponentially:

- *Text*: report, I-search, white paper, essay, biography, article, brochure, press release, résumé, instructions, song, poem, dramatization
- *Visual*: poster, painting, book jacket, collage, display, storyboard, timeline, cartoon, photo journal, concept map, transparency
- *Oral*: report, debate, skit, booktalk, oral history
- *Video*: commercial, documentary, booktalk, interview, drama
- *Audio*: narrative, monologue, booktalk, soundscape documentary
- *Digital*: web page, WebQuest, webliography (annotated bibliography of websites), multimedia presentation, computer-aided design, spreadsheet, database, simulation, e-story

Particularly in online or distance education, writing constitutes the main communication—and assessment—vehicle because of its flexibility, portability, and low-end technical requirements. Here are some interactive ways to use writing as an assessment tool:

- *Journaling*: commenting on readings, commenting on information-related processing, commenting regularly on information-related issues and concerns that arise in a course, describing one's "life of information"
- *Narrative inquiry*: describing and analyzing critical incidents related to information literacy

- *Writing to prompts*: responding to information and sources, demonstrating declarative knowledge about a subject, creating one-minute papers on a topic
- *Reciprocal teaching and learning*: posing case studies or problems for peers to analyze or solve
- *Peer review*: using rubrics to assess peer's work, using word processing features (e.g., tracking, highlighting) on a peer's writing to aid criticism

Assessors need to maintain student confidentiality and be sensitive to student self-disclosure. Students should be able to "pass" on discussing personal matters, exploring relevant published accounts instead.

In assessing these products, both the end results and the supporting processes should be considered. Rubrics serve as a customizable tool for assessing the different elements—either holistically to get a general picture or analytically to examine each factor—both during the production process, as a means to make adjustments, and at the end. Both formative and summative assessment rubrics provide qualitative and quantitative descriptors for each identified key criterion.

Typically, assessors build on sample work, identifying the key features that distinguish high-quality products from mediocre ones. The rubric is then constructed by specifying the assessment indicators, each criterion measuring one unique aspect. The rubric should be pilot-tested with additional work samples and refined. As much as possible, students can learn how to use rubrics to guide their efforts by calibrating their assessments using exemplar samples. With practice, students can develop their own rubrics. The following websites on rubric creation offer a good start by detailing how rubrics work, giving guidelines for developing high-quality rubrics, supplying exemplar rubrics, and providing rubric templates.

- Rubistar: rubistar.4teachers.org/
- Kathy Schrock's Guide for Educators: school.discovery.com/schrock guide/assess.html
- Teachnology: The Online Teacher Resource: www.teach-nology.com/ web_tools/rubrics/
- Authentic Assessment Toolbox (links "Rubrics" and "Portfolios"): jonathan.mueller.faculty.noctrl.edu/toolbox/

When examining products, a host of assessments may be used throughout the process, as exemplified here. One of the more typical information literacy tasks is a research report. The following steps show what assessment might be used and what actions may be taken after analyzing the data.

1. From the very beginning, prior student content knowledge can be diagnosed using a K/W/L chart (what I know, what I want to know, what I learned) of a presearch concept map. If prerequisite concepts are not in place, then the classroom teacher may need to redefine the information task and the teacher librarian may need to provide basic background resources.

2. Similarly, students can create a flow chart or a quick write about their intended research strategies. Teacher librarians can discover how students plan to proceed; if no sense of direction is apparent for many of the class, then teacher librarians can scaffold student approaches to locating relevant information.

3. Reviewing student note-taking efforts, be they on cards or in the form of Cornell notes (one half of the page includes notes, and the other half of the page includes student commentary), gives an indication of students' ability to identify main ideas and extract relevant details; students may need some guidance on how to use textual clues (e.g., boldface, headings, summaries) to choose important data. Students may also need instruction in how to decipher graphical information or interpret visual messages.

4. Another point for assessment is examining students' bibliographies, which reveals students' choices of resources; if a student lists Google and Wikipedia as their only sources, then an intervention for teaching more effective searching is called for.

5. A useful assessment practice is to require students to have a research conversation with the teacher librarian, which students can schedule according to their own needs: as they start, when they hit an obstacle, or toward the end as they identify research gaps; the timing as well as the content in discussion provide authentic assessment information, and the teacher librarian can offer effective feedback to help students succeed in their final product.

An authentic way to provide ongoing assessment is to assign an I-search paper, where students self-select a topic for investigation and journal about their efforts. Students can self-monitor their information literacy skills; the classroom teacher and teacher librarian should also examine those journals along the way in order to provide timely feedback and redirection so students can be successful. However, care should be taken in evaluating these journals since students take a variety of routes to knowledge; students should be given enough leeway to pursue different avenues according to their way of thinking. It is also important to differentiate between process and product: sometimes students are not very efficient in their time management or research efforts but may end up with an acceptable product; on the other hand, students can make great efforts but may confront obstacles that impact the final results. Thus, it is important to assess both process and product.

Questionnaires

Questionnaires are a popular way to gather descriptive data quickly. They capture data about perceptions, broaden the basis for decision making, and demonstrate an interest in the school community. Designing valid and reliable questions is key in getting good data. Here are some guidelines:

- Determine the objective and target audience for the questionnaire.
- Decide whether there is a need for anonymity.
- Ask questions regarding issues that are under the library program's control; be prepared to act upon the responses.
- Force respondents to take a side; do not use five-point scales where someone can answer three throughout.
- Group questions by theme, such as demographics, reading preferences, and so forth.
- Start with objective, uncontroversial questions and ask sensitive questions late in the questionnaire.
- Avoid leading questions, such as "Why do you like libraries?"
- Avoid asking two questions in one, such as "How often do you read in school and at home?"
- Keep questionnaires short.
- Pilot-test the questionnaire for clarity and validity (getting at the needed information).
- Analyze the data quickly, and provide feedback to the respondents so they know that their opinion matters.[6]

Questions can take a variety of formats, each best suited to get specific types of information.

- *Dichotomous*: to ask closed questions with only two options (e.g., yes/no, male/female)
- *Multiple choice*: to ask closed factual questions that are mutually exclusive and cover all options (e.g., grade in school, country of origin)
- *Rank ordering*: to ask closed questions that force one to prioritize different options (e.g., favorite genres, reasons for reading)
- *Rating scales*: to ask closed questions to capture sensitivity flexibly (e.g., relative importance of library services)

- *Open-ended*: to ask questions that provide opportunity for self-elaboration

Eventual data analysis should drive the format and wording of the questions. For instance, if limited human resources exist for data transcription or if technology does not handle open-ended questions easily, then closed questions should be used for large-scale questionnaires.

Several free and low-cost online questionnaire tools exist—of varying quality. Several factors should be considered when deciding which program to use.

- How are security and confidentiality addressed?
- How is authentification insured?
- How are forms and data imported and exported?
- How are data accessed and controlled?
- What back-up and disaster-recovery provisions are available?
- How long can data be kept?
- How much storage space is available?
- Where are servers located?
- What kind of technical service is provided?
- How much does technical or processing service cost? Do different levels of service exist?
- What third-party audit procedures insure quality?[7]

Surveys are particularly useful for determining respondent perceptions and for educating those participants about those topics raised in the questionnaire. For instance, teacher librarians can ask what kinds of resources are used by students when they conduct research. Based on those answers, teacher librarians can determine which resources and information-seeking strategies to promote. Finding out what kind of technology and what kind of Internet connection is available to students outside of school (e.g., home, public libraries) can enable teacher librarians to justify longer library hours of public operations so that students can access computers to find needed information.

Interviews

Interviews provide an easy and flexible way to assess nuanced knowledge and perceptions. The format of the interview can range from a highly structured framework of consistently asked closed questions with preset response checklists to a very loose event where a few starting questions such as "What is information literacy?" can lead to unknown topics; typically interviews use a semistructured agenda with closed and open-ended questions. Basically, interviews are informed conversations that require intense active listening skills and good communications skills to keep the interviewee on topic as needed. It should be noted that related costs are deceptive: while the only equipment needed is an audiotape recorder, the labor costs for interviewing and transcribing can potentially run up quite a bill.

Assessment-oriented interviews require careful planning because the resulting data need to be examined and compared. After determining the reason for the interviews, the assessor needs to identify the most effective interviewee pool. The time frame for the interview needs to be determined, usually sixty to ninety minutes to get at deeper issues, taking into consideration the characteristics of the potential interviewee and the environment (i.e., a shorter interview might be appropriate for younger children or to accommodate shorter school periods). Scheduling also has to be negotiated. Questions have to be developed to address the intended assessment objective. Unlike text-based questions, interview questions should include a subset of follow-up-related questions based on the interviewee's response that can probe for more details. For instance, if the interviewee states that she feels comfortable searching on the Internet, then follow-up questions might ask for example searches and reasons why she feels comfortable. A good practice is to pilot-test the interview to see what issues or misunderstandings emerge. Permissions for audiotaping should be secured ahead of time, and equipment should be checked to make sure it is in good operating condition before the interview (and back-up batteries should be secured).

Several factors can make or break the actual interview. Here are some tips:

- Arrive on time. Introduce yourself and restate the purpose of the interview.
- Interview in a comfortable setting that permits unobtrusive audiotaping (carry a back-up audiotape).
- Listen sensitively, noting the interviewee's strengths and interests; guide gently.
- Disclose personal information as needed to help draw out the interviewee, but avoid interrupting the interviewee.
- Take notes even if taping to record the conversation and to help remember points to bring up later in the interview; review and clarify notes immediately after the interview.
- Thank the interviewee for her or his time and information; follow up with a thank-you note.[8]

Too often teacher librarians and classroom teachers may make inaccurate assumptions about students' information literacy. Interviews provide an open-ended way to test those assumptions. For instance, high school teachers may think that their students' tendency to plagiarize indicates that they have not received instruction about plagiarism; in an interview, however, those same high schoolers may well say that they have heard many lectures about plagiarism and intellectual property and may give other reasons for their plagiarism: poor time management, lack of self-confidence to write originally, or thinking they will not be caught. Knowing the bases for plagiarism helps teacher librarians address the issue at the level that students can understand and accept.

Interactive Software

Technology has enabled assessors to use interactive software programs that measure learners' information competency through performance. These programs set up scenarios with decision points that the user acts upon. At the least, the program facilitates documentation of the performance through graphic organizers or a dialogue box. Many programs branch to different tasks or assessments based on the user's decisions, thus tracking the mental processing. Upper-end programs export the user's decision points into a database file for later assessment.

WebQuests exemplify this interactive assessment quality. As structured online resource-based learning activities, WebQuests usually frame an essential question as a compelling scenario leading to an authentic task to be achieved in small collaborative groups. Each person assumes a role and investigates predetermined relevant resources in order to generate a group solution. Each step is recorded, later to be assessed using a rubric. Hunt's WebQuest on information literacy models and explains how to create one's own WebQuest (www.mla.mb.ca/infolit/WebQuest/index.cfm).

Many libraries, particularly in higher education, use digital information literacy tutorials as assessment tools. Typically, the user follows a sequence of research process steps. Questions or "quizlets" check for understanding at the end of each section, with answers provided in one of two ways: sometimes clues are given based on the user's input so that he or she can guess again, and sometimes the correct answer is simply listed regardless of how the user guessed. Occasionally, the user's responses are recorded and exported for further analysis and instructional improvement, such as California State University, Long Beach's SURF (Students Understanding Research Fundamentals) interactive program (www.csulb.edu/projects/surf/).

Increasingly, librarians are exploring the use of virtual learning environments as a means to assess information literacy. A closed virtual universe is created in which artifacts reside. Scenarios are posed for the user to engage in, and their steps are recorded as a means of assessing information competency. One such prototype is being developed by Newell.[9] The advantage of such a simulated environment is that learners can participate independently at their own convenience, thus freeing the teacher librarian to provide just-in-time specific interventions. The data collected should also be analyzed; if these virtual environments can be used to diagnose learner gaps and provide guidance for that specific subtask, then assessment can be used formatively in an efficient and individualized manner. With the increasing interest in role-playing digital games, librarians should consider this venue as a viable way to record learner behavior.[10] Such developments will probably have to involve partnerships with software developers because the programming aspects are quite complex. On the other hand, if such a game were created, the market could be very lucrative.

In all of these interactive technology approaches, the development of simulations can use rapid design prototyping steps, which incorporate user feedback early on in the process.

1. Define the concept.
2. Develop a skeletal system.
3. Get user feedback to refine the concept.
4. Implement refined requirements of the program.
5. Get user feedback.[11]

This kind of approach works particularly well for information literacy since ongoing assessment improves the product and optimizes learning.

One main advantage of WebQuests and online interactive tutorials is their ability to capture and export data for analysis. As students work through information tasks, these digital tutorials can identify decision points where students go astray so that targeted interventions can make maximum positive impact. For instance, if given a list of sources to use for research a significant number of students choose the biased ones, then it is obvious that teacher librarians need to focus on this aspect of information literacy instruction.

Videos

Video has reemerged as a viable assessment tool. Video has been used for decades to accurately capture an event such as a presentation or skit. The persons being videotaped can examine their own behaviors, noting delivery as well as content. They can also control the tape in order to replay a critical scene or pause to spot some specific detail. Videotaping can occur in situ, offering an opportunity for evaluators and peers to observe critically in an asynchronous fashion.

With the advent of digital video and built-in computer video editors (e.g., iMovie and MovieMaker), learners can edit their own videos relatively easily in order to identify key learning moments and comment on their decision-making process. Likewise, evaluators can select video clips that exemplify high-quality—or low-quality—information literacy performances. In either case, learners and assessors can insert video clips into authoring programs and on-line environments at pivotal points for group discussion.

While video is an attractive tool, several caveats are in order before implementing this medium. The two main obstacles are resources and training. Digital camcorders are becoming less expensive but may still be out of financial reach for many students. Libraries should provide this equipment for circulation purposes, realizing that borrowers need to be trained in its use and care. If analog camcorders are used, then software and peripherals need to be acquired to transform analog signals into digital ones; again, training is required, and results can be disappointing because synching of audio and video can be problematic with low-end products. Even when the source material is in digital format, learning how to select and edit material can be a frustrating and time-consuming process at the start. Furthermore, video requires extensive storage space and sufficient bandwidth to transmit satisfactorily, either of which might be unavailable to learners. If final products are being shared outside of the classroom, written permission from distinguishable individuals in the videos is also required. When all of these factors are added up, both learners and assessors may wonder what is being evaluated: the performance itself, selection and organization of information, or technical skill. Even though all three of these competencies reflect some aspect of information literacy, separate assessment tools should be considered for each of these processes.

The PT3 (Preparing Tomorrow's Teachers to Use Technology) project, funded by the U.S. Department of Education, developed technology-based assessment instruments and methodologies. Video was recognized as a viable assessment tool. The project's site includes several examples of the use of video for assessment purposes (www.ed.gov/programs/teachtech/index.htm). California State University, Long Beach, a lead grantee, adapted a number of rubrics to assess video-based products (www.csulb.edu/colleges/colled/pt3/resources.htm#assessment). One of the rubrics used was developed by Warsaw Community Schools (Indiana) for use in K–12 settings (www.warsaw.k12.in.us/edcom/rubrics/video.pdf). Thus, video can be used to diagnose information literacy behaviors, to identify best practices, and as assessment source material.

Portfolios

Portfolios have become a popular way to assess competencies over time. Basically a collection of sample work, portfolios address the problem of single assessments. Instead, multiple efforts can reflect a complex set of competencies. While it is possible to collect *every* piece of evidence (sometimes done as learning records), one of the values of portfolios is selection, which is a key information competence. Learners choose those pieces that best demonstrate competency, and they typically write a reflection about their choices. Portfolios also require organization, another important information skill. Thus, portfolio form and function meld well to show information literacy. Furthermore, portfolios can assume a variety of formats: print, audio-visual, and digital. The third, though, offers the greatest flexibility in data storage and retrieval because learners can repurpose and link evidence to the relevant standards or outcomes.

As with other assessment tools, portfolios need to be carefully designed.

- What is the purpose of the portfolio? Entrance diagnostic? Benchmark assessment? Exit outcome?
- What kind of evidence is expected? What learning activities will be provided so learners can create artifacts demonstrating information literacy?
- How selective should the evidence be? What is the time frame for the work to be collected? What reflective components are needed?
- What organization is required? To what extent will organization impact assessment results?
- How will the portfolio be assessed? What actions will occur as a result of the assessment?

Because portfolios usually represent substantial effort over time, coordination of the stakeholders and the learning environment is needed from the start. Learners should be informed of the outcome, portfolio requirements, and assessment methods early on so they can begin to collect and think about their work. This awareness also encourages learners to try hard and progress over time. Getting students' best efforts also enables their evaluators, principally classroom teachers, to identify trends across students that can lead to targeted interventions such as guidance on selecting portfolio entries or organizing portfolio evidence for optimum presentation.

ADMINISTRATION ISSUES

Assessment occurs constantly. As teacher librarians observe students searching on the Internet or note what books are borrowed, informal assessment occurs. Likewise, teachers can tell when a class is off task or doesn't understand an assignment. Anyone can conduct an assessment. It just takes an assessor, a target population, an assessment instrument, and the means to administer the assessment. Data analysis also occurs on a daily basis as the teacher librarian moves a computer station to improve supervision or as the teacher reexplains a misunderstood concept.

Typically, the organizational level of the assessment aligns with the assessment decisions. For instance, the classroom teacher decides how to administer a class quiz. The department chair decides how to administer a curriculum satisfaction survey. As soon as assessments require cooperation or coordination between people, then a more systematic approach is needed. Between two individuals, these procedures can be accomplished without undue formality. For instance, the teacher librarian may want to hold a class focus group on reading habits; scheduling time for a class visit is often the hardest part. Within a grade or department, discussion usually focuses on articulation and coordinated scheduling. If a standardized test is to be taken by all students simultaneously, then the entire school staff will be involved. In each case, these people should tell their superiors about their assessment plans so no surprises occur.

When addressing assessment on a schoolwide basis, several decisions need to be made before actually administrating the assessment. First of all, an individual or group has to be designated "in charge"; someone has to have ultimate authority (the final decision maker) and someone has to have final operational responsibility. Other individuals need to be involved as well: stakeholders should have some say in the decisions, and the chief implementer must have broad-based support in order to delegate tasks successfully. Establishing an assessment team provides flexibility and accountability.

Assuming the population has been determined, the assessment team needs to determine if everyone will be assessed or if a representative sample will be used. This sampling can be chosen by classes (i.e., a consistent percentage of classes per grade), by subject (i.e., a consistent percentage of classes per subject matter), by teacher (i.e., a consistent percentage of classes per teacher), by grade point average (i.e., a consistent percentage of students within each grade point), by gender (i.e., the same percentage of males and females as represents the total population), by ethnicity (i.e., the same percentage of each ethnicity as represents the total population), by time frame (i.e., a consistent percentage of classes per period), or by another variable that might be significant. Random numbers or every x number can be used to derive the sampling. Sometimes convenience overrules randomness; nevertheless, consideration of fair representation should be maintained. Schools should probably obtain blanket parental permissions at the beginning of the school year to facilitate assessment efforts such as videotaping.

The conditions for administrating an assessment can impact results. Therefore, as much as possible, the environment should have a neutral or positive feeling. Those being assessed should feel comfortable and at ease so their anxiety will not interfere with the measurement of their knowledge and attitude. Students bring their own beliefs about and perceptions of the assessment to the event, which can impact their responses, so clear discussion of the assessment is important.[12] All supplies for assessing should be made available, such as writing utensils and forms to be scanned. If assessments are done digitally, then the accompanying equipment and connectivity should be checked ahead of time to minimize distractions or aberrations. Directions also need to be given in a clear, neutral manner so assessees will know how to respond appropriately.

Some kinds of assessments, such as interviews, require training. Protocols need to be followed to insure consistent interaction with participants. When several people are involved in interviewing or reviewing of work, these assessors need to be calibrated to insure consistency. The easiest way to do this is to use exemplar works to get all assessors to agree on the assessment.

MAKING USE OF THE DATA

It is not enough to collect data or to administrate an assessment instrument. The results need to be analyzed and acted upon. Ultimately, the point person in control of the assessment should also be the person who directs the data analysis. However, several steps need to be accomplished along the way:

1. Review the research question.
2. "Skim" the data to see if possible trends or questions emerge.
3. Organize the data: cluster, categorize, and classify them to align with the research question.
4. Determine which analytic method to use to make sense of the data; this step may involve reorganizing the data.
5. Apply the analytic method (usually qualitative or quantitative statistics).
6. Contextualize the findings in terms of the situation, the setting, long-term implications, and relevant theories.
7. Explain the findings and represent them in accessible terms: graphs, charts, tables, images.
8. Identify missing data that need to be addressed and other limitations of the analysis.[13]

Data analysis should lead to conclusions and recommendations that may be acted upon. Stakeholders should participate in the data analysis and conclusions, and all participants should be informed about the results so they can feel that their input is recognized and utilized for school improvement. In cases where no action is taken, the report should still be communicated, and the justifications for nonaction should be explained.

Data Organization

Assessment involves gathering a lot of data. Piles of student work, videos, and survey forms have to be sorted out and organized so that the data can be compiled and compared. The type of data determines what statistical method should be used to analyze the data and make meaning of them. Along the way, some data may need to be rejected because they are incomplete or not indicative of the person's true performance or feelings (e.g., marking all Cs in a multiple-choice test or writing jokes in an open-ended survey).

To begin with, data documents can be stored in the order received and checked against a list of targeted participants (e.g., homerooms, teacher list). Once the data are collected, they have to be organized and presented in a way that can be analyzed. Most data can be described in terms of characteristics or "fields" (e.g., demographic information, test scores, time on task, degree of agreement about a statement). Typically, the fields are determined when an instrument is selected; when observations or other qualitative methods are used, the fields "emerge" as the resultant data are being analyzed.

Numerical data are typically inputted into a spreadsheet, and qualitative data are usually inputted into a database; both of these methods of representing and organizing information allow one to sort the data by different fields. Scantron forms can be "programmed" for easier data presentation. Depending on how online questionnaires are developed, the responses can be exported into spreadsheet or statistical programs. In many cases (such as responses on a paper survey), however, data have to be tallied manually so careful attention has to be made to insure accuracy; it is a good idea to "test" the intended tallier on a small data set (such as a handful of surveys) to make sure no errors are made. Charting the resultant data summaries can facilitate understanding; most spreadsheet programs can transform numerical data into graphs for easier interpretation.

As much as possible, data should be disaggregated by demographics such as sex, age, ethnicity, socioeconomic background, and feeder school in order to help identify at-risk groups; if possible, data can also be disaggregated by preferred learning style or preferred subject matter. For example, boys tend to have lower reading scores so interventions should be custom designed to motivate and help that group. Another way to disaggregate data is by quartiles or other score rankings; one cost-effective practice is to focus on those groups who *almost* meet a standard, because a specifically targeted intervention may be relatively easy to implement and result in a significant return on investment.

As data are organized, missing data may also be identified. Referring back to the original research question can uncover data gaps. Perhaps educational background of the students' parents might be relevant in determining factors for reading success. At this point, it might be possible to gather and incorporate the additional data, but even if it is too late for new data to be added, the omission can be noted for the next round of assessments and data gathering.

Choosing the Statistical Method

Once the data have been organized, then statistics may be applied. The inquiry question to be answered, the objectives of the assessment, the type of data to be gathered, the choice of assessment tool, and the analytic method all need to be aligned. Thus, the type of assessment instrument generally dictates what kind of statistical method will be used to analyze the data. For example, videotaping student information-seeking behaviors might be used to observe student interaction; qualitative content analysis would be used to ascertain patterns. On the other hand, standardized reading scores lend themselves well to quantitative analysis methods.

Quantitative analysis. Increasingly, schools are called upon to make decisions based on scientifically based evidence. The "gold standard" for such research include

- randomized controlled trials, whereby conditions are controlled as much as possible and the randomly chosen subjects are treated the same except for the independent variable under investigation (and, furthermore, attrition and disruption are minimized); and
- quasi-experiments, whereby the selected sample is not randomly selected, but the two control and treatment groups being compared are equated (e.g., same demographic academic balance); alternatively the same subjects might be assessed over time between treatments.[14]

Data collected from these studies need to be measurable and quantifiable. Often the sample population is small enough that only descriptive statistics may be used: frequency, range, mean, median, mode. These figures can still give the audience an idea of the scope of the findings and enable them to see if two sets of findings reflect similar or different populations. Tables 6.1–6.4 provide an example of descriptive data about a class's reading performance.

Table 6.1. Student Reading Rubric Scores and Number of Books Read

Student	Number of Books Read	Reading Rubric Score
Ann	6	4
Bob	0	1
Carl	1	1
Dan	1	1
Eva	4	3
Fawn	10	3
Greg	2	2
Hans	2	1
Issa	2	2
Jana	10	4

Table 6.2. Frequency Count of Number of Books Read

Number of Books Read	Frequency
0	1
1	2
2	3
4	1
6	1
10	2

Table 6.3. Frequency Counts of Rubric Scores

Reading Rubric Score	Frequency
1	4
2	2
3	2
4	2

Table 6.4. Descriptive Statistics for Books Read and Rubric Score

	Number of Books Read	Reading Rubric Score
Range	0–10	1–4
Mean (Average)	3.8	2.2
Median (Middle Score)	2	2
Mode (Score with the Highest Frequency)	2	1

* Number of data points = 10.

Analyzing the statistics above, several findings emerge:

- The class reflects a relatively wide range of reading performance.
- The majority of students read two or fewer books, but two students read ten books in the same time frame.
- Four students had low reading scores; the rest of the students had reading scores spread across the remaining three levels (which cannot be interpreted as two, three, or four times better).
- Students who read four or more books had reading rubric scores of three or four.
- Boys tended to read less than girls and tended to have lower reading rubric scores.

Inferential statistics usually make or *infer* generalizations about significantly large populations based on sampling; typically, analysis tries to find correlations between two variables, such as number of books read and reading comprehension ability. Looking at table 6.1, one can see a possible correlation between gender and reading performance. Looking at the scatter plot in figure 6.1, one can see a possible positive correlation between the number of books read and reading rubric score. However, the number of students is too low to make statistically significant conclusions.

The most important statistical consideration is the characteristic of the derived numerical data; misaligning a statistical method with number property causes misleading conclusions. The chief "offender" is ascribing

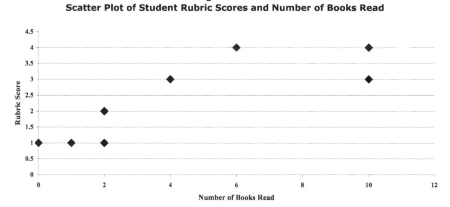

Figure 6.1. Reading Performance Scatter Plot of Student Rubric Scores and Number of Books Read

mathematical equations to emotions (e.g., one person is 2.5 times as satisfied as another person).

- *Nominal scale:* numbers that act as symbols (e.g., room 27, 1 = girls). Mathematical operations may not be performed on them.
- *Ordinal scale:* numbers that can be ranked but usually not measured equally by units (e.g., 5 = most important, 1 = highly agree). Ordinal numbers are found frequently in questions, using Likert scales (e.g., rating a competency from 1 to 5).
- *Interval scale:* numbers on a uniform scale (e.g., circulation figures). Differences between numbers can be calculated.
- *Ratio scale:* interval numbers that include absolute zero (e.g., time).

Data may also be distinguished as discrete (whole numbers, such as the number of students) or continuous (analog, such as length). Most numbers in assessment are the discrete ordinal or interval kinds.[15]

A statistics specialist can serve as a short-term consultant to "grind out" the numbers and give meaning to the generated statistics. Nevertheless, teacher librarians should learn enough about statistics that they can serve as educated consumers of statistical analysis. This skill is especially important because any data analysis needs to be contextualized in terms of the environment or time frame. An outside consultant may have no idea of how the local system works and may make faulty inferences; the assessment team needs to work closely with such outsourced experts.

Qualitative Analysis.   Some data cannot be captured in numbers: images, narratives, gestures. Qualitative analysis gets at the quality and context of data, be they perceptions or unconscious behaviors. Here are a few of the typical qualitative methods.

- *Participant observation:* Teacher librarians often observe information literacy behaviors in the library. They are part of the scene so are not entirely objective. On the other hand, having an insider's perspective can lead to more informed data gathering and analysis.
- *Ethnography or field research:* Assessors observe behaviors in natural settings, such as the school library or computer lab, getting information from the user's point of view. Assessors have to take accurate notes describing the situation and sometimes have to infer behaviors.
- *Case study:* A single case, or limited number of cases, is explored in depth to serve as a microcosm or representative sample for a larger population. For instance, the teacher librarian might follow one or two stu-

dents' information-seeking behaviors in order to determine possible bottleneck decision points.

- *Unobtrusive measures:* This approach examines evidence without impacting the target population. The goal is to gather data that would not be "tainted" by someone's awareness of being assessed. Two typical types of data are accretion (what people leave behind) and erosion (what people wear down). Examples of the former include student locker rubbish and discarded note cards; examples of the latter include worn furniture and keyboards. Examining student work or retrieving website histories also constitute unobtrusive measures.

Qualitative data such as open-ended questions or videotaped incidents are more problematic to manipulate. Interviews should be recorded (either on audiotape or videotape) and then transcribed; typically, it takes six to eight hours to transcribe one hour's worth of recording. Responses need to be coded to generate patterns. The data analyzer should read over the responses to get an overall sense of the data as well as to start picking up reoccurring phrases or themes; jotting down notes while examining the responses helps generate useful categories. A second closer reading can verify and refine the initial categories. Creating a concept map can help visualize relationships among data.

At this point, a grid may be generated, cross-referencing the content with demographics; for instance, do males search the Internet differently from females? (They do.) Subsequent readings can pick up nuances. While software programs such as Nudist and Atlas/ti can help in this process if items are already in digital form, it should be remembered that these programs work based on word-frequency and word-proximity algorithms, so they may be somewhat arbitrary in their associations; they are best used as a starting point.

Table 6.5 provides an example of a qualitative method of identifying patterns, codifying them, and then developing an assessment instrument that captures in situ data. The teacher librarian observed student information literacy processing and took copious needs. Based on analysis of the notes, she conducted a focus group to validate possible patterns and generate appropriate categories that could then be used to develop a self-assessment survey of information literacy. The resultant survey could be administered to a larger population, and respondent data could be analyzed to make more generalizeable conclusions.

It can be easy for data analyzers to make overarching inferences about these "thick" data sets, so care must be taken to stay close to the data. Close attention should be paid to the nuances of language; in that respect, "inside" assessors have an advantage if they understand the unspoken connotations of

Table 6.5.   Information Literacy Challenge/Support Matrix

		Classroom teacher	Other teacher	Teacher librarian	Paraprofessional library staff	Other student	Tutor	Other student	Public librarian	School/district tech support	Phone or online help	Family	Other
	RANK							SUPPORTS					
Rank													
	Interactions with												
	teachers												
	students												
	library staff												
	Resources												
	location												
	evaluation												
	selection												
	comprehension												
	interpretation												
	Technology												
	computers												
	telecommunications												
	images												
	Time management												
	setting priorities												
	scheduling												
	Production												
	organizing												
	synthesis												

CHALLENGES

the words used by the target population. Date analyzers also need to be aware of silence, ambiguity, and contradiction of language. Analyzing qualitative data requires intuition and creativity to "connect the dots." It also requires analyzers to recognize personal bias as well possible contexts made when interacting with the data, such as gender bias or disadvantaged communities. Analyzers should also link their data interpretations to relevant literature.

For example, in examining videos of students seeking information, teacher librarians can look at student interactions with resources, peers, and adults. The analysis should take into consideration time frames, teacher instructional design and delivery, information literacy instruction and other available learning guides, behaviors that facilitate or impede research efforts, and environmental impact on information-seeking (e.g., other students, heating, time of day, Internet speed, availability of resources, etc.). Teacher librarians might or might not know about students' personal factors (e.g., current stress, health, motivation, reading ability, physical/mental differences, etc.). Parsing the contributing factors can be challenging.

Acting on Findings

By analyzing the data derived from assessments, the assessment team can make recommendations to address the emergent issues. For instance, if student bibliographies cite web pages inaccurately, then more emphasis on that source can be made in lessons or guide sheets. If subscription databases show low usage, then either they need to be mentioned explicitly in library instruction or made more visible on websites; follow-up assessment can determine the basis for low usage. Both process-based and product-based interventions should be considered. In identifying an effective solution, the entire system should be examined since any of the entities might impact the outcome.

Assessment findings, analysis, and recommendations should be communicated with all stakeholders and those being assessed in order to show that their interest and participation made a difference. These groups can also provide input to refine recommendations. The communiqué should include the background need, the results, and the intended recommendations. Representative formats of the findings include a one-page executive summary, three-fold flyer, brief and extended report, and multimedia presentation. Visual aids such as graphs and diagrams can facilitate understanding and increase the assessment's impact. Technology can facilitate broadcasting and repurposing of information.

The ultimate use of assessment, though, is improvement of information literacy. Resources, both material and human, need to be determined for the intervention to be implemented. And assessment continues to play a central role as the cycle of inquiry is reiterated to the next level, particularly in measuring the impact that the intervention makes on the population being assessed.

CASE STUDIES

Does assessment of information literacy make a difference? It can if the process is well done and acted upon. The following case studies represent the efforts of several levels of education.

MIICE Project: Measurement of the Impact of ICT on Children's Education

The University of Edinburgh's Scottish Interactive Technology Centre studied sixteen local primary, secondary, and special schools to develop a set of information and communication technology outcomes and components that could assess best practices of using information and communication technology (ICT) in teaching and learning. Seven outcomes focused on learner abilities and attitudes, three focused on the management of learning, and three focused on the teacher's ICT-related professional development. These assessments aligned with national educational standards so schools could leverage their improvement efforts. Each outcome and its associated components were listed one per page; teachers were asked to choose only one-third of the outcomes to observe and comment upon, which lowered their feeling of being overwhelmed, gave them control for assessment, and revealed individuals' values. Eleven educational authorities identified a cross-section of sixty-eight schools and 242 teachers to participate in the assessment effort. Some of the strengths of this assessment effort included site-controlled input and implementation: to determine educational targets, to plan professional development, to help communicate with parents, and to develop individualized educational programs. Overall, use of this assessment changed perceptions about teaching and learning, and revealed educational trends and needs (www.miice.org.uk/)

Hong Kong Information Literacy Framework

To address the knowledge needs of twenty-first-century Hong Kong students, four institutions of higher education (University of Hong Kong, Chinese University of Hong Kong, Baptist University, and the Hong Kong Institute of Education) collaboratively assessed the perceptions of key stakeholders with respect to a draft information literacy framework and its implementation in primary and secondary schools. Seventeen focus groups and eleven in-depth interviews were conducted, with participation by associations in education; education bodies; secondary, primary, and international schools; and expert panels on information literacy. Follow-up questionnaires were sent to 1,300 local schools. The value and need for information literacy and supportive professional training were strongly evidenced. Based on this systematic assessment process, a substantive information literacy framework was developed, and ways for professional development, teachers' assessment, students' assessment and support, and implementation policies and strategies were suggested. To advance the project's agenda, a pilot study was proposed to further explore important implementation issues with respect to information literacy.[16]

Primary School Students' Interaction with Library Media

In New Zealand, Penny Moore conducted a two-part information literacy assessment: one geared toward classroom teachers and the other geared toward primary school students. Perception questionnaires and interviews were held with teaching staff in four suburban elementary schools, revealing different definitions of information literacy and different expectations of children's abilities to evaluate and use information. Based on the "information climate" assessment, a series of workshops on information problem solving was developed and implemented for teachers in three schools. Student observations and interviews were then conducted to explore children's interaction of library media before and after training. As a result of the assessments, teachers became much more aware of the assumptions hidden behind resource-based learning, both on the part of the teacher and of the student.[17]

Santa Maria College Information Literacy Project

Each year, for four years in a row, year seven students in this all-girls college preparatory school in Northcote, Victoria, Australia, explained how they did a research assignment, and their information and cognitive skills were assessed according to a forty-point scale. These skills were aligned with established key learning areas. After the first assessment, research-based learning activities were collaboratively designed by teacher librarians and classroom teachers, and research templates were produced to scaffold student learning. Postassignment assessment showed significant student improvement; longitudinal studies showed cumulative progress. By the third year, scaffolding was withdrawn, and students were also assessed in terms of their ability to learn independently; gains continued to be significant. Assessments were used as diagnostic tools, and professional expertise was enhanced. Student-centered communication and collaboration also increased.[18]

Pierce College

Librarians at this Pierce County (Washington) college collaborated with departments to integrate information literacy across the curriculum. Using learning outcomes as their lodestone, instructors developed goals and assessment tools, and librarians created student self-assessment instruments for each research process. Competency progress was measured for the relevant semester and used as the basis for instructional improvement. As a result of this collaborative effort, faculty have more buy-in into the process, and the library is serving more students.[19]

NOTES

1. American Association of Higher Education Assessment Forum. *9 Principles of Good Practice for Assessing Student Learning* (Brevard, NC: Policy Center on the First Year of College, 2003).

2. Gordon Mowl, *Innovative Assessment* (New Castle, UK: University of Northumbria, 1996).

3. Violet Harada and Jane Yoshina, *Assessing Learning: Librarians and Teachers as Partners* (Westport, CT: Libraries Unlimited, 2005).

4. Educational Testing Service, *Digital Transformation: A Framework for ICT Literacy* (Princeton, NJ: Educational Testing Service, 2002).

5. Peggy Maki, "Developing an Assessment Plan to Learn about Student Learning," *The Journal of Academic Leadership* 28, no. 1 (2002): 8–13.

6. Jeffrey Parsons, "Effects of Local versus Global Schema Diagrams on Verification and Communication in Conceptual Data Modeling," *Journal of Management Information Systems* 19, no. 3 (2002): 155–83.

7. Mary Abbott, Charles Greenwood, Yolanda Tapia, and Cheryl Walton, "Research to Practice: A Blueprint," *Exceptional Children* 65 (1999): 339–62.

8. Martin Terre Blanche and Kevin Durrheim, *Research in Practice: Applied Methodologies for the Social Sciences* (Cape Town, South Africa: University of Cape Town Press, 1999).

9. Terrence Newell, "Thinking beyond the Disjunctive Opposition of Information Literacy Assessment in Theory and Practice," *School Library Media Research* 7 (2004), www.ala.org/ala/aasl/aaslpubsandjournals/slmrb/slmrcontents/volume72004/beyond.cfm (accessed July 31, 2007).

10. Helmut Klaus, "Information Literacy Education and Experiential Learning: Application of the Simulation Technique," *Education for Library and Information Services* 16, no. 2 (1999): 33–45.

11. Steven Tripp and Barbara Bichelmeyer, "Rapid Prototyping: An Alternative Instructional Design Strategy," *Educational Technology, Research and Development* 38, no. 1 (1990): 31–44.

12. Karen Moni, Christina Van Kraayenoord, and Carolyn Baker, "Students' Perceptions of Literacy Assessment," *Assessment in Education*, 9, no. 3 (2002): 319–42.

13. Lesley Farmer, *How to Conduct Action Research: A Guide for Library Media Specialists* (Chicago: American Association of School Librarians, 2003), 17.

14. U.S. Department of Education, "Evidence Standards for Reviewing Studies," What Works Clearinghouse, http://ies.edu/gov/ncee/wwc/pdf/study_standards_final.pdf (accessed September 14, 2007).

15. Farmer, *How to Conduct Action Research*, 31.

16. Siu Kong, James Henri, Fong Lee, and Siu Li, "A Study on the Development of an Information Literacy Framework for Hong Kong Students," http://ies.edu/gov/nceet/wwct/pdf/study_standards_final..pdf (accessed September 14, 2007).

17. Penny Moore, "Information Problem-Solving: A Wider View of Library Skills," *Journal of Contemporary Educational Psychology* 20 (1995): 1–31.

18. Sandra Ryan and Vicki Hudson, "Evidence-Based Evidence, Transformational Leadership and Information Literacy at Santa Maria College," *Synergy* 1 (2003): 29–41.

19. Christie Flynn, Lynn Olson, and Judy Kvinsland, "Connecting the Dots: Using the Assessment Cycle to Foster Student Success" (paper presented at the ACRL conference, Charlotte, NC, April 2003).

· 7 ·

Problems in Assessing Information Literacy

$\mathcal{A}$ssessing information literacy may sound like a good idea, but actually implementing it and using the results to improve practice can be difficult if for no other reason than it needs support from the rest of the school community to be effective. Particularly as library programs change in response to technology-based information, new educational organizational structures, and increased demand for accountability, new problems emerge along with age-old obstacles of time and money.[1] The definition and deconstruction of information literacy itself has changed in recent years, and finding feasible assessment instruments that measure each aspect of information literacy validly can be problematic. Assessing information literacy should be part of the total system assessment plan; the data gathered needs to be analyzed and acted upon in light of that system. Therefore, decisions on how to address possible barriers to information literacy assessment must be made and supported at several levels, potentially: within the library, within a grade or content area, across an educational system, across a region, and across the nation.

FROM AD HOC TO SYSTEMATIC ASSESSMENT METHODS

One of the advantages of working in a school library is the ability to see how students are learning and using information literacy skills. The library offers a model of performance-based assessment. How do you know if a student understands the library catalog? If the student can independently locate the desired item on the shelf based on the catalog information. How do you know if a student can read a map? If he or she can point out the tallest mountain, the capital, the distance between two towns. Likewise, if students are aimlessly flipping through a *Time* magazine and you ask why, their response that they are trying to find an article on seaweed habitats probably indicates that they do not know how to locate appropriate articles.

Every day, teacher librarians see students in action and work with them to improve their information competence. They can tell by students' body language if there is a problem, and students may also ask questions that indicate some kind of learning obstacle. Through training and years of experience, teacher librarians can usually diagnose the problem and help students resolve it. This kind of just-in-time instruction can be a very valuable way to help students, and, on their part, students usually appreciate focused intervention that helps them accomplish their specific task.

However, in such an approach to assessment, teaching and learning is not very cost-effective or systematic. Putting out individual intellectual brushfires does not go very far to address wildfires in a forest of ignorance. Nor does it offer an efficient way to prevent mental burn-out (to continue the metaphor). For every student who is helped, dozens are overlooked due to constraints in staffing and time.

On such ad hoc bases, about the best that the teacher librarian can do is to observe patterns of information-related behaviors of a class or grade over time, and then work with the associated classroom teacher to address the learning gap. For instance, the teacher librarian may observe students printing vast amounts of paper instead of skimming website summaries for possible relevance before downloading them. A quick lesson on previewing potential information sources can help students hone their evaluation skills. Similarly, a teacher may observe that several students are citing sources inaccurately and can show them bibliographic style sheets and have them practice this specific skill.

On the other hand, observation and responsive guidance do not adequately address information literacy needs, if for no other reason than the fact that information-related competencies are complex and nuanced. If a student's research paper is feebly done, there may be several reasons for failure: from poorly designed questions to bad note taking, from inadequate organizational skills to poor time management. Even the specific skill of using key words for searching depends on several subskills: identifying main ideas, knowing or finding synonyms, drawing from prior knowledge. When one considers how detailed reading diagnostic tests can be, it is little wonder that students do not display great information-seeking and -using strategies: few teacher librarians or other educators parse information literacy that finely or spend the corresponding time in diagnosing and instructing in such a systematic way. Still, some satisfactory middle ground must exist.

In the final analysis, for assessment to make a significant difference in the instruction and practice of information literacy, a systematic approach to the process is vital. Even if the scope is limited to one class or one site, scrupulous and systematic consideration of the aspects involved in assessment needs to be exercised throughout the process.

As mentioned in earlier chapters, several questions need to be asked in preparing for assessing information literacy:

- What is the purpose of the assessment: diagnosis, intervention, summative information, instructional design, curricular design, strategic planning?
- What is the scope of the information literacy competency: one distinct subskill for one set of competencies (e.g., identifying key terms), one set of literacy skills (e.g., evaluating the quality of information sources), or a set of information literacy processes (e.g., conducting a research project)?
- What is the population: one student, one student group, one class, one grade, one content area, one position (e.g., administrators), one school, one district, one geographical region, a whole nation?
- What is the time frame: one minute, one class period, one learning activity, one curriculum unit, one grading period, one year, several years?
- At what point in the learning process should assessment occur: upon entrance into the learning environment, at the start of a learning activity, in the middle of learning, at the end of the learning activity, when exiting the learning environment?
- What material and human resources are available: existing assessment instruments, trained assessors, facilities for administering the assessment, record-keeping resources (e.g., videotape, audiotape, transcribers, spreadsheet or statistical software)?
- What is the context of the assessment: teacher librarian job evaluation, collaborative learning, curriculum review, student graduation, whole-school reform, governmental mandate?
- How does the assessment fit with other assessments: isolated, part of a student's cumulative record, one source of a course's set of evaluations, part of reading fluency assessments, complementing technology competency evaluation, part of student graduation requirements, one aspect of professional development, one factor in a grant award?

All of these factors need to be considered and combined in order to choose an appropriate and feasible assessment instrument, administer it, analyze it, and act on the findings. For instance, requiring an e-portfolio with edited video clips is not feasible presently for a regional assessment used for diagnostic purposes. On the other hand, a multiple-choice test must be very carefully constructed and validated if it is to capture the essence of a learner's information competence regardless of the person's context, a task that the U.S. Educational Testing Service (ETS) is now addressing.

Whatever the assessment chosen, the data gathered should be such that it can be effectively acted upon. For example, assuming that the ETS test is found to be valid and reliable, the results can be used as a starting point for higher education and secondary schools to design curriculum and delivery systems that can help students become information literate, and subsequent test results can serve as a placement device for college-age students to take those appropriate courses. At the class level, evaluating a history of Internet links used while students search for information about a topic might be enough to ascertain students' search processes, although a think-aloud transcript would offer a fuller picture about student decision-making processes. The data can be analyzed to reveal students' misconceptions about search strategies so that explicit instruction can be provided to help students become more efficient information seekers.

When sets of assessment instruments and collected data can be compared and complemented, they can deepen the impact of resultant information literacy interventions. The data gain credence when different perspectives lead to the same conclusion; the data are said to be triangulated. Thus, if all secondary school staff focus on reading assessments, they can each stake out their niche: each content teacher can examine how students comprehend specialized vocabulary and evaluate content-specific information, language arts teachers can link reading and writing critical skills, teacher librarians can focus on voluntary and personal reading habits, special education teachers can develop individualized reading interventions specific to each student's disabilities, administrators can evaluate teaching strategies related to reading. Data from class observations, student products and presentations, standardized tests, writing prompts, attitudinal surveys, focus group discussion, reading contests can all be analyzed to paint a rich picture of reading's role in information literacy throughout the school. The ensuing interventions to improve reading can then impact the total school community to leverage learning efficiently.

Unfortunately, schools and districts have tended to assess what is easy to assess—lower level skills—and to use existing assessment tools, such as state-mandated standardized tests and textbook predesigned examinations. High-stakes testing such as exit examinations have further exacerbated this situation. Sad to say, as of 2000 only three of the U.S. fifty states required preservice principals to be competent assessors.[2] No wonder that assessment is not used more effectively.

STAGES OF INFORMATION LITERACY ASSESSMENT IMPLEMENTATION: AN ACTION RESEARCH MODEL

By now teacher librarians should know about information literacy and support its use for lifelong learning and contextualization within the educational community. However, most of the rest of the school community may be ignorant of information literacy, although they may well be aware of elements or aspects of information literacy, such as

- library skills,
- research skills,
- problem solving,
- critical thinking, and
- process of designing products or solutions.

For that reason, teacher librarians should focus more on the ultimate goal of student learning and weave in information literacy concepts as a means to coordinate and optimize students' engagement with information across the curriculum. To this end, teacher librarians should examine relevant educational goals, standards, and indicators, and then match those elements with information literacy concepts. Having done this background research, teacher librarians can then communicate with the rest of the school community in terms they can understand as well as serve as the source for a lingua franca among those members. In short, teacher librarians should know their own domain well before asking others to accept and use it. In the process, information literacy can then be presented as an umbrella term encompassing these already accepted ideas.

At this point, information literacy might be regarded as an agreeable set of skills and processes to be addressed by teacher librarians. For information literacy to impact the rest of the school community, some kind of need on that community's part must emerge; the status quo cannot remain comfortable. At this point, a needs assessment, even if it consists of faculty discussion, should be conducted. Since a main goal of education is to prepare students to meet specified standards of learning outcomes, a needs assessment can examine the school's conditions for learning. Indeed, the process of assessment provides an authentic venue for communication and involvement. The following research-based model looks at the school's infrastructure and culture.[3, 4]

Instructional Program: This part of the model focuses on the conditions and structures that enable students to meet identified student outcomes.

- Are educators highly qualified and competent?
- Is the curriculum characterized as rich and challenging?

- Is there a shared belief in high academic standards and expectations for students?
- Are classes and the school as a whole well organized and managed?
- Is the curriculum coordinated and supported by strong leadership?

Student Motivation and Engagement: This part of the model focuses on students and encompasses their affective domain.

- Are students actively involved in concrete, authentic learning experiences?
- Do enrichment activities outside school hours and beyond the campus enhance learning?
- Do educators draw upon a wide repertoire of teaching strategies in response to identified needs?

Student and Family Needs: This part of the model acknowledges the context of students' personal lives.

- Does the school address the physical and emotional health needs of students?
- Are appropriate interventions and special assistance given to students and families with special needs?
- Does the school provide a safe, supportive, and respectful climate?

Collaboration among School, Home, and Community: This part of the model recognizes that schools are community based.

- Do professional teaching and learning teams further school efforts?
- Does the school model a learning community?
- Are school efforts monitored, assessed, and acted upon to optimize impact?
- Are families actively engaged in their children's education?
- Does the school provide opportunities for students to connect to the broader learning community?

Baseline Data

Baseline data may be gathered through questionnaires and surveys, focus group discussions, content analysis of student and school community products and publications, peer observation, and self-assessment. Indiana University's *College*

Student Expectation Questionnaire provides a holistic picture of collegiate attitudes about engagement, including the use of libraries, which can be adopted for high school assessment purposes to get at student-centered needs. The survey comprises eighty-five questions along five dimensions: college activities, conversations, reading/writing, college environment, and estimate of personal gains. By thoughtfully considering these elements, the school community should be able to identify some issues that can be addressed through the incorporation of information literacy.[5]

In 2006, for instance, the California State University (CSU) system randomly sampled their freshmen and senior undergraduate students. The Long Beach site found that, relative to their CSU counterparts, their freshmen students perceived

- slightly *greater* academic challenge,
- about the *same* level of active and collaborative learning,
- moderately *less* student-faculty interaction,
- moderately *more* enriching educational experiences,
- a slightly *more* supportive campus environment, and
- substantially *greater* opportunities to communicate with students of different race or ethnicity.

CSULB (California State University, Long Beach) seniors reported

- moderately *less* academic challenge,
- moderately *less* active and collaborative learning,
- substantially *less* student faculty interaction,
- moderately *less* enriching educational experiences,
- about the *same* level of supportive campus environment, and
- moderately *greater* opportunities to communicate with students of different race or ethnicity.

Because the campus had focused on the incoming experiences of students, the strengths of support and active learning did not extend through the senior year. The findings were incorporated into CSULB's accreditation study, in which the governing body prioritized more interactive instruction throughout undergraduate education, additional guidance for students who transfer into CSULB as juniors, increased percentage of permanent faculty to teach upper-division courses, and multiple curricular/extracurricular and research opportunities for students. University librarians, in particular, recognized the need to target transfer students relative to information literacy skills and access to library resources.[6]

Interventions

At this point, teacher librarians can present information literacy best practices that model ways to meet those needs: through readings, presentations, workshops, and interactive WebQuests. For instance,

- information literacy can be used as a means to coordinate curriculum;
- information literacy provides a concrete means for students to engage in personally meaningful learning activities;
- information literacy facilitates learning that crosses school-community lines;
- information literacy helps students find information that can help their personal needs;
- information literacy is most effective when taught collaboratively; and
- families can reinforce and use information literacy skills at home.

Teacher librarians can also note valid research-based assessments to use with these models.

To facilitate change, action research groups can explore possible solutions to meet the identified needs, most likely one group per need. This approach supports those "early adopters" who like to take intellectual risks and publicly rewards their efforts.[7] For teacher librarians, the most difficult problem with this approach is a feeling of conflict trying to decide which group to join; having already established good working relationships with other school-community members can help because another person can speak knowledgeably about a specific aspect of information literacy within another action research initiative. Furthermore, teacher librarians can serve as consultants and literature review coordinators. Based on the research and best-practice experiences, action research groups can then posit different interventions and test the most likely ones; assessment instruments need to be determined alongside any interventions in order to align efforts with impact. One of the advantages of action research is that it helps the school community address issues systematically and explicitly rather than by guesswork; as the action research group evaluates the intervention, they model self-reflective practice that facilities an ongoing cycle of inquiry.

Because schools are organic and dynamic systems, one intervention might impact the rest of the school in unpredictable ways; changing the school's schedule to block periods might preclude some students from participating in intramural sports programs, for instance. Therefore, any action research effort should include communication: among the group, with the entities being impacted by the action research, with other action research groups, with administrators, and with any other stakeholders. If the common ground is information literacy, then teacher librarians need to be part of the communication loop, at the very least. This communication aspect helps each group define its role within the larger school community, provides evidence for accountability, minimizes duplicative or conflicting efforts, and facilitates possible coordination with other bodies. For example, the same assessment instrument might be used by two groups, or two groups might design a common assessment instrument that can measure the impact of two different interventions. That assessment can also help action research groups redirect their efforts to avoid conflicts with other groups or to improve their final outcome.

Even if the intervention is ineffective or, worse, negatively impacts student performance, the action researchers can study the reasons for failure and learn from their experiences. They can posit whether a larger test group would have made a difference, in which case they can work on persuading others to join in the project. Perhaps the intervention required more resources, which would make a strong case for allocating additional funds to the effort. Perhaps the school community was not ready for the change, be it because of lack of training or insufficient attention to group norms; prerequisite interventions might be called for in this situation. And if the idea was a total flop, at least the whole school doesn't have to suffer.

On the other hand, if rigorous assessment and analysis reflect that the intervention *does* improve student performance, then the action research has a strong case for wider school participation and adoption. Using a model of the learning community, the action research group acts as the veteran experts who can help mentor and support the new participants. Again, the factors for success, including ways to overcome obstacles, need to be determined in order to optimize outcomes on a broader base. At this point in organization change, a formal proposal can be developed by key personnel, to be put into place via approved policies and procedures. Effort needs to be made to prepare potential participants so they will be ready and prepared to implement the plan of action: through staff development in-services, tutorials, guidelines, and coaching. Adequate resources—including materials, facilities, and human—need to be allocated and insured in order to start, implement, and sustain the effort. Influential leaders, particularly the principal, need to catalyze the school community into action. Again, teacher librarians can take leadership in this process by training their colleagues, suggesting relevant learning resources, and culling best practice.

Making Action Reseach Systematic

Only through systematic preparation and support can change be implemented successfully. Moreover, ongoing assessment is crucial for systemic change because attention needs to be paid to each element in the plan, from time management to teaching strategies. Setting assessment-goal benchmarks provides a means for reflecting on and celebrating process at key junctions, not just at the end. Especially as the number of successful participants grows, individual assistance can be given to those having trouble with change so they will have the inner and outer resources to persevere past the obstacles. As part of that effort, teacher librarians can help manage the growing knowledge base so all can access important learning.

As the school community experiences the benefits of the action plan, they start to value and internalize it. Summative assessment can provide empirically based evidence of improvement, and longitudinal students can demonstrate positive change over time. The "new" procedures become the de facto norm, the new status quo. When new individuals join the school community, they are oriented to these actions as part of the school routine. Sustained change needs to transcend any vanguard personalities or situational variations; otherwise, the effort will regress to the former status. If, for instance, a change in library staffing results in the information literacy "ball" being dropped, then that is a sign that the school community really hasn't developed a sense of ownership for it. One of the most telling pieces of evidence of such ownership is prioritization of resource allocations; when the now accepted process or policy is challenged, as the school community affirms its value, then it has a good chance for institutional survival.[8, 9] The learning community can continue to grow.

A Case Study of Action Research

Redwood High School, a suburban school north of San Francisco (California), typifies how an action research model can incorporate assessment to improve information literacy and lead to school improvement. In gathering baseline data, the following information was found (organized by the model elements discussed earlier):

Instructional Program: The school was known for its high-achieving students and sound instructional program. Curriculum was rich, and management was generally sound. However, curriculum was not consistently coordinated; some departments had varying expectations and student outcomes, and little cross-discipline coordination existed.

Student Motivation and Engagement: Students were usually actively involved in authentic learning experiences, but some students did not read the requiring texts and seemed disengaged in learning.

Student and Family Needs: The school dedicated staff to support students' physical and emotional health, and the site was a magnet school for students with special needs. The general climate was safe and respectful.

Collaboration among School, Home, and Community: The school modeled a learning community and actively encouraged parental involvement. While the community offered enrichment activities, student awareness and participation depended more on familial pro-action than on school announcements. Based on the above data, the school focused on on-site efforts, and some students were not succeeding. Almost 30 percent of seniors did not pass the reading/writing exit exam. In the library, students often asked low-level critical-thinking questions such as how to find a magazine article, and they spent valuable time in the library just getting organized to start their research efforts. Classroom teachers commented on student plagiarism and low levels of access skills. Although an information literacy scope-and-sequence set of skills was approved by the department chairs five years prior, little follow-up occurred.

One of the key elements that facilitated change to support information literacy was the school's administration, who were encouraging and supporting reading-related action research projects that year through release time and joint planning time. Recognizing a window of opportunity, the teacher librarian aligned information literacy to reading achievement, asserting that evaluation and use of information supported reading efforts. She identified a colleague with strong collaborative potential: a young, reputable science teacher. Together, they proposed a research skills study (RSS) Group, consisting of cochairs and a representative from each subject matter department. The RSS group goal was to enable students to become information literate. At the time, few classroom teachers heard of the term *information literacy*, and the American Association of School Librarians (AASL) information literacy standards were just in draft form (1997), so the term *research skills* was used to describe the knowledge and skills set.

The group gathered a variety of baseline data using several assessment methods:

- *Student learning outcomes relative to research skills*: through a literature review; focus group interviews of faculty, students, and feeder school teacher librarians; faculty consensus of research skills
- *Current student level of research skills*: through focus group interviews of faculty, students, and feeder school teacher librarians; survey of faculty and students, analysis of sample middle school and high school student work (including bibliographies); library observation
- *Current instructional practice relative to research skills*: through focus group interviews of faculty, students, and feeder school teacher librarians; survey of faculty and students; analysis of assignment handouts and citation style sheets; library observation; examination of the current library skills handbook (twelve years old)

The RSS group analyzed the data and reported the results at a faculty meeting, where participants discussed the implications and possible interventions. As a body of the whole, the school developed and implemented the following interventions:

- A revised research skills scope-and-sequence curriculum, approved by all faculty, that would be taught in all departments with required courses, in collaboration with the teacher librarian
- Agreement between the high school and feeder school teacher librarians on research skills to be expected of incoming freshmen
- Incorporation of Internet use instruction into the required computer literacy course
- Increased consistency in assignments across sections of the same course, and greater articulation of assignments across groups within departments
- Faculty in-service training on using the Internet and on creating plagiarism-proof assignments
- Parent training on family use of the Internet
- Revised research handbook aligned with AASL information literacy standards that could be used by students independently as well as by classrooms, which would be available in print and online
- Consistent citation style guide sheets with examples of works cited at the end and within a paragraph (science agreed to use American Psychological Association citation style, and the rest of the faculty agreed to use Modern Language Association citation style)
- Development of a library portal that would focus on research and reading guidance: online research handbook, subject- and assignment-specific webliographies, reading promotion, and links to other sources of information (e.g., libraries and metasites)

The trainings and documents were developed by the RSS group. The computer teacher, technology specialist, Web-design students, and the teacher librarian developed the library portal. Throughout the process, the administration and the staff development coordinator provided time for faculty professional development. The RSS group cochairs also received one period a day to oversee the action research project.

The impact of the action research interventions were measured in the same manner as the baseline assessment.

- *Student level of research skills*: bibliographies improved in citation accuracy and in the quality of the sources cited, and plagiarism declined;

students were more prepared to do research when they came to the library and asked the higher-level questions; the passing rate for the exit reading exam rose five percent the first year

- *Research-related instructional practices*: greater consistency in assignments within departments; more faculty interaction across disciplines; more explicit incorporation of research skills in student assignments; incorporation of Internet use instruction in the required computer literacy course; greater and deeper faculty collaboration with the teacher librarian; regular use of the library portal, including increasing requests for project-specific webliographies

Even though the outside community was not a central focus of the action research, the effectiveness of the collaboration between the high school and feeder school teacher librarians led to articulation meetings for *all* faculty at the two levels. Additionally, a small study found that during their first semester of high school, students who had certificated teacher librarians at their middle school earned grade point averages a full point higher than their peers who did *not* have a middle school teacher librarian. When this finding was reported to the feeder school principals, one of them immediately hired a teacher librarian so that his site's students would be more academically prepared for high school.

As mentioned in this case study, several conditions led to effective incorporation of information literacy and impact on student learning:

- Focus on student achievement
- School culture of improvement
- Alignment of information literacy to school priorities
- Administrative leadership and support
- Broad participation by the school community and deep involvement by key stakeholders
- Allocation of human and material resources: time, professional development, technological expertise, and telecommunications
- Continuous communication and collaboration
- Effective assessment, planning, and implementation[10]

Did these results depend on assessment? Certainly. Could these results have happened without the pro-activity of the teacher librarian? Highly unlikely. Did this action research benefit the library program? Indeed! Did the library program impact student learning? Demonstratively so. The following section details how to optimize information literacy assessment through systematic efforts.

WORKING ON AN INDIVIDUAL BASIS

An initial barrier to assessing information literacy may well be defining the need for such assessment. If this process is considered one more workload demand, then any kind of organized effort will be hard to establish. As the logical point person for information literacy, teacher librarians might take it upon themselves to administer some kind of student test or observation checklist as the basis for a needs assessment. For their own self-knowledge, they may design interventions to address the emergent need and even assess how effective that intervention might have proved. However, it is difficult—and ineffective—for teacher librarians to function independent of the rest of the school. Moreover, as long as information literacy is considered the teacher librarian's "problem" or domain, no one else will probably care, and any cooperation they exert will probably be deemed a favor to redeem at some future time.

As a lead in to school community awareness and discussion, teacher librarians *can* share their assessment efforts, (1) showing evidence of students' gaps in learning some aspect of information literacy, such as using Boolean expressions when searching for articles; (2) designing an intervention to address the learning need, such as a Web tutorial and guided class exercise, based on a literature review of best practices for this situation; and (3) comparing later student work that resulted in more relevant citations because these students used Boolean-based search strategies.

Such a string of events is possible if the library program includes stand-alone class sessions. However, this promising practice will probably not have any lasting effect without at least some minimal cooperation of a classroom teacher. The concept of "It's Tuesday so it's Magazine Index Day" with its iso-lationist philosophy needs to die at this point in educational history. While it might be argued that classroom teachers would be happy to let the teacher librarian handle information literacy needs separately, those same teachers might well resent the teaching time taken away from them with the mandate for high-stakes testing and standards-based student outcomes. On the other hand, classroom teachers may also feel uncomfortable *sharing* their teaching time with the teacher librarian.

Quite frankly, classroom teachers need to be convinced that information literacy assessment will benefit them and their students to the point that it merits the necessary allocation of time and effort. Again, this act of persuasion *can* be done on an individual basis between the teacher librarian and a classroom teacher, but it requires an element of personal trust and professional comfort. To begin with, the teacher librarian may need to spend more time in building social capital and listening than in touting information literacy. The teacher librarian needs to find the connection between the classroom teacher's content-related knowledge structure and information literacy processes in order to develop a mutual understanding about teaching and learning: focusing on students. This process can occur with homogeneous groups such as departments or grade levels who possess a common vocabulary and value set. In either case, information literacy should not be considered an add-on, one more thing for the teacher to do; rather, it should be couched in terms of what teachers do—or hope to accomplish—more effectively. The underlying idea is to work smarter, not harder. For example, the teacher librarian might point out the fact that assessing students' ability to ascertain main ideas may help explain students' failure to understand a curriculum unit can; with that knowledge, classroom teachers and teacher librarians can collaboratively design learning activities that help students acquire this skill in order to improve their understanding of ideas across the curriculum.

Another way to work on an individual basis is to try to influence site administrators, particularly the principal, who usually serves as instructional and visionary leader. Perhaps more than teachers because of information literacy's relatively short existence as a formal concept, most principals have little knowledge of information literacy and need to be educated as to its value and implementation. Thus, the personal approach outlined above with respect to classroom teachers applies to administrators as well. Since principals tend to think of schools as an entire entity, the underlying philosophy of cross-curricular information literacy has potential to resonate with principals. As teacher librarians can "translate" elements of information literacy into content-specific vocabularies, principals are more likely to see how such processes and mind-sets can permeate and, indeed, provide intellectual "glue" for schoolwide academic efforts. Interesting the principal is not enough in itself, though; principals need to model and advocate for information literacy assessment. Since that may seem to be "one more thing" to do—another "problem"—teacher librarians would do well to suggest solutions on ways to facilitate systematic adaptation:

- Conduct an information literacy "audit" (a useful quick snapshot assessment is found at www.ala.org/ala/acrl/acrlissues/acrlinfolit/professactivity/iil/immersion/infolitiqtest.htm). This quick on-page survey addresses the interdependence of the librarian, the importance of information literacy, the teaching/learning environment, and the information infrastructure. Based on the results, the assessment suggests actions that are appropriate at each stage. For instance, if few conditions are in place, discussion is needed before a committee would be useful.

- *Present research-based evidence of information literacy's impact on learning*: Indicators of impact include correlations between ability to read statistical tables and standard testing scores, ability to select online resources and grades on reports, ability to categorize and science classification skills, ability to work cooperatively in small groups and sports teamwork ability, and so forth.
- *Demonstrate model, empirically based programs that address information literacy*: These might include reading across the curriculum, articulated research process units, research-based science fair projects, student writing initiatives, capstone senior projects, student e-portfolios, and so forth.
- *Provide professional development opportunities*: In-services could include attending workshops on evaluating resources, promoting student-generated data sets to test hypotheses, using visual images to teach propaganda concepts, doing content analysis of newspapers to identify gender bias, demonstrating video editing as a way for students to identify key decision points, and so forth.
- *Provide resources and other supports for information literacy initiatives*: Resources might include library collections, Internet websites, software programs, equipment, and local expertise. Services that support information literacy initiatives might include bibliographies, videotaping services, and technology coaching.
- *Create pilot programs or action research projects*: Examples could include developing a summer school book club for English learners, pairing high schoolers and middle schoolers as research buddies, comparing intrinsic and extrinsic motivation in prescriptive reading programs, examining online reference transactions with students, and other plans.
- *Develop an assessment plan to measure impact of site efforts*:
  1. Form an assessment committee of site stakeholders.
  2. Identify existing goals, objectives, indicators, and site efforts.
  3. Identify existing assessment instruments that could be used to measure impact of site efforts.
  4. Map the instruments and identify remaining assessment gaps.
  5. Locate or create relevant assessment instruments.
  6. Determine target assessment audience and assessors.
  7. Administer assessments.
  8. Analyze assessment data in light of site efforts.
  9. Report findings and recommendations to the school community.
  10. Modify site efforts as appropriate.

CHANGING THE COMMUNITY

Eventually a one-to-one approach to information literacy instruction and assessment can work, rather like eating an elephant one bite at a time. However, to insure sustained and systematic assessment that results in targeted action, the school community as a whole should support this initiative. In this regard, incorporating information literacy assessment as part of the curriculum becomes a kind of action research project, empowering the community who participate in the process and improving the school overall. For such initiatives to be successful, several elements need to be in place:

- Willingness to change
- Group participation with the intent to improve education by changing it
- Collaboration among those who are responsible for improving education
- Self-reflective and self-evaluative communities of learning
- Internalized theory and practice
- Accountability in terms of documenting plans, actions, data analysis, and changes

In sum, for meaningful assessment to occur, people must see an overriding need to change in order to improve instruction and effective learning. Not only should they find a common motivation and common vocabulary to use assessment for improvement, but they should also be aware of its costs in time and effort because change redistributes resources and influence. A simple exercise to help assess a group's readiness for change is to identify possible problems to assess and then brainstorm potential solutions. Next, have the group determine how feasible the solution would be to implement; would they then choose to act on that solution? If the answers are "no" for the latter part of the exercise, then the effort is probably not worth the effort; if the latter answers are "yes," then a cost-benefit analysis is in order.[11]

Particularly since teacher librarians usually do not have authority over the school community at large, they need to align themselves with key decision makers and existing prioritized efforts. Teacher librarians should also significantly participate in governance committees so their expertise will be heard and considered seriously—and so they assess the ease with which information literacy and its assessment can be meaningfully infused throughout the educational process.

SOCIAL AND CULTURAL CONSIDERATIONS

Because different cultures and societies teach and learn in different ways, assessments may vary as well. Where collaborative learning is encouraged, normed standardized tests given to each student might be threatening. When individualism is king, getting a group grade may seem unfair. If deadlines are considered more as guides, marking down late work might be culturally insensitive (although frustrating for the assessor). If saving face is paramount, then confidentiality needs to be insured. If students are supposed to spend their out-of-school time helping the family, then take-home assessments might not measure performance fairly. If gender impacts class participation, then writing assessments might be more appropriate. If book ownership is limited because of family finances, then measuring student reading habits by the number of books purchased can be embarrassing and misleading, especially if good local libraries exist. If Internet connectivity is scarce, requiring online assessments is frankly embarrassing. Fortunately, most schools know their students' backgrounds and community values so they can make assessment adjustments accordingly. However, in large heterogeneous districts, having one set of standardized assessment instruments and administrative processes requires those elements to be equitable; otherwise, data analysis needs to take into consideration the varying contexts of learners' lives.

For these reasons, people prefer internal assessment ("one of us") to external assessment ("one of them"); they often feel that outsiders cannot accurately capture their contextualized reality and do not have to live with the consequences of the assessment thereafter. In this regard, teacher librarians may well be considered outsiders to classroom teachers if common ground is not established. Certainly, teacher librarians may feel threatened being assessed alongside classroom teachers, noting their distinctive roles in collection management and supervision. Inside assessments are usually more aware of subtle organizational behaviors and values and may be able to elicit deeper data. However, external assessments can provide a more impartial and independent point of view, bring in expertise, and offer new insights unhampered by prior connotations. In any case, group-based cultural and social norms must constitute part of the assessment equation.

This issue becomes critical when comparing information literacy across cultures and nations. Indeed, in very stressed environments in developing countries or where natural disasters must be addressed, information literacy may have to take a backseat to temporary relief; comparisons in these cases are rather unfair and certainly uninformed. The follow-up research to the TIMMS (Trends in International Mathematics and Science Study) report by

Stigler and Hiebert asserted that no one universal teaching approach guaranteed student achievement in mathematics and science; rather, teaching and learning are culturally defined and contextualized. Indeed, if one teaches in a mode that is not aligned with cultural expectations, then the learning results will be inconclusive at best.[12] A useful assessment tool that measures an organization's cultural competence was developed by the Ministry for Children and Families in British Columbia (Canada); its elements can help institutions plan strategically while remaining culturally sensitive.[13]

Using that argument, it is unlikely that one size fits all in terms of information literacy instruction or assessment. For that reason, if for no other, assessment barriers and ways to overcome those obstacles need to be addressed within the cultural context. Unfortunately, such variations may preclude valid information literacy assessment analysis across cultures except at the most basic levels; in those cases, teacher librarians have to settle for the benefits of thorough and systematic assessment strategies for a well-defined population. It must be noted, though, teacher librarians around the world do hold a set of deep common values: equitable access to information and ideas, critical thinking, and lifelong learning. In some societies, such beliefs may be considered revolutionary or treacherous, so in that respect, information literacy assessment risks the danger of upsetting the status quo.[14] In the final analysis, information literacy *is* a powerful mechanism for change, regardless of social or cultural conditions.

MEETING AND OVERCOMING RESISTANCE TO ASSESSMENT

The idea of assessment can be threatening to people; it conjures up images of punishment, rejection, loss—of something wrong. Even when assessment is used to diagnose current status, a tacit assumption of correction is often implied. Even when change is considered positive, people resist, so it is no wonder that those same people put up barriers when confronted with the possibility of assessing information literacy.

Resistance to assessment exists in many forms. Determining the basis for resistance can help find a solution to overcome it. Here are some possible dimensions:

- Overt (what one can see) vs. covert (what is being said or done behind one's back)
- Intentional (conscious effort) vs. unintentional (subconscious or side effect)

- Rational (logical stance) vs. irrational (usually, emotional basis)
- Active (contrary action) vs. passive (failure to act)

People often will not confess that they are resistant to assessment, either because they do not want to hurt/embarrass the assessment proponent *or* because they do not want to hurt/embarrass themselves (e.g., jeopardize their own standing). Instead, they may show surface compliance. If they do not follow up with action or do not ask probing questions that indicate reluctance, then it is probably a good idea to provide an atmosphere of trust and openly acknowledge the possible risks so people can feel comfortable enough to sound their issues. Isolating the problem can then lead to effective solutions.[15]

ASSESSMENT BARRIERS AND WAYS TO OVERCOME OBSTACLES: Q & A

The following issues reflect actual barriers to information literacy and assessment experienced by teacher librarians and others in the education community. Each issue is parsed into several specific obstacles, indicated by ▲. Following each one are suggested ways to overcome it, indicated by ▼.

Time

The underlying issue is time management, whether it relates to scheduling or to prioritization of tasks.

▲ There is no joint planning time.

▼ Plan before and after school or at lunchtime; use e-mail and synchronous online chat; work with preexisting planning documents; create assessments jointly by using the tracking features of word processing program.

▲ There is not enough time to create assessments.

▼ Examine current lesson plans, curriculum, or student work and suggest assessment instruments to address pedagogical issues; locate and adapt existing assessment instruments.

▲ Class time is too short to administer assessments.

▼ Focus on just one concept or skill; subdivide assessment into smaller steps; have students do some of the assessment outside class time; if feasible, share time with another teacher; teacher librarians and classroom teachers can collaborate to develop an online assessment that students can do at their convenience.

▲ It takes too much time to analyze data.
▼ Use online assessment tools that create statistics automatically; enter data into a spreadsheet program that generates graphs; invest in computer-based statistical software programs that analyze data more quickly (e.g., SPSS, SAS); locate a data analyzer through the district or local community; have high school or college statistics students analyze data as part of their coursework; collaborate with university faculty to facilitate data analysis.

▲ Insufficient time exists to follow up on data analysis.
▼ Calculate the time and money already invested in assessing, noting how it is not leveraged to make improvements; calculate the time saved when diagnosis can facilitate targeted interventions that result in significant improvement in student performance; provide summer grants or institutes to plan modifications (e.g., curriculum, resources, instruction) that will improve student information literacy.

Money

The underlying issue is current money management, particularly prioritization of allocations, potential money management: grantsmanship.

▲ Assessment instruments cost money.
▼ Locate free assessment instruments, which can be used as or modified easily; use free online assessment tools; administer assessment instruments via e-mail to avoid paper costs.

▲ Analyzing data costs money.
▼ See ideas about time-savers (e.g., have students analyze data); use free statistical packages such as those listed in "The Impoverished Social Scientist's Guide to Free Statistical Software and Resources" (data.fas .harvard.edu/micah_altman/socsci.shtml).

Resources

The underlying issue is the lack of access to resources to support information literacy assessment efforts, which is usually management based.

▲ Few well-aligned assessment instruments exist.

▼ Locate appropriate free or low-cost instruments; customize existing assessment instruments to align with local needs; create well-aligned assessment instruments.

▲ Little technical support exists for assessment.
▼ Find other schools who have successful technical support and see if their person is available on a commission, consultant, or part-time basis; have an existing staff person trained in giving technical support; use assessment instruments that do not require technical support.

▲ Access to the library and its resources is limited.
▼ Increase library access hours; increase library staff hours; adjust the school schedule to facilitate regular class and individual access; acquire equipment and connectivity cables to expand access to online resources; establish on online library presences; provide subscription database access via intranet and/or extranet connectivity; teach/assist the school community how to use technology to access information.

▲ Resources do not meet information literacy needs.
▼ Conduct a needs assessment of resource needs; use prior assessment of student performance to guide collection development strategies; share control of collection development.

Lack of Knowledge

The underlying issue is that people often do not want to admit their ignorance, or they want to stay in their comfort zone.

▲ What is information literacy?
▼ Translate information literacy concepts and terms into language/vocabulary that school community members already know; share information literacy definitions and standards via documents and presentations; analyze existing learning activities and student products in terms of information literacy, marking the relevant points; give concrete examples of information literacy in practice.

▲ Information literacy definitions are fuzzy.
▼ Explain that information literacy is nuanced and complex and that its definition can be operationalized in terms of its context; enable the school community to define information literacy in terms that they understand and can accept; parse "large" information literacy competencies into concrete manageable skills.

▲ Why should information literacy be assessed as part of the curriculum?

▼ Show how information literacy—and assessment thereof—is already embedded into the curriculum; share economic reports about the need for information literacy in the workplace; share studies that demonstrate that information literacy helps students transfer learning in new situations and courses; discuss the value of assessment in general, noting how it improves teaching and learning.

▲ How do you align/meld information literacy and content area assessment?

▼ Translate information literacy standards and indicators into content area language; examine current content area assessment instruments and extract information literacy elements.

▲ How do you teach information literacy?

▼ Conduct in-service workshops on information literacy instruction; locate or create an information literacy handbook and other learning aids; team-teach so classroom teachers can learn techniques for teaching information literacy; encourage teachers to attend conferences and other professional development venues that address information literacy instruction.

▲ How do you assess information literacy?

▼ Locate assessment instruments and articles/websites about information literacy assessment; conduct in-service workshops about assessing processes for school community members; match assessment methods with information literacy "levels" (e.g., portfolio assessment for research projects).

▲ What is the role of the teacher librarian?

▼ Share examples of model library programs; refer to professional library organization position statements about the role of teacher librarians; share research on the impact of teacher librarians based on their roles within the school; encourage decision makers to attend library professional events; make sure the teacher librarian participates in curriculum and other decision-making committees.

▲ Information literacy is considered the teacher librarian's "thing" or curriculum.

▼ Give concrete examples of how information literacy permeates teaching and learning; foster the concept of preparing all students to be self-monitoring lifelong learners; incorporate information literacy throughout preservice teacher curriculum development and design courses.

Lack of Collaboration

The underlying issue has two levels: personal and schoolwide. The former has several facets: education, control, habit. The latter is largely due to leadership practices.

▲ People do not know how to collaborate.

▼ Provide evidence that collaboration is a cost- and time-effective way to assess; locate and share models of collaboration for assessment; provide readings and online tutorials on collaborative assessment techniques; conduct in-service workshops on collaborative assessment practices.

▲ People have had negative experiences in collaborative assessment.

▼ Explore the reasons for past negative collaborative assessment experiences and find ways to overcome those obstacles; recall positive collaboration assessment experiences and build on factors that facilitate collaboration; keep an open mind to assessment methods.

▲ Assessments are already designed for one-person delivery.

▼ Locate and share examples of collaboratively designed and delivered assessment; in pairs review and revise an existing assessment to incorporate collaborative elements; conduct in-service workshops on collaborative assessment techniques.

▲ Assessment is inconsistent across staff members.

▼ Use validated, objective assessment instruments; have several staff members design and test the assessment tool together; use exemplar sample work to anchor assessment; calibrate assessors through training and recalibration "refresher" sessions.

▲ People do not want to share control when assessing.

▼ Locate and share testimonials of collaborators that show the productivity and learning benefits of joint assessment processes; separate ego from professional efforts; start by doing a single cooperative assessment effort such as analyzing data from an assessment measurement and build on successes.

▲ Personality conflicts arise.
▼ Distinguish between working and personal relationships; learn to negotiate differences; work in small teams in order to diffuse personal issues; focus on student achievement goals that override personal agendas.

▲ Little overlap exists between information literacy and course content or assignments.
▼ Compare standards and find commonalities; locate and share learning activities that meld information literacy and course content; review and revise assignments to optimize alignment.

▲ Administrators do not support collaborative assessment.
▼ Locate and share scientifically based research that supports collaborative assessment as an effective way to improve student achievement; calculate the cost-benefits of collaborative assessment practice; point to model or rival schools who use collaborative assessment practices effectively; work with teacher organizations or district personnel to find ways to reschedule the school day to facilitate collaborative assessment, establish telecommunications to facilitate joint planning time for assessments, and recognize/reward collaborative assessment efforts.

▲ The school culture does not value collaboration in general.
▼ Start collaborative assessment efforts on an individual or small-group basis and build on success; compare the assessment data of student achievement, especially information literacy improvement, between classes where collaboration occurs and those without collaboration; encourage/support administrators and other decision makers to attend conferences and other professional development venues that show how to collaborate.

No school is perfect; not all students succeed. Therein lie opportunities for change—and for the incorporation of information literacy assessment. Teacher librarians need to examine the forces that can foster—or impede—the conditions for information literacy. Teacher librarians need to understand the total school organization and culture and identify the site's priorities so that information literacy can be aligned with those supported efforts. Moreover, teacher librarians need to be an integral part of the school culture, building on excellent library service as a way to build credibility. Only through a strong programmatic foundation and positive, meaningful interactions with the rest of the school community can librarians serve as proactive advocates for student lifelong learning. Only through careful collaborative assessment, planning, and implementation can that schoolwide goal of student success be achieved. Everyone, from the entering student to the retiring staff, is an agent of change—hopefully, for the better.

NOTES

1. Leena Jansson, "Fifty Decades Information Seeking Skills for Customers in Public Libraries" (paper presented at the Research in the Field of Public Libraries workshop, Riga, Latvia, September 16, 2004).

2. Richard Stiggins, "Building a Productive Assessment Future," *NASSP Bulletin* 85, no. 621 (2001): 2–4.

3. Coalition for Community Schools, *The Five Conditions for Learning* (Washington, DC: Coalition for Community Schools, 2003).

4. Carmel Hill and Peter Hill, "Evaluation of a Whole-School Approach to Prevention and Intervention in Early Literacy," *Journal of Education for Students Placed at Risk* 3, no. 2 (1998): 133–57.

5. College Student Experiences Questionnaire Research Program, *College Student Experiences Questionnaire* (Bloomington: Indiana University, Bloomington, 2005).

6. California State University, Long Beach. *2006–07 Resource Planning Process: Strategic Planning Priorities and Goals* (Long Beach: California State University, Long Beach, 2006).

7. Everett Rogers, *Diffusion of Innovation*, 4th ed. (New York: Free Press, 1995).

8. Karen Glanz, Frances Lewis, and Barbara Rimer, *Health Behavior and Health Education: Theory, Research, and Practice*, 2nd ed. (San Francisco: Jossey-Bass, 1996).

9. John Biggs, "The Reflective Institution: Assuring and Enhancing the Quality of Teaching and Learning," *Higher Education* 41 (2001): 221–38.

10. Lesley Farmer, "Building Information Literacy through a Whole School Reform Approach," *Knowledge Quest* 29, no. 3 (2001): 20–24.

11. Thomas Angelo, "Doing Assessment as if Learning Matters Most," *AAHE Bulletin* 51 (May 1999): 3–6.

12. James Stigler and James Hiebert, *The Teaching Gap* (New York: Free Press, 1999).

13. Ministry for Children and Families, *Cultural Competency Assessment Tool* (Victoria, British Columbia: Ministry for Children and Families, 2001), www.mcf.gov

.bc.ca/publications/cultural_competency/assessment_tool/tool_4.htm (accessed May 8, 2007).

14. Lyn Robinson and David Bawden, "Libraries and Open Society; Popper, Soros and Digital Information," *Aslib Proceedings* 53, no. 5 (2001): 167–78.

15. Stephen Ehrmann, "Diagnosing and Responding to Resistance to Evaluation," *Flashlight Program*, www.tltgroup.Flashlight/Handbook/Resistance.htm (accessed September 14, 2007).

· 8 ·

Existing Information Literacy Assessment Instruments

$\mathcal{A}$s education increasingly has to address issues of accountability and as librarians increasingly have to justify their impact on the educational system, assessments have correspondingly increased. Assessment of information literacy has become a natural focus since it offers a complex set of knowledge, skills, and dispositions that comprise much of learning in general.

Current thinking and practice–related information literacy assessment instruments notes several trends:

- Preference for performance assessment
- Transition from tool-based to problem-based assessment
- Transition from library-centric to content-centric assessment
- Transition from multiple-choice standardized tests to portfolios of evidence
- Tension between high-stakes testing and ongoing assessment
- Acknowledgment of the affective domain's role in information literacy assessment
- Collaborative assessment between teacher librarian and classroom teacher
- Use of multiple measures
- Use of simulations
- Incorporation of technology
- Embedded assessment within tutorials to give instant feedback and targeted remediation
- Investigation of systemwide conditions for information literacy learning (e.g., organizational structure, school norms and culture, curriculum, resources, instructional strategies)

This chapter mentions representative assessment tools and practices along two major spectrums: information literacy components and levels of systems.

APPROACHES TO INFORMATION LITERACY ASSESSMENT

For as long as library skills, per se, have existed, so have assessment methods. As mentioned previously, the individual's ability to locate a resource and extract information from that resource constitutes concrete performance-based assessments. If in following courses and grades those same people continue to locate and extract information, then one can be fairly certain that the learning has been internalized. Since the assessment process has as one intention facilitating the transfer of knowledge to real situations, these kinds of authentic activities can offer valid and reliable data for both short-term and long-term analyses.

However, such close observation and possible discussion with each person as he or she practices information literacy skills are very time-intensive efforts for teacher librarians. Often, teacher librarians assess by exception, rather like a manager may do in a business setting. That is, once teacher librarians demonstrate a skill and explain how to do it, they usually have the learners practice the skill. By observation, teacher librarians can often tell if the learners understand the concept and can carry out the task; those individuals who have difficulty can then be given further instruction and assistance. If people continue to have problems performing the task in subsequent sessions, teacher librarians may conduct an on-the-spot diagnosis to determine at which point the person is frustrated, and then try to break down the task into small enough steps that he or she can understand the idea and perform it successfully. If an entire group still has problems understanding the concept or doing the task, then the teacher librarian usually assumes that additional instruction is needed. Teacher librarians may also provide reference or guide sheets to help people recall the steps necessary to perform satisfactorily; the best-known example is a bibliographic style sheet.

While direct observation and interaction with library users constitutes the most obvious means for teacher librarians to assess information literacy, it is hard to document and is not very systematic. Additionally, information literacy may be learned and practiced in any setting at any time. For that reason, print-based assessment instruments have been the main method of collecting data about student information literacy. These paper assessments may take several forms: multiple choice, fill in the blank, matching, short answer, short essay, or graphic representation. These instruments are often chosen for convenience sake; they are easy to locate, easy to administer, and easy to grade. In some cases, teacher librarians adapt standardized tests to fit local resources and curriculum. Through item analysis, teacher librarians can discover what concepts are not well understood and can focus on those details in a follow-up session.

These types of assessments tend to measure simple skills and facts, which may be fine for introductory literacy; however, they seldom capture complex thought or critical thinking. In general, assessment instruments should align in design with the intended outcome, and it should not be so difficult to decipher that it distracts from the knowledge, skills, or dispositions being measured (e.g., editing video clips of critical incidents). Thus, a portfolio of evidence over time would constitute a more valid and accurate measure of one's ability to manipulate information for a variety of purposes than a simple essay. Collecting all the paperwork involved in creating a research paper or presentation provides more insight than the end product itself because it documents the person's processing; if such documentation is supplemented with a research log and final reflection, a rich set of data may be analyzed (recognizing that the presenter may omit embarrassing or culpable details from this paperwork). This thick data set may take extensive time to analyze, though, which is a true constraint for the overworked teacher librarian and classroom teacher; checklists, rubrics, and holistic grading can ameliorate the workload.

It should be noted that up to this point in this chapter, the learner has not been identified explicitly. Observation of any school community member's action, be it by a student or adult, constitutes a valid assessment method, and specific coaching also works with all ages. However, few adults are administered print-based assessment instruments related to information literacy beyond simple self-assessments. To an extent, adult school community members are not given the same tests as students because it might be considered condescending. Typically, it is assumed that adults in educational settings (1) are information literate and (2) can accurately assess their own knowledge base and skills.

These two assumptions are often erroneous. Personal information literacy does not necessarily equate to instructional information literacy. Focusing on technology-related information literacy, for example, one may be able to word process and telecommunicate, but might not know how to incorporate technology into collaborative-based student learning activities. In addition, self-assessment tools have been found to be inaccurate measures for incompetent people; that is, the less one knows about a subject, the less accurate will be that self-assessment. In general, males tend to overrate their knowledge, and women tend to underrate their knowledge. Even when one is shown models of expertise, the ignorant person might not be able to assess himself or herself accurately; instead, the individual needs to be taught that skill explicitly.[1] In fact, one interesting way to use self-assessment is to compare an expert's assessment of the learner and that learner's self-assessment. When both agree that the learner knows a subject matter, then it really is likely to be true.

ASSESSMENT AT DIFFERENT INFORMATION PROCESSING POINTS

One of the advantages of information literacy assessment is that it can be accomplished through authentic assessment. From simple location skills to sophisticated research projects, students' products can provide firsthand evidence of their work. Of course, the more steps and tools used to accomplish the task, the harder it is to assess the underlying process competencies. Just as a substantial piece of writing may be judged in several ways—grammar, structure, word choice, organization, content, depth of thought, editing—so too may sophisticated research products be examined from several angles: choice of topic, resources used, data extraction and analysis, organization and synthesis, presentation elements. For that reason, assessment choices must depend on the immediate objective and the overall assessment plan. Ideally, students should have multiple opportunities to learn and practice a set of information-related skills in different contexts and combinations *in an articulated* curriculum, so small-scale assessments can be used for diagnostic purposes to provide timely interventions that are easy to implement and check afterward. By systematically helping students build up a repertoire of strategies, educators can then match assessment scale to the task at hand rather than be bogged down in trivial measures of in-depth knowledge.

Research Processing

The classic indicator for information literacy is the ability to conduct research. Indeed, the terms *information literacy* and *research skills* are often used interchangeably, although information literacy is a broader concept. Several research process models exist, although rigorous assessment instruments for those models usually were not designed concurrently. Instead, indicators for targeted behaviors typically accompany the model.[2] Nevertheless, educational and professional entities have developed process-based assessment tools, usually in the form of rubrics. Here is a representative sampling:

- The Australian School Library Association and Australian Library and Information Association developed an information and ICT (information and communication technology) literacy matrix of student learning at six levels (alia.org.au/advocacy/literacy.kit.pdf).

- Wisconsin's model academic standards meld information and technology literacies throughout the curriculum and benchmarks targeted performances at fourth, eighth, and twelfth grades (www.waunakee.k12.wi.us/DPI_Standards/matrix.htm).
- The Kansas State Department of Education aligned its information literacy standards to the American Association of School Librarians', and developed benchmark indicators for each standard (www.ksde.org/Default.aspx?tabid=146).
- Mankato (Minnesota) area schools have developed grade-level targeted performance standards for information and technology skills (www.isd77.k12.mn.us/resources/infocurr/benchmarks.pdf).
- TRAILS (Tool for Real-time Assessment of Information Literacy Skills) is a federally funded project to create a standards-based, free tool for teacher librarians and high school teachers to assess students' info lit skills (www.trails-9.org).

Access Skills

Traditional library skills tended to focus on locational skills, which are relatively easy to assess. If students independently locate the desired physical book, article, or digital source in a timely manner, then that is usually good evidence that they understand access tools and strategies. If they find the specific intended fact or passage within a resource, that is also direct evidence of access skills. Teacher librarians can observe students having difficulties and can ask where the stumbling block occurs; responsive, specific guidance usually bridges the knowledge gap for straightforward skills. Students can also do think alouds in the teacher librarian's presence—or hand in a recorded version—so the teacher librarian can identify points of misunderstanding and give corrective information to redirect the students' efforts. For more complex information problems, students can journal their access efforts for the teacher librarian to review and comment on. This kind of skill reflects a tool-based approach to information organization:

- How are groups of resources arranged: by format, by subject, by author, by use?
- What access tools aid in locating a resource: catalog, index, directory, search engine?
- How is information presented in different types of resources: print encyclopedias, atlases, almanacs, newspapers, magazines, videotapes, CDs, DVDs?

- What access mechanisms aid in locating information with a resource: table of contents, index, logical sequence of content (e.g., alphabetical, chronological), find function, search engine, key/legend?

Assessing these closed-ended rote bits of knowledge can be done through objective, short-answer quizzes and may be found in standardized tests under the heading of "study skills." Easy to grade, they are most helpful for diagnosing a specific need for remedial instruction or other targeted intervention, such as better directions.

It should be noted that one important information skill associated with the above tasks is determining what terms are associated with the resource or piece of information. Beyond the basic concept of key words, implementing this skill calls for critical thinking and draws upon prior content knowledge, particularly the vocabulary of synonyms or related words. Using key words, especially in combination, is an open-ended process. Some assessments can capture the essence of simple information tasks, such as underlining key words in a topical sentence or listing ways to generate key words (e.g., using a thesaurus, looking at headings in an encyclopedia article). Authentic assessment, whereby a student either locates—or doesn't—the desired information, has to be followed up when a student fails to produce a relevant source: was the issue one of poor key word choice, misuse of Boolean operations, misspelling, poor selection decisions, lack of persistence, and/or lack of background content knowledge? Multiple-choice tests do not suffice for this kind of analysis. Ways to get at this processing situation include step-by-step think alouds or other self-documentation such as online search histories. Discovering the student's learning obstacles can be time-consuming and difficult, but an accurate diagnosis quickly followed by a well-targeted intervention can be a powerful investment in learning.

A more complex set of skills relates to strategizing how to access unknown information; it is the difference between "finding a book on snakes" and "finding out how snakes transmit poison." The former task requires one to *recall* how books are arranged and what tool marks their physical location. The latter task requires one to *critically decide* (1) what kind of information is needed, and (2) what kind of resource contains that specific information. As with key words, knowing what informational questions to ask and categorizing those informational needs depends on one's existing knowledge base as well as the ability of one to contextualize for the information need (e.g., match the strategy with the desired end product). Thus, the end product may measure success but fail to measure *lack* of success adequately.

Even the deceptively simple task of asking good questions requires explicit instruction and careful assessment. In his book on Socratic circles, Copeland provides very specific guidelines for posing and assessing questions

and also structures students' reflections of the experience (www.stenhouse
.com/pdfs/0394ch05.pdf).[3] Richard Paul developed a taxonomy of Socratic
questions, which has been adapted into a rubric (ed.fnal.gov/trc/tutorial/
taxonomy.html).[4] The former examines the conditions leading to good ques-
tioning, such as reading preparation, engagement, encouraging thinking and
listening, supporting ideas, and accepting different viewpoints; the latter focuses on new vocabulary and strategies for comprehension and analysis, individual and group performance, and the meaning and importance of ideas expressed. Janssen posits a four-dimensional scale for assessing the value of
information literacy questions: (1) the complexity of the search needed to answer the question, (2) interest, (3) fact/explanation, and (4) knowledge ad-
vancement. The last dimension has proven to be the most useful measure.[5]

On a basic level, students typically learn to link different kinds of resources and different kinds of information: primary sources for firsthand accounts, almanacs for current facts and figures, maps for geographic locational
information, government documents for laws and regulations, scholarly journals for research studies. This associative process is often taught using a tool-
based approach, just as students learn to use different mathematical formulas
to solve different kinds of problems. Authentic assessment works for this case:
does the student find relevant information? However, more specific assessment follow-up is again needed if the student fails in this task. While less
time-consuming, multiple-choice tests only give a rough idea of a person's
knowledge, and standardized tests may be inappropriate if they note resources
unavailable to the testee. In general, single-answer responses do not reflect the
reality that information can be found in many different ways in many different
kinds of sources.

- Copeland has guidelines for posing and assessing questions (www
.stenhouse.com/pdfs/0394ch05.pdf).
- Illinois Mathematics and Science Academy developed an interactive key
word assessment (21cif.imsa.edu/tutorials/challenge/Q2Q/Keyword
Challenge.swf).
- Moore lists significant elements for educators to observe in children's
problem-solving efforts (www.ifla.org/IV/ifla63/63moop.htm).[6]
- Shambles lists several useful tools for assessing information and com-
munications technology competency (www.tepaonline.net/pages/staff/
AssessIT/).

Evaluation Skills

This aspect of information literacy has become the core assessment activity for
school library information literacy "curriculum." Prior to the Internet, the

school library's collection was generally a closed universe; the teacher librarian selected and controlled the access to the materials. Users evaluated materials in terms of their relevancy and readability (in the broad sense); they needed to determine the author's point of view because the teacher librarian tried to provide a balanced collection, but users could be fairly certain that obvious untruths (e.g., that the earth is made of tigers) would not be confronted. In the digital world, the school library provides access to information—and misinformation—worldwide; the teacher librarian maintains only some control over the quality of accessible information. Therefore, users need to know how to critically select and evaluate potential sources.

To this end, teacher librarians have spent much time instructing in this area. In most cases, they start with print resources with young children, and then progress to articles and then online information as students gain more experience. At the beginning, evaluation criteria need to be explained and modeled explicitly with carefully chosen materials; once the door is open to any type of resource, it can be difficult to ascertain how learners interpret information critically. Penny Moore's investigation into primary students' evaluation of materials reveals the complicated assumptions that teachers and students bring to the task, particularly when confronted with conflicting information (e.g., color coding differences between texts, statistics with different significant digits, contextualized multiple definitions of a term). Poor reading skills, developmental immaturity, and inadequate knowledge also limit the ability of learners to evaluate information. Piaget, for instance, demonstrated that young children do not understand the concept of volume conservation; he posited that formal logical operations might not be in place until mid-adolescence. Furthermore, individuals have different ways of processing information, so a source that might be rejected by learner A with reason might be used productively by learner B.[7]

Therefore, assessing learners' ability to evaluate information needs to take these developmental and experiential issues under consideration. Assessment methods are relatively simple:

- Marking phrases that reflect content accuracy, perspective, authenticity
- Explaining why a specific source was selected or rejected in terms of the criteria, preferably documenting the decision-making process
- Using evaluation rubrics to analyze a source (e.g., Kathy Schrock's extensive list at school.discovery.com/schrockguide/eval.html)
- Applying critical-thinking skills to problem solving (www.denison.k12 .ca.us/ms/courses/rain/rubric.htm).

With sources pre-chosen by the teacher librarian or classroom teacher, analyzing how students engage with this material is straightforward since the assessor already knows the material and what to look for. When information has not been preselected, the basic criteria may hold, but the learners' choice of resources reflects their unique interaction and evaluation so the assessor may have a difficult time capturing this decision-making process and analyzing its implications.

Basically, no one source is the best for all learners, which is actually good news for teacher librarians and affirms the need for a rich collection. The more important question may be how well learners can evaluate their own stage of knowledge and ability to use information so they can choose the most appropriate information for a specific task in a specific context. Chico (California) Unified School District uses an authentic task to assess students' ability to evaluate websites (www.cusd.chico.k12.ca.us/~jasnault/website_evaluation_assessment.htm).

Communication Skills

Just as reading and writing are two sides of orthographic literacy, so too is communication another aspect of information literacy. Knowledge-building requires communicating the knowledge one learns. Therefore, learners need to identify the most appropriate medium for communicating specific kinds of information for specific objectives to specific audiences. Then they need to organize their information so it can be transmitted effectively relative to those dimensions. The following approaches address those different aspects of communication.

- With Socratic circles, students discuss their insights on their reading and model intellectual dialogue. The National Teaching and Learning Forum provides a rubric for assessing several facets of participation (www.ntlf.com/html/lib/suppmat/1306a.htm).
- The Victorian Curriculum and Assessment Authority, State Government of Victoria (Australia) created a communication rubric that integrates oral, visual, and written communication (vels.vcaa.vic.edu.au/assessment/ppoint/communication/index.html).
- Schools of California Online Resources for Education (SCORE), which uses California content standards, has developed a simple collaboration rubric (www.sdcoe.k12.ca.us/score/actbank/collaborub.html).
- Rourke et al. have developed a useful coding scheme that captures assessment data about affective, cohesive, and interactive responses to thematic content, specifically in asynchronous learning environments (cade.athabascau.ca/vol14.2/rourke_et_al.html).[8]

Metacognition Skills

According to Mueller, metacognition involves at least three critical stages: an awareness of one's own cognitive ability, a proficiency in explaining tasks that improve performance, and an ability to suggest alternative strategies when existing practice proves ineffective.[9] Although students in this study demonstrated varying levels of progress, most of them became more aware of their thinking processes through journal writing. They made strides in paraphrasing and elaborating on steps in the information search process. They also grew in their ability to identify techniques for self-improvement. If a student knew that she had a poor memory for deadlines, for example, she created a timeline. As they worked on their final products, many students employed fallback strategies when technical problems arose.[10]

Good readers know how to monitor their own reading and have a variety of coping strategies to enable them to solve reading problems independently. So too do information literate people know how to identify and overcome obstacles in information processing. One of the underlying assumptions, which is seldom discussed, is self-awareness: what do I know and what do I not know? Armour posits five levels of ignorance:

4. Not knowing what ignorance is
3. Lacking a process for finding out you are ignorant
2. Not knowing that you don't know
1. Knowing that you don't know something, and knowing how to eliminate that ignorance
0. Knowledge[11]

When students and teachers agree on the degree of ignorance (or knowledge), the next step is usually clear: teachers can help students reach the next level. When students perceive that they are knowledgeable but teachers disagree, the perception gap must the bridged. This issue focuses on self-efficacy and highlights the problem that students who are incompetent but think themselves otherwise do not compare themselves accurately with other students in response to model student work/products; instead, teachers have to diagnose the specific area of weakness and teach that specific skill or knowledge set.[12] This targeted approach appears to have more success than teaching general metacognitive skills. Nevertheless, an individual's overall mind-set about learning and studying *does* impact task-specific efforts.

- Biggs' revised study process questionnaire gives valid information about a student's level of motivation and use of study strategies (teaching .polyu.edu.hk/datafiles/R75a.doc).

- Learning and Teaching Alberta supplies two self-assessments for capturing learner perceptions and for collecting evidence of attainment (www.education.gov.ab.ca/k_12/curriculum/bySubject/focuson inquiry.pdf).

Self-documentation has another severe limitation: knowing how to assess oneself and accurately stating what actually occurs may differ dramatically. Students may record what they think the teacher wants to see rather than honestly telling the story; students may even delude themselves, thinking that they reviewed all their notes, for instance, when in actuality they merely gathered them together. Videotapes and observation can overcome that obstacle because they show a person's actual behavior, but they do not capture well that person's internal processing. A better approach is to provide a safe learning environment and multiple opportunities for students to make their internal thinking processes visible. MRIs would be a valid assessment method in this regard, but not very cost-effective at this point in time.

A more realistic approach is multiple measures; one promising assessment approach is to conduct interviews about information literacy strategies, and then assess how students' behaviors change in light of the conversation. MacLeod, Butler, and Syer's metacognitive questionnaire has been validated and captures the essence of three key metacognitive elements that apply well to information literacy: task analysis, strategy understanding, and managing learning.[13] Since then, Butler and Cartier have developed a research-based inquiry learning questionnaire that takes into consideration contextual issues; it reliably measures self-competence, attributions, emotions, problem solving, planning, strategies, self-monitoring self-assessment, "fix-up," and criteria.[14]

Cheuk developed an indicator-based scheme for assessing information behavior (including physical, cognitive, and affective domains) for a given task. She identified the following information seeking/using situations: task initiating, focus formulating, assuming ideas, confirming ideas, rejecting ideas, finalizing ideas, passing on ideas. For each situation, she noted the choice of information sources, judgment of information relevance, information organizing strategies, information presentation strategies, feelings, and definitions of information. One strength of this instrument is that it enables one to consider decisions for each information seeking/using situation; one does not have to pursue all seven situations. While Cheuk extracted this information through an interview protocol, she has provided enough specific observable indicators to enable assessors to compare observation with self-revelation. Of course, the ultimate goal is alignment between what learners say they do and how they actually behave.[15]

Assessing metacognitive differences over time or differentiating metacognitive processes of two parallel activities is probably an easier task because one can compare two concept maps, reflective journals, or think alouds of private speech of the same person in a straightforward manner, taking into account that with practice one tends to improve the self-documentation. Comparing two different learners in the same task can be enlightening but misleading if a value rating is applied beyond rudimentary assessment (i.e., data in one is very skimpy and vague while the other shows complex processing and specific supporting details); moreover, valuing a sequential developmental process over a global holistic process may well reflect societal or cultural norms more than learning efficacy.

Collaboration Skills

Ultimately, learning is a social activity; people learn from one another, even if the only point of contact is the written page. Thus, the American Association of School Librarians includes the ability to work cooperatively as one information literacy standard. It should be noted that collaboration involves both an intellectual task and a social task, so both aspects need to be assessed.

Several authors lead the field in assessing aspects of collaborative learning in school settings: Costa, Johnson and Johnson, Kagan, Kallick, and Slavin. Assessment of student collaboration usually includes the following guidelines: be specific, be descriptive, address both process and product, be clear, be truthful, focus on behaviors within the person's control, be timely but wait until the person is receptive, check for understanding and verification. Clear expectations about collaborative tasks and assessment methods need to be in place from the start so learners can self-monitor and peer-monitor throughout the process, thus providing opportunities for learners to make effective, timely adjustments. A good practice is to have one person serve as an observer of the group, noting behaviors that advance and impede collaboration. Other typical assessment tools include individual and group questionnaires and checklists, reflective documentation, and authentic assessment of group projects.

- The International Association for the Study of Cooperation in Education (www.iasce.net/resources.shtml) offers resources from the leading researchers in the field.
- The Center for the Study of Learning and Performance at Concordia University in Canada, for instance, is listed on this site and has a very useful set of assessment tools for students and teachers (doe.concordia.ca/cslp/RS-Instruments.php).

- San Diego (California) State University's College of Education developed a simple rubric to assess student collaboration (edweb.sdsu.edu/triton/tidepoolunit/Rubrics/collrubric.html).
- Las Cruces (New Mexico) and Kyrene de las Brisas Elementary (Arizona) public schools targeted their collaboration rubric to elementary students (www.zianet.com/cjcox/edutech4learning/cincorubric.html and www.kyrene.org/schools/brisas/sunda/litpack/collaboration_rubric.htm).

Increasingly, handheld devices have been used to assess student collaboration because the technology is relatively inexpensive and can provide timely feedback. Project WILD (Wireless Internet Learning Devices; ctl.sri.com/projects/displayProject.jsp?Nick=wild) lists several educational assessment efforts that incorporate this tool; from these projects, a useful software program was developed by the U.S. Department of Education, which is freely accessible at www.teamlab.org/.

Appreciation Skills

Is appreciation of creative expression considered an information literacy competency? The American Association of School Librarians reckons it as one element therein. The critical feature in such a competency is esthetic, which includes very individualistic and psychological aspects. A useful philosophy to apply to this competency is connoisseurship, promoted by esthetic theorist Elliot Eisner. He asserted that connoisseurship served as private esthetic appreciation and that criticism acted as public disclosure. While connoisseurship may bring to mind art collecting, Eisner applied its philosophy to "any realm in which the character, import, or value of objects, situations, and performances is distributed and variable, including educational practice."[16]

The extent to which one can understand the language or protocol of the communications medium, understand the content, and critically compare it with other works from an esthetic viewpoint impacts the degree to which one can appreciate a creative expression. Those capabilities can be taught and assessed. Even if quality might be debated, the basis for the decision can be justified according to agreed-upon criteria. Leder et al. developed an information processing model of esthetic experience that confirms the above suppositions and addresses the emotional aspect of the esthetic experience.[17] Basically, cognitive and emotional evaluation impact each other throughout the engagement with a creative expression. To have an esthetic experience, one usually contextualizes it in terms of the environment, such as a museum or classroom. One then preclassifies the object of the experience—sculpture, haiku,

Beethoven symphony, and so forth—which sets up the first response (i.e., I hate organ music, or I love Picasso). Then one analyzes his or her perceptions in terms of complexity, contrast, order, grouping, and so forth. If the object is too complex, one becomes confused, and if the object is too simple, one becomes bored, so some novelty or complexity can evoke a positive emotional state. One then integrates the perception with prior experience and then explicitly classifies it in terms of style and content based on declarative knowledge (i.e., facts) and domain-specific knowledge (e.g., science fiction genre literature or art), personal taste, and interest. At that point one interprets the object and relates it to oneself, and then evaluates it for understanding and emotional satisfaction. As one gains competence, this esthetic process becomes more cognitive based; "naïve" individuals tend to base their experiences on feelings of pleasure.

- Kansas State Department of Education has developed a rubric that addresses basic appreciation elements across the creative arts (www.ksde.org/LinkClick.aspx?fileticket=HDanx08Pf5k%3d&tabid =1713).
- Art educator Marvin Bartel has explored the status of art and esthetics in education and daily life. Among his assessment instruments is a multifaceted rubric that assesses discussion and writing on art and esthetics. With just a few changes in terms, it can be used for creative expressions in any format (www.goshen.edu/art/ed/rubric3.html).
- Lynchburg College's Division of Fine and Performing Arts examines art processes that involve ways of thinking and expressing oneself. Their rubric can be applied to active appreciation as well (www.lynchburg .edu/facresources/Gen%20Ed%20Page%20files/Rubrics/Fine Arts%20Rubric.doc).
- Museums often have educational services to help young people develop an appreciation of the arts. The Kennedy Center in Washington, D.C., has an extensive Web presence, which includes ways to assess art appreciation (artsedge.kennedy-center.org/content/3338/).
- As with visual arts, music appreciation includes both universal elements such as tonality, rhythm, and tempo, as well as culturally defined norms of quality (e.g., Cantonese opera versus Italian opera). Music appreciation can also impact other literacies; for instance, nonnative speakers can learn another language with the use of that country's music. Orlova developed a three-stage music appreciation assessment plan for English learners (iteslj.org/Techniques/Orlova-Songs.html).[18]
- The Australian Children's Television Foundation lists indicators of insightful television and film appreciation that can be applied to K–12

settings (www.actf.com.au/learning_centre/school_resources/teaching
_kits/btv/units/btv_lp.htm).

ASSESSMENT AT DIFFERENT SYSTEM LEVELS

Library Level

Information literacy is a core element of school library programs, and its implementation can be assessed in several ways: in terms of student outcomes, in
terms of conditions for learning, in terms of instruction, in terms of resources
and their use. Even though the library staff cannot control outside influences,
they can identify those factors and figure out ways to work with other people.

- Reflecting the complex nature of library programs, the Department for
  Education and Skills and the School Libraries Working Group (UK) developed two series of scenarios that teacher librarians can use to assess
  their programs, one for primary and one for secondary settings (www
  .teachernet.gov.uk/teachingandlearning/resourcematerials/school
  libraries/?3300545056b4385-a1d7191d-3302-4529-8db5-17
  eb5900db37).
- Berea College Hutchins Library uses a number of useful forms to assess bibliographic instruction program (faculty.berea.edu/henthorns/
  bieval/).
- Bertland maintains links evaluation forms for school library programs
  and teacher librarians (www.sldirectory.com/libsf/resf/evaluate.html
  #forms).
- Maxfield (Montana) Library has quick forms for both students and teachers to assess library instruction (www.lib.umt.edu/research/eval.htm).

Classroom Level

At the classroom level, teachers can examine their courses, instruction, learning activities, and student work to see how information literacy is being addressed and achieved. As much as possible, teachers should try to help their
students make their thinking visible so instructional strategies can be individualized for maximum impact.[19] Assessment can be conducted continuously,
and feedback can be provided in a timely manner to improve student learning. Classroom teachers can also assess their collaboration with other school-
community members in producing these deliverables.

The teacher librarian can collaborate with the classroom teacher to align content standards with information literacy standards and then project out to investigate what learning assignments incorporate information literacy. A good practice is to code student assignment handouts, noting the phrases referring to information literacy concepts. Which of those assignments assume prior knowledge of information literacy and which need explicit instruction? In the former case, articulation of information competencies should exist and be accessible for consultation. In the latter case, the instructor should be identified: classroom teacher, teacher librarian, technological specialist, reading specialist, other school-community member.

- Turner and Riedling identify three dimensions of instructional consultation: amount of interaction (from none to extensive), purpose of interaction (noting degree of impact on teacher's knowledge, experience, and values), and number of instructional design components involved.[20]
- The Indiana State University library portal includes a self-assessment tool to determine to what extent a course needs library instruction; although targeted for college faculty, most of the questions can be easily adapted for secondary school settings (library.indstate.edu/about/units/instruction/assess.html).
- Alberta (Canada) Learning's 2004 publication *Focus on Inquiry* helps teachers to incorporate technology for inquiry-based learning and to meld information literacy; the twelve appendices include useful assessment tools for both teachers and students (www.education.gov.ab.ca/k_12/curriculum/bySubject/focusoninquiry.pdf).
- Fink offers a system of assessment techniques relative to teaching practice: self-monitoring, taping, student evaluations, student work, and outside observation (honolulu.hawaii.edu/intranet/committees/FacDevCom/guidebk/teachtip/evaluate.htm).[21]
- Seufert's 2002 assessment instrument measures the beliefs and practices related to interactive learning systems and can be used to compare different educators' approaches (www.scil.ch/seufert/docs/cultural-perspectives.pdf).[22]
- New Zealand's Ministry of Education constructed a literacy assessment rubric targeted to classroom teachers (www.tki.org.nz/r/assessment/atol_online/self_review_e.php).
- Heckman and Annabi provide a detailed coding scheme for a content analysis assessment of learning processes; it consists of indicators for social processes, cognitive processes, discourse, and instruction (jcmc.indiana.edu/vol10/issue2/heckman.html).[23]

Probably the most telling evidence, however, is sample student work. Does student work demonstrate information competency? Such assessment not only points out students' competencies but also reflects the quality of instructional strategies and supporting resources. Both the classroom teacher and teacher librarian can examine bibliographies (at least as a first step to assess citation style and inclusion of feasible sources, realizing that students might not have actually used those materials), theses statements, development of arguments, and possible supporting documentation such as notes, outlines, and document commentary. While research process worksheets can lead to one-way thinking or nonrecursive *re*searching, these guides do provide a structure for novice researchers. Tamalpais (California) Union High School District's High School's research handbook serves as a consumable guide in this respect (rhsweb.org/library/researchhandbook.htm). One way to address the affective domain is to have students and teachers select a critical incident and reflect on the nature of their engagement and learning.

Research project rubrics provide a concrete way to assess student work; both the process and product should be assessed.

- Rochman's rubric, based on the information literacy standards of the Association of College and Research Libraries (ACRL), is a good start (www.calstate.edu/LS/1_rubric.doc).
- New Jersey City University's information literacy rubric is also based on ACRL's information literacy standards and was included in Middle States Commission on Higher Education's 2003 publication on curricular incorporation of information literacy (www.njcu.edu/Guarini/Instructions/instructions.htm).[24]
- From New Zealand comes another simple rubric to assess information processing skills (www.in2edu.com/downloads/infolit/inforubric.PDF).
- The Australian Library and Information Association has developed an information literacy toolkit, which includes an ICT literacy matrix of student learning (www.alia.org.au/advocacy/literacy.kit.pdf).
- The Northwest Regional Educational Laboratory's research rubric assesses student work from three perspectives: technology use, researching, and presentation (www.ncrel.org/mands/FERMI/prairie/9prairie/9rub1.html).
- Joyce Valenza's research "checkbric" can be used by students and adults alike (mciu.org/~spjvweb/checbric.html). Her research project rubric aligns with standard research process models (mciu.org/~spjvweb/resrub.html).

- California State University, Long Beach, developed an analytic writing rubric, which reflects information literacy elements (www.csulb.edu/divisions/aa/personnel/fcpd/resources/ge/analytic/index.html).
- Kansas City Public School District's science report rubric (kancrn .kckps.k12.ks.us/science/assessment/secondaryrubric.htm) points out the critical features of technical writing.
- Redwood (California) High School's research process rubric may be used by students to diagnose their research behaviors before and during a research project (rhsweb.org/library/research_rubric.htm).
- The following research product rubric (see table 8.1), developed at Redwood (California) High School and based on the Kansas State Department of Education research product model, may be used jointly by classroom teachers and teacher librarians.

Site Level

As the school community examines information literacy assessment plan, it needs to inventory present practices at the teacher, grade, department, and school level: objectives, personnel, resources, preparation, methods, timing, data analysis, accountability. Part of the inventory needs to address articulation coordination throughout the school. Gaps in assessment can then be identified and addressed, taking into account existing and feasible resources.

A good practice is a systemwide information audit, used to identify resources and services that can contribute to information literacy planning and implementation. At the operational level, it can help streamline procedures, minimize duplicative effort, and aid in prioritizing the allocation of resources. Some of the factors to consider include

- identifying resources and services that support information literacy;
- identifying gaps and dysfunctional use of information literacy–related resources;
- identifying needs of key information literacy stakeholders;
- mapping information flow within the system and between the system and its surrounding environment;
- linking information literacy and governance issues; and
- identifying existing and needed information literacy–related policies.[25]

The New South Wales (Australia) Department of Commerce's Office of Information Technology offers guideline for conducting an information audit, which can provide a framework for an information literacy assessment plan (www.oict.nsw.gov.au/docs/IM_Audit.pdf).

Table 8.1. Research Product Rubric

Target Indicators	Adherence to Assignment	Organization	Proof and Justification/ Commentary	Use of Language and Strategies	Spelling and Grammar
6. Exceptional	All aspects of assignment are covered in depth. Bibliography and citations are done according to format without errors. Assignment is free of plagiarism.	Well-organized structure and paragraphs that support insightful, defined thesis.	Substantial and appropriate proof with convincing justification and commentary.	Language is mature and clear. Sentence structure is varied and well developed.	Errors are rare.
5. Accomplished	All aspects of assignment are covered. Bibliography and citations are done according to format with few or no errors. Assignment is free of plagiarism.	Organized structure and paragraphs that support clearly defined thesis.	Suitable proof with convincing justification and commentary.	Language is effective and clear. Sentence structure is varied.	Errors are infrequent.
4. Competent	Most aspects of assignment are covered. Bibliography and	Organization and paragraphs that support simplistic thesis.	Adequate proof with somewhat convincing justification and	Language is adequate. Sentence structure varies somewhat.	Errors appear occasionally.

(continued)

Table 8.1. (*continued*)

Target Indicators	Adherence to Assignment	Organization	Proof and Justification/ Commentary	Use of Language and Strategies	Spelling and Grammar
	citations are done according to format with some errors. Assignment is free of plagiarism.		commentary.		
3. Emerging	Some important aspects of assignment are missing. Bibliography and citations contain frequent, distracting errors. Assignment is free of plagiarism.	Unorganized structure and paragraphs with underdeveloped or vague thesis.	Inadequate proof with underdeveloped or vague justification and commentary.	Language is awkward. Sentence structure is simplistic.	Errors appear often and distract the reader.

2. *Rudimentary*	Many important aspects of assignment are missing. Bibliography and citations are incomplete. Assignment contains uncited information.	Unorganized structure and paragraphs with no apparent thesis or focus.	Inadequate proof with little clear or related justification or commentary.	Language is unclear or repetitive. Sentence structure is simplistic and lacks control.	Errors appear continuously and distract the reader.
1. *Unsatisfactory*	Most important aspects of assignment are missing. Bibliography and citations are missing or incomplete. Assignment contains plagiarism.	No organization is present. Product lacks thesis.	Clearly lacking proof with little or no justification or commentary.	Language is ineffective or repetitive. Sentence structure is confused.	Errors make comprehension difficult.

Increasingly, schools and districts are developing information literacy and information technology plans, which include a series of questions about existing vision, resources, services, and capacity, as well as identified directions with appropriate support. These plans give teacher librarians an opportunity to provide input and leadership about directions for change. Particularly since technology continues to be a priority in education, linking information literacy to such initiatives can leverages the library's role effectively.

- The ACRL (of the American Library Association) has designed an information literacy IQ (institutional quotient) test and scoring guide to determine an institution's readiness for integrating information literacy into the curriculum; the emphasis is on systemwide conditions and steps toward capacity building (www.acrl.org/ala/acrl/acrlissues/acrlinfolit/ professactivity/iil/immersion/infolitiqtest.cfm).
- New Zealand's Ministry of Education developed a literacy leadership tool for elementary schools that includes a planning vision, literacy review tool, and school action plan (www.tki.org.nz/r/literacy_numeracy/ lit_lead_tools_1_8_e.php).
- Colorado's Department of Education now mandates district technology and information literacy plans and provides forms and guidelines to help staff in this process (www.cde.state.co.us/edtech/plng-etil.asp).
- The North Central Regional Educational Laboratory offers a self-assessment tool for school leaders to examine technology and transformation; it may be adapted for information literacy issues (www.ncrel .org/engauge/).
- California's Technology Information Center for Administrative Leadership provides several templates and guidelines for site and district technology plans, which include information literacy aspects (www.portical .org/contents2.html?mode=TT).

Each school has a mission and a vision for education; even the lack thereof indicates a site's values. Those schoolwide goals are manifested in the curriculum, both in terms of content and delivery. The role that information literacy plays in the curriculum can serve as a bellwether about the school community's attitudes about education and vice versa. For instance, a skills-based approach to information literacy is likely to reflect a skills-based curriculum in other areas. Lecture-based instruction based in textbook readings typically undervalues resource-based learning and constructivist philosophies.

Three major models for information literacy have emerged: a compartmentalized approach, an integrated approach, and a mixture of the two. In the first model, information literacy curriculum exists as a separate course and unit with its own stand-alone standards and indicators. This model tends to be skill and tools based. The teacher librarian usually controls the content and the delivery. The second approach embeds information literacy within one or more courses. This approach requires extensive coordination and collaboration, and it can be difficult to determine each person's instructional and assessment role. The focus is usually content, with information literacy used as a series of processes to learn specific domain knowledge. Usually, content standards are used to address information literacy issues. In the mixed model, information literacy instruction includes some tools-based modules such as use of reference resources and content contextualized processes. As with the integrated model, careful coordination is vital, but it is sometimes easier to assign and clarify roles.[26] The mixed model tends to be the preferred one in K–12 education, with earlier grades emphasizing tools and older grades emphasizing integration with domain-specific information processing.

Whatever the approach, the curriculum leads to instructional approaches, supporting learning activities, and assessment. Usually, teaching and learning reflect each other: lecture methods often lead to parroting essays and multiple-choice tests, seminar-based instruction often leads to discussion and debate, demonstration often leads to tool-based hands-on practice and performance, constructivist approaches often lead to project-based learning and assessment. When curriculum, teaching, learning, and assessment are *not* aligned, each element is not well leveraged and learners may well become confused. The U.S. National Center for Education Statistics developed a questionnaire that examines information literacy instructional programs (nces.ed.gov/surveys/SASS/pdf/0304/sass_ls1a.pdf).

Regardless of the information literacy curriculum model, each site must determine the roles and responsibilities of each school-community member. Typically, the teacher librarian focuses on tools and generic processes, and classroom teachers focus on context contextualized processing and application. To that end, classroom teachers need to be information literate themselves so they can apply those literacies within their subject domain through appropriate learning activities. Both bodies can share issues of assessment. The following assessment (see table 8.2) helps school community members, particularly teacher librarians and classroom libraries, examine their collaborative practice.

Part of site-based assessment, which is often overlooked or assumed to be unnecessary, is evaluating the staff's own information competency. At the very least, they can self-identify their strengths and weaknesses according to the agreed-upon information standards. To a certain extent, the lessons and learning activities planned by classroom teachers is a fair indication of their comfort with locating and using a variety of reputable resources. Surprisingly,

Table 8.2. Partnership Rubric

Activity	Exemplary	Good	Fair	Limited
Assessment	Partners use various assessment strategies to evaluate students/services. Assessment drives curricular program. Assessment is used to improve resources/instruction.	Partners regularly assess students/services. Assessment informs curricular program. Assessment informs resources/instruction decisions.	LMT or partner sometimes assesses students/services. Assessment sometimes impacts curricular or instructional decisions.	Partners do not share assessments. Assessments seldom inform curriculum decisions.
Planning	LMT is full curriculum development partner. Full range of info lit skills are integrated into curriculum. All activities involving the library are planned cooperatively. LMT is involved throughout planning process.	LMT helps develop curriculum. Most info lit skills are integrated into curriculum. Many activities involving the library are planned cooperatively. LMT plays significant role in planning.	LMT supports curriculum development. Some info lit skills are integrated into curriculum. Some activities involving the library are planned cooperatively. LMT plays a limited role in planning.	LMT follows curriculum development. A few info lit skills are integrated—or are taught in isolation. Few activities involving the library are planned cooperatively. LMT isn't part of plan.
Implementation	Partners usually team-teach. Partners use a variety of strategies and resources. Partners assess student achievement regularly. Partners modify plan as needed in collaboration with others.	Partners sometimes team-teach. Partners share several strategies and resources. Partners sometimes assess student achievement. Partners make some plan changes as needed.	Partners decide who teaches. Partners share some resources or strategies. Partners assess student achievement unevenly. Partners occasionally change plans.	LIT doesn't teach. Resources and strategies aren't shared. LMT does not access student work. Partners seldom change plans.
Commitment	Partners communicate regularly with each other and with the school community. Partnership is long term and close. Peer coaching is ubiquitous.	Partners communicate regularly with each other. Partners have worked together and coached each other regularly.	Partners sometimes communicate and work together usually for short-term activities. Peer coaching is spotty.	Partners seldom communicate, coach, or work with each other. Activities are one time only.

Source: Lesley Farmer, *Partnerships for Lifelong Learning,* 2nd ed. (Worthington, OH: Linworth, 1999), 77. Reprinted with permission.

some staff are not as well versed in information skills as might be expected considering their professional preparation.[27]

Under the auspices of the International Federation of Library Associations, a survey about on-site teacher librarian and principal perceptions was offered. Although the website has not been maintained since the original initiative, the template can be used to collect valuable information (farrer.riv.csu .edu.au/principal/survey/canada.html); results from the earlier surveys have been analyzed by Henri and Bonanno.[28]

The North Central Regional Educational Laboratory maintains a website on twenty-first-century skills, which includes information literacy. Their approach to student success is systemwide conditions for learning. To this end, their enGauge assessment tool may be given to individual administrators, teachers, and students to survey their practice within the learning environment; the accumulated data generates a profile of the school's readiness to develop and sustain a technology-rich environment that supports information literacy among other literacies (www.ncrel.org/engauge/intro/ intro.htm).

Washington State University's Transformative Assessment Project similarly supports the idea of systemwide assessment for transformative change. Their rubric provides a guideline for this process (www.educause.edu/ir/ library/pdf/EDU0251.pdf). The project also describes lessons learned from trying to transform teaching and learning.

The Center to Advance Palliative Care also recognizes the need for organizational change in order to establish and sustain meaningful initiatives. Their rubric about states of organizational change offers a simple starting point for assessing a school's status relative to developing an information literacy reform (64.85.16.230/educate/content/development/organizationalchangestages.html).

WEB-BASED TUTORIAL ASSESSMENTS

While information literacy gaps can be addressed "just in time" on an individual basis as teacher librarians and classroom teachers design learning activities, a more systematic approach to information literacy professional development can optimize results. One nonthreatening approach is to identify instructional supports that would help learners throughout a research process: reference pages, citation guides, web tutorials, graphic organizers, worksheets. This product-based orientation offers several opportunities for information literacy instruction: in getting input as those materials are developed, in training classroom teachers in the use of these support materials, and in assessing their use by students as a means to improve instruction—and the quality of those support materials.[29] While several of these websites are maintained by universities, their links may be easily applied to information literacy in secondary school settings.

The following information literacy metasites include assessments and serve as good starting points for locating instructional aids. Several include interactive web tutorials (e.g., University of Washington, ACRL) with embedded assessments that check for understanding and give instant feedback.

- International Association for School Librarianship, "Information Skills Resources in the Internet": www.iasl-online.org/advocacy/resources/infoskills.html
- American Association of School Librarians, "Information Literacy": www.ala.org/ala/aasl/aaslissues/aaslinfolit/informationliteracy1.htm
- ACRL, "Information Literacy": www.ala.org/ala/acrl/acrlissues/acrlinfolit/informationliteracy.htm
- National Coalition on Information Literacy: www.infolit.org/
- City University of New York Office of Library Services, "Information Literacy (ACRL)": libraries.cuny.edu/infolit/infolitresources.htm
- Council of Australian University Libraries, "Information Literacy Links": www.caul.edu.au/info-literacy/links.html
- Florida International University Libraries, "Information Literacy on the WWW": www.fiu.edu/~library/ili/iliweb.html
- University of Washington Libraries, "UWill": www.lib.washington.edu/uwill/learn.htm
- Lesley Farmer, "Information Literacy for K–16 Settings": www.csulb.edu/~lfarmer/infolitwebstyle.htm
- Daybreak Education, "Information Literacy": www.daybreakeducation.com.au/lit/infolit.html
- Marilyn Arnone and Ruth Small, "S.O.S. for Information Literacy": informationliteracy.org/default.php
- Barbara Humes, "Understanding Information Literacy": www.libraryinstruction.com/infolit.html
- Sue Spence, "Information Literacy—Useful Links": www.teachers.ash.org.au/rblonline/informationliteracy/infolitlinks.htm

Several educational institutions and information specialists have developed information literacy web tutorials, some of which are interactive. These websites can be linked from library web portals for independent use. To maximize their benefit, teacher librarians can present them as part of class information literacy instruction or a staff development workshop.

- Alberta (Canada) Education, "Focus on Inquiry: A Teacher's Guide to Implementing Inquiry-Based Learning": www.learning.gov.ab.ca/ K_12/curriculum/bysubject/focusoninquiry.pdf
- Bellingham (Washington) School District, "Online Research Investigations": www.bham.wednet.edu/studentgal/onlineresearch/newonline/ online.htm
- California State University, Long Beach Library, "SURF: Students Understanding Research Fundamentals": www.csulb.edu/projects/surf/
- North Carolina State University Libraries, "LOBO: Library Online Basic Orientation": www.lib.ncsu.edu/lobo2/
- Queensland University of Technology, "PILOT: Your Information Navigator": pilot.library.qut.edu.au/
- York College (Pennsylvania), "Information Literacy 101": www.ycp .edu/library/ifl/etext/ethome.html
- Michelle Dodds, "Information Literacy & Learning": www.edu.pe.ca/ bil/bil.asp?ch1.s5.gdtx
- Rosalind Kentwell, "An Interactive Guide to the Research Process": www.mhs.vic.edu.au/home/library/infoproc/index.htm
- Big6: www.big6.com/
- AT&T Knowledge Network Explorer, 21st Century Literacies, "Information Literacy": www.kn.sbc.com/wired/21stcent/information.html
- McDougal Littell, ClassZone, "Web Research Guide": www.classzone .com/books/research_guide/page_build.cfm?state=none&CFID=108 34320&CFTOKEN=4baebcb-00066781-ea17-14a6-bb6f -831b0f1f0000

UNIVERSITY-GENERATED ASSESSMENTS

Universities have taken the lead in assessing students' information competency. The initiative has largely come from university librarians, who increasingly serve as instructional consultants for academic faculties. Since the days of bibliographic control and stand-alone orientation worksheets, librarians have tried to help students learn how to navigate the world of scholarship, using assessment as a diagnostic tool and check for understanding. With the advent of the recent term *information literacy*, librarians have had to find common language with academians in order to discuss the underlying concepts; critical thinking, source discernment, design briefs, and information processing constitute several of existing collegiate terms intersecting information literacy. For the last five years, the ACRL has surveyed higher education institutions about their information literacy initiatives. Only about 15 percent of responses had a formal assessment in place; most use pre- and posttests and course-related assignments. Nevertheless, university librarians are participating in campus policy committees in an effort to develop graduation requirements that involve information literacy, frequently using technology skills as the "hook" to attract attention to the issue.

The Technology Applications Center for Educational Development at the University of Texas, Denton (www.tcet.unt.edu/START/assess/tools.htm), maintains a strong list of tested assessment tools that focus on technology competency. Several of these instruments can be used to assess information literacy skills that use technology. Instruments include self-assessments about technology skills and system support, educational leadership, attitudes about technology, technology collaboration, technology integration, technology prerequisite skills, and technology program evaluation.

The California State University (CSU) system launched an information competency initiative in 1995 (www.calstate.edu/LS/infocomp.shtml). Each year, individual campuses compete for mini-grants to improve student competency through assessment-driven interventions on a program, faculty, or campus basis. The most established and validated online assessment was developed by CSU Pomona (www.csupomona.edu/~library/hsi/informationliteracy.html), much of which can be adapted to secondary school settings. However, the system has decided to partner with the Educational Testing Service for their assessment instrumentation.

Indiana University Bloomington Libraries developed a campuswide information literacy plan that defines basic and advanced information literacy and learning strategies in terms of goals and specific objectives with supporting measurement techniques (www.indiana.edu/%7Elibinstr/Information_Literacy/assessment.html).

Weber State University (Utah) requires information literacy instruction across the curriculum in a planned manner, from freshman orientation through upper division integration, supporting the initiative through subject librarians collaborating with content faculty. Their online exam consists of multiple-choice items and ten exercise questions based on an Internet search (programs .weber.edu/cil/Overview.htm).

Several university libraries have developed online tutorials that include assessment exercises for assessing students' knowledge. These programs provide immediate feedback for the learner, but generally do not include reports that the instructor can use to help design effective interventions. Nevertheless, these kinds of interactive lessons and quizzes can be very helpful for self-paced learning. University of California, Berkeley, maintains a clearinghouse of online bibliographic instruction tutorials at www.lib.berkeley.edu/Teaching

Lib/BIResources.html#tutorials. Other representative specific information literacy tutorials include

- James Madison University: www.lib.jmu.edu/instruction/default.aspx;
- Purdue University: gemini.lib.purdue.edu/core/login/login.cfm;
- Cornell University: www.library.cornell.edu/t/help/res_strategy/tutorial/tutorial.html; and
- University of Texas: tilt.lib.utsystem.edu/.

PROFESSIONAL ORGANIZATION–GENERATED ASSESSMENTS

Library associations provide a means for information professionals to network and develop broad-based information literacy standards and assessment tools. These groups can leverage subject expertise through their membership to impact decision makers up to the international level. When these efforts involve wide representation of stakeholders (e.g., site librarians, district leaders, library educators, policy makers, researchers, and library literature authors), the resultant instruments are more likely to reflect rigorous input and peer review so that measurements will be valid and reliable.

American Library Association (ALA) divisions and committees have developed several initiatives related to information literacy assessment. The most overarching effort is the ACRL Institute of Information Literacy. Their website (www.ala.org/ala/acrl/acrlissues/acrlinfolit/informationliteracy.htm) provides standards and indicators, resources, and professional activities. Probably the most useful part of the site is the list of performance indicators that students should be able to demonstrate if they are information literate; these indicators can be used as starting points for designing appropriate learning activities and authentic assessments that combine content and information literacy standards. The ACRL website also discusses assessment issues and provides links to useful instruments.

In 1998, another ALA division, the American Association of School Librarians, developed information literacy standards with content-specific benchmark performance indicators for primary, intermediate, and secondary students that can be used to design authentic assessment activities (www.ala.org/ala/aasl/aaslproftools/informationpower/InformationLiteracyStandards_final.pdf).

NATONAL ASSESSMENTS

National information literacy assessment efforts tend to reflect national curricula and centralized governments. In some cases where local education is not well developed, national direction can offer a useful structure to follow. As with universities, national initiatives have often blended information and technology literacy, particularly in developing countries that are creating telecommunication infrastructures to advance their economies. Thus, ICT is seen as an economic necessity.

ICT Literacy Assessment

The U.S. Educational Testing Service mounted an ambitious initiative in 2002 (www.ets.org/portal/site/ets/menuitem.435c0b5cc7bd0ae7015d9510c39215 09/?vgnextoid=b8a246f1674f4010VgnVCM10000022f95190RCRD): to develop and validate a standardized, normed online two-hour test of ICT literacy skills that can be used by secondary schools as an exit proficiency assessment and by higher education for diagnostic, placement, and curriculum development purposes. The test is divided into three types of assessments: (1) problem scenarios presented with tools (e.g., word processing, spreadsheets) that assess results of information processing; (2) problem scenarios that focus on tasks involving individual ICT components (assessing, managing, evaluating, integrating, and creating information); and (3) diagnostic scenario tasks that focus on underlying cognitive and technical skills and can be deconstructed to find specific gaps. The breakthrough aspect of this online assessment is its real-time measurement of testees' processes and adjustment of tasks to uncover specific skills. A simulation demonstration of the test can be found at www.ets.org/ictliteracy/demo.html.[30]

INTERNATIONAL ASSESSMENTS

Performance Indicators on ICT for Education Matrix

UNESCO Bangkok wanted to assess the impact of ICT impact in education and to develop an indicators database based on an Asian-Pacific regional survey. The assessment initiative is planned to provide a longitudinal picture of progress that can also be used to make adjustments of ICT efforts to optimize results. To this end, UNESCO Bangkok collected existing national ICT standards developed for students, teachers, and administrators. Realizing that impact can only be realized when policies, infrastructure, resources, and teacher competence are in place, this headquarters identified five indicator components targeted to ministers of education, systems, administrators, teachers, and students. Each indicator defines concrete behaviors and resources, gives the purpose for the element, notes sources of data, and suggests methods for collecting data. Benchmark country data have been collected and are available to leverage work (www.unescobkk.org/index.php?id=662).

PISA Framework for Assessment of ICT Literacy

Wouter van Joolingen University's Graduate School of Teaching and Learning saw a need to assess secondary school graduates in terms of their preparation to succeed in today's digital workplace. They developed an online assessment test that uses real-life scenarios for students to respond to, describing their use of ICT tools and strategies to solve the simulation problem. This instrument has been pilot-tested in Australia, Japan, and the United States (www.ictliteracy.info/rf.pdf/PISA%20framework.ppt).

NOTES

1. David Dunning et al., "Why People Fail to Recognize Their Own Incompetence," *Current Directions in Psychological Science* 12, no. 3 (2003): 53–57.

2. American Association of School Librarians and Association for Educational Communications and Technology, *Information Power: Building Partnerships for Learning* (Chicago: American Library Association, 1998).

3. Matt Copeland, *Socratic Circles* (Portland, ME: Stenhouse, 2005).

4. Richard Paul, *Critical Thinking: What Every Person Needs to Survive in a Rapidly Changing World* (Rohnert Park, CA: Sonoma State University, 1990).

5. Tanja Janssen, "Instruction in Self-Questioning as a Literary Reading Strategy: An Exploration of Empirical Research," *Educational Studies in Language and Literature* 2, no. 2 (2002): 95–120.

6. Penny Moore, "Teaching Information Problem Solving in Primary Schools: An Information Literacy Survey" (paper presented at the annual conference of the International Federation of Library Association, Copenhagen, August 31–September 5, 1997).

7. Penny Moore, "Information Problem-Solving: A Wider View of Library Skills," *Journal of Contemporary Educational Psychology* 20 (1995): 1–31.

8. Liam Rourke et al., "Assessing Social Presence in Asynchronous, Text-Based Computer Conferencing," *Journal of Distance Education* 14, no. 3 (1999): 51–70.

9. Richard Mueller, *Instructional Psychology: Principles and Practices* (Champaign, IL: Stipes Publishing, 1992).

10. Violet Harada, "Personalizing the Information Search Process: A Case Study of Journal Writing with Elementary-Age Students," *School Library Media Research* 5 (2002), www.ala.org/ala/aasl/aaslpubsandjournals/slmrb/slmrcontents/volume52002/harada.cfm (accessed July 31, 2007).

11. Phillip Armour, "The Five Orders of Ignorance," *Communications of the ACM* 43, no. 10 (2000): 17–20.

12. Patricia Larres, Joan Ballantine, and Mark Whittington, "Evaluating the Validity of Self-Assessment: Measuring Computer Literacy among Entry-Level Undergraduates within Accounting Degree Programmes at Two UK Universities," *Accounting Education* 12, no. 2 (2003): 97–112.

13. W. MacLeod, Deborah Butler, and K. Syer, "Beyond Achievement Data: Assessing Changes in Metacognition and Strategic Learning" (paper presented at the annual conference of the American Educational Research Association, New York, April 1996).

14. Deborah Butler and Sylvie Cartier, "Multiple Complementary Methods for Understanding Self-Regulated Learning as Situated in Context" (paper presented at the American Educational Research Association conference, Montreal, April 2005).

15. Bonnie Cheuk, "Modelling the Information Seeking and Use Processing in the Workplace," *Information Research* 4, no. 2 (1998), informationr.net/ir/4-2/isic/cheuk .html (accessed July 31, 2007).

16. Elliot W. Eisner, *The Enlightened Eye: Qualitative Inquiry and the Enhancement of Educational Practice* (Upper Saddle River, NJ: Merrill, 1998), 63.

17. Helmut Leder et al., "A Model of Aesthetic Appreciation and Aesthetic Judgments," *British Journal of Psychology* 95 (2004): 489–508.

18. Natalia Orlova, "Helping Prospective EFL Teachers Learn How to Use Songs in Teaching Conversation Classes," *Internet TESL Journal* 9, no. 3 (2003), iteslj.org/ Techniques/Orlova-Songs.html (accessed July 31, 2007).

19. Anthony Pelligrini and Peter Smith, eds., *Major Writings in the Psychology of Education* (London: Routledge, 2000).

20. Philip Turner and Ann Riedling, *Helping Teachers Teach* (Westport, CT: Libraries Unlimited, 2003).

21. L. Dee Fink, "Evaluating Your Own Teaching," in *Improving College Teaching*, ed. Peter Seldin, 191–204 (Bolton, MA: Anker, 1995).

22. Sabine Seufert, "Cultural Perspectives," in *Handbook of Information Technologies for Education and Training*, ed. Haimo Adelsberger, Betty Collis, and Jan Powlowski, 411–24 (Munich: Springer-Verlag, 2002).

23. Robert Heckman and Hala Annabi, "A Content Analytic Comparison of Learning Processes in Online and Face-To-Face Case Study Discussions," *Journal of Computer-Mediated Communication* 10, no. 2 (2005), jcmc.indiana.edu/vol10/issue2/ heckman.html (accessed July 31, 2007).

24. Middle States Commission on Higher Education, *Developing Research and Communication Skills: Guidelines for Information Literacy in the Curriculum* (Philadelphia: Middle States Commission on Higher Education, 2003).

25. Sue Henczal, *The Information Audit: A Practical Guide* (Munich: K. G. Saur, 2001).

26. Lawrie Merz and Beth Mark, *Assessment in College Library Instruction Programs* (Chicago: American Library Association, 2002).

27. Moore, "Information Problem-Solving."

28. James Henri and Karen Bonanno, *The Information Literate School Community: Best Practice* (Wagga Wagga, Australia: Charles Sturt University, 1999).

29. Alexius Mackin and Michael Fosmire, "A Blueprint for Progress: Collaborating with Faculty to Integrate Information Literacy into the Curriculum at Purdue University," in *Libraries within Their Institutions: Creative Collaborations,* ed. W. Miller and R. Ella, 43–56 (Binghamton, NY: Haworth Press, 2005).

30. Educational Testing Service, *Digital Transformation: A Framework for ICT Literacy* (Princeton, NJ: Educational Testing Service, 2002).

Bibliography

Abbott, Mary, Charles Greenwood, Yolanda Tapia, and Cheryl Walton. "Research to Practice: A Blueprint." *Exceptional Children* 65 (1999): 339–62.

Adler, Mortimer. *The Paideia Proposal: An Educational Manifesto.* New York: Macmillan, 1982.

Akin, Lynn. "Information Overload and Children: A Survey of Texas Elementary School Students." *School Library Media Research* 1 (1998). www.ala.org/aasl/SLMQ/overload.html (accessed July 31, 2007).

American Association of Higher Education Assessment Forum. *9 Principles of Good Practice for Assessing Student Learning.* Brevard, NC: Policy Center on the First Year of College, 2003.

American Association of School Librarians and Association for Educational Communications and Technology. *Information Power: Building Partnerships for Learning.* Chicago: American Library Association, 1998.

American Library Association. *Presidential Committee on Information Literacy: Final Report.* Chicago: American Library Association, 1989.

Angelo, Thomas. "Doing Assessment as if Learning Matters Most." *AAHE Bulletin* 51 (May 1999): 3–6.

Armour, Phillip. "The Five Orders of Ignorance." *Communications of the ACM* 43, no. 10 (2000): 17–20.

Asselin, Marlene. "Teaching Information Skills in the Information Age." *School Libraries Worldwide* 11, no. 1 (2005): 17–36.

Aufderheide, Patricia, ed. *Media Literacy: A Report of the National Leadership Conference on Media Literacy.* Aspen, CO: Aspen Institute, 1993.

Bateson, Gregory. *Steps to an Ecology of Mind.* London: Paladin, 1973.

Bawden, David. "Progress in Documentation: Information and Digital Literacy: A Review of Concepts." *Journal of Documentation* 57, no. 2 (2001): 218–59.

Beal, Carole. "Development of Knowledge about the Role of Inference in Text Comprehension." *Child Development* 61 (1990): 1011–23.

Bellinger, Gene. "Knowledge Management—Emerging Perspectives." Systems Thinking. www.systems-thinking.org/kmgmt/kmgmt.htm (accessed July 22, 2006).

Bereiter, Carl, and Marlene Scardamalia. "Rethinking Learning." In *The Handbook of Education and Human Development*, edited by David Olson and Nancy Torrance, 485–513. Cambridge, MA: Basic Blackwell, 1996.

Biggs, John. "The Reflective Institution: Assuring and Enhancing the Quality of Teaching and Learning." *Higher Education* 41 (2001): 221–38.

Blake, Brett, and Robert Blake. *Literacy and Learning: A Reference Handbook*. Santa Barbara, CA: ABC-CLIO, 2002.

Blanche, Martin Terre, and Kevin Durrheim. *Research in Practice. Applied Methodologies for the Social Sciences*. Cape Town, South Africa: University of Cape Town Press, 1999.

Bloom, Benjamin, ed. *Taxonomy of Educational Objectives; the Classification of Educational Goals, by a Committee of College and University Examiners*. New York: Longmans, Green, 1956.

Board on Children, Youth, and Families. *Engaging Schools: Fostering High School Students' Motivation to Learn*. Washington, DC: National Academies Press, 2003.

Boswell, James. *The Life of Samuel Johnson*. London: Baldwin, 1791.

Bouazza, Abdelmajid. "Information User Studies." In *Encyclopedia of Library and Information Science*, vol. 44, suppl. 9, edited by Allen Kent, 144–64. New York: Dekker, 1989.

Bruce, Christine. "Information Literacy: A Framework for Higher Education." *Australian Library Journal* 44 (August 1995): 158–69.

———. "Information Literacy Research: Dimensions of the Emerging Collective Consciousness." *Australian Academic and Research Libraries* 31, no. 2 (2000): 91–109.

Buckland, Michael. "Information as Thing." *Journal of the American Society of Information Science* 42, no. 5 (1991): 351–60.

Bundy, Alan. "For a Clever Country: Information Literacy Diffusion in the 21st Century." Background and issues paper for the First National Roundtable on Information Literacy, Australian Library and Information Association, Melbourne, Australia, February 2001.

———. "Growing the Community of the Informed: Information Literacy—a Global Issue." Paper presented at the Standing Conference of East, Central and South Africa Library Associations, Johannesburg, South Africa, April 2002.

Butler, Deborah, and Sylvie Cartier. "Multiple Complementary Methods for Understanding Self-Regulated Learning as Situated in Context." Paper presented at the American Educational Research Association conference, Montreal, April 2005.

California Department of Education, Elementary Teaching and Learning Division and the High School Teaching and Learning Division. *Check It Out!* Sacramento: California Department of Education, 1998.

California Library Association. "Competencies for California Librarians in the 21st Century." www.cla-net.org/resources/articles/r_competencies.php (accessed July 31, 2007).

California State University, Long Beach. *2006–07 Resource Planning Process: Strategic Planning Priorities and Goals*. Long Beach: California State University, Long Beach, 2006.

Campbell, Barbara. "High School Principal Roles and Implementation Themes for Mainstreaming Information Literacy Instruction." PhD diss., University of Connecticut, 1994.

Candy, Philip. "Major Themes and Future Directions." In *Learning for Life: Information Literacy and the Autonomous Learner: Proceedings of the Second National Information Literacy Conference Held in Adelaide, Australia, 30 November–1 December 1995,* edited by D. Booker, 135–49. Adelaide: University of South Australia, 1995.

Chartered Institute of Library and Information Professionals. "Information Literacy: Definition." www.cilip.org.uk/professionalguidance/informationliteracy/definition/ (accessed December 22, 2006).

Cheuk, Bonnie. "Modelling the Information Seeking and Use Processing the Workplace." *Information Research* 4, no. 2 (1998). informationr.net/ir/4-2/isic/cheuk.html (accessed July 31, 2007).

Chickering, Arthur, and Zelda Gamson. "Development and Adaptation of the Seven Principles for Good Practice in Undergraduate Education." *New Directions for Teaching and Learning* 80 (1987): 75–81.

Chipman, Susan, Judith Siegal, and Robert Glaser, eds. *Thinking and Learning Skills: Current Research and Open Questions.* Hillsdale, NJ: Erlbaum, 1984.

Chrislip, David. *The Collaborative Leadership Fieldbook.* San Francisco: Jossey-Bass, 2002.

Clarke, John. "Using Visual Organizers to Focus on Thinking." *Journal of Reading* 34, no. 7 (1991): 526–36.

Coalition for Community Schools. *The Five Conditions for Learning.* Washington, DC: Coalition for Community Schools, 2003.

College Student Experiences Questionnaire Research Program. *College Student Experiences Questionnaire.* Bloomington: Indiana University, Bloomington, 2005.

Copeland, Matt. *Socratic Circles.* Portland, ME: Stenhouse, 2005.

Council of Australian University Librarians. *Information Literacy Standards.* Canberra: Council of Australian University Librarians, 2001.

Crevola, Carmel, and Peter Hill. *Children's Literacy Success Strategy: An Overview.* Melbourne, Australia: Catholic Education Office, 1998.

Cushman, Kathleen. "The Cycle of Inquiry and Action: Essential Learning Communities." *Horace* 15, no. 4 (1999). www.essentialschools.org/cs/resources/view/ces _res/74 (accessed July 31, 2007).

Dervin, Brenda. "Information as a User-Construct: The Relevance of Perceived Information Needs to Synthesis and Interpretation." In *Knowledge Structure and Use: Implications for Synthesis and Interpretation,* edited by Spencer A. Ward and Linda J. Reed, 154–83. Philadelphia: Temple University Press, 1983.

———. "Useful Theory for Librarianship: Communication, Not Information." *Drexel Library Quarterly* 13 (1977): 16–32.

Dewey, Melvil. "The Profession." *American Library Journal* 1 (September 1987): 5, 6.

Doyle, Christina. *Information Literacy in an Information Society: A Concept for the Information Age.* Syracuse, NY: ERIC Clearinghouse on Information and Technology, 1994.

Dunning, David, K. Johnson, J. Ehrlinger, and J. Kruger. "Why People Fail to Recognize Their Own Incompetence." *Current Directions in Psychological Science* 12, no. 3 (2003): 53–57.

Ecological Society of America. "Inquiry Framework: Levels of Student Ownership." tiee.ecoed.net/teach/framework.jpg (accessed July 3, 2007).

Educational Testing Service. *Digital Transformation: A Framework for ICT Literacy*. Princeton, NJ: Educational Testing Service, 2002.

Ehrmann, Stephen. "Diagnosing and Responding to Resistance to Evaluation." Flashlight Program. www.tltgroup.Flashlight/Handbook/Resistance.htm (accessed September 14, 2007).

Eisenberg, Michael, and Robert Berkowitz. *Information Problem-Solving: The Big Six Approach to Literacy and Information Skills Instruction*. Norwood, NJ: Ablex, 1990.

Eisner, Elliot W. *The Enlightened Eye: Qualitative Inquiry and the Enhancement of Educational Practice*. Upper Saddle River, NJ: Merrill, 1998.

Eraut, Michael. "Informal Learning in the Workplace." *Studies in Continuing Education* 26, no. 2 (2004): 247–73.

Facione, Peter, Noreen Facione, and Carole Giancarlo. "The Disposition toward Critical Thinking: Its Character, Measurement, and Relationship to Critical Thinking Skill." *Informal Logic* 20, no. 1 (2000): 61–84.

Fairthorne, Robert. "Information: One Label, Several Bottles." In *Perspectives in Information Science*, edited by Anthony Debons and William Cameron, pp. 144–64. Norwell, MA: Kulwer Academic Publishers, 1975.

Farmer, Lesley. "Building Information Literacy through a Whole School Reform Approach." *Knowledge Quest* 29, no. 3 (2001): 20–24.

———. *Collaborating with Administrators and Educational Support Staff*. New York: Neal-Schuman, 2006.

———. *Collaborative Leadership and Support: How Library Media Specialists Can Work with Administrators and Service Personnel* (New York: Neal-Schuman, 2006).

———. *Cooperative Learning Activities in the Library Media Center*. 2nd ed. Westport, CT: Libraries Unlimited, 1999.

———. "Developmental Socio-Emotional Behavior and Information Literacy." In *Information and Emotion: The Emergent Affective Paradigm in Information Behavior Research and Theory*, edited by Diane Nahl and Dania Bilal, 99–120. Medford, NJ: Information Today, 2007.

———. *How to Conduct Action Research: A Guide for Library Media Specialists*. Chicago: American Association of School Librarians, 2003.

———. *Partnerships for Lifelong Learning*. 2nd ed. Worthington, OH: Linworth, 1999.

———. *Student Success and Library Media Programs: A Systems Approach to Research and Best Practice*. Westport, CT: Libraries Unlimited, 2003.

Fink, L. Dee. "Evaluating Your Own Teaching." In *Improving College Teaching*, edited by Peter Seldin, 191–204. Bolton, MA: Anker, 1995.

Fjällbrant, Nancy, and Ian Malley. *User Education in Libraries*. 2nd ed. London: Clive Bingley, 1984.

Flynn, Christie, Lynn Olson, and Judy Kvinsland. "Connecting the Dots: Using the Assessment Cycle to Foster Student Success." Paper presented at the ACRL conference, Charlotte, NC, April 2003.

Forkosh-Baruch, Alona, David Mioduser, and Rafi Nashmias. "Diffusion Patterns of ICT-Based Pedagogical Innovations." Paper presented at the Ed-Media conference, Orlando, FL, June 2006.

Gagne, Robert. *The Conditions of Learning and Theory of Instruction.* 4th ed. New York: Holt, Rinehart and Winston, 1985.

Garner, Sarah. *High-Level Colloquium on Information Literacy and Lifelong Learning.* Alexandria, Egypt: International Federal of Library Associations, 2005.

Gendina, Natalila. "Information Literacy for Information Culture." Paper presented at the annual conference of the International Federation of Library Associations, Buenos Aires, August 2004.

Glanz, Karen, Frances Lewis, and Barbara Rimer. *Health Behavior and Health Education: Theory, Research, and Practice.* 2nd ed. San Francisco: Jossey-Bass, 1996.

Glasser, William. *Choice Theory in the Classroom.* New York: Harper, 1998.

Gonzales, Patrick, et al. *Highlights from the Trends in International Mathematics and Science Study (TIMSS) 2003.* Washington, DC: National Center for Education Statistics, 2004.

Haberma, Jurgen. *Knowledge and Human Interests.* Boston: Beacon Press, 1971.

Harada, Violet. "Personalizing the Information Search Process: A Case Study of Journal Writing with Elementary-Age Students." *School Library Media Research* 5 (2002). www.ala.org/ala/aasl/aaslpubsandjournals/slmrb/slmrcontents/volume52002/harada.cfm (accessed July 31, 2007).

Harada, Violet, and Jane Yoshina. *Assessing Learning: Librarians and Teachers as Partners.* Westport, CT: Libraries Unlimited, 2005.

Heckman, Robert, and Hala Annabi. "A Content Analytic Comparison of Learning Processes in Online and Face-To-Face Case Study Discussions." *Journal of Computer-Mediated Communication* 10, no. 2 (2005). jcmc.indiana.edu/vol10/issue2/heckman.html (accessed July 31, 2007).

Heinstrom, Jannica. "Fast Surfing, Broad Scanning and Deep Driving: The Influence of Personality and Study Approach on Students' Information-Seeking Behavior." *Journal of Documentation* 61, no. 2 (2005): 228–47.

Helwig, Charles, and Susan Kim. "Children's Evaluations of Decision-Making Procedures in Peer, Family, and School Contexts." *Child Development* 70, no. 2 (1999): 502–12.

Henczal, Sue. *The Information Audit: A Practical Guide.* Munich: K. G. Saur, 2001.

Henri, James. *The School Curriculum: A Collaborative Approach to Learning.* 2nd ed. Wagga Wagga, New South Wales, Australia: Center for Library Studies, 1988.

———. "Understanding the Information Literate School Community." In *Leadership Issues in the Information Literate School Community*, edited by James Henri and Marlene Asselin, 11–26. Westport, CT: Libraries Unlimited, 2005.

Henri, James, and Karen Bonanno. *The Information Literate School Community: Best Practice.* Wagga Wagga, New South Wales, Australia: Charles Sturt University, 1999.

Herring, John. *Teaching Information Skills in Schools.* London: Library Association Publishing, 1996.

Hill, Carmel, and Phillip Hill. "Evaluation of a Whole-School Approach to Prevention and Intervention in Early Literacy." *Journal of Education for Students Placed at Risk* 3, no. 2 (1998): 133–57.

Hong Kong Education and Manpower Bureau. "Empowering Learning and Teaching with Information Technology." www.emb.gov.hk/index.aspx?langno=1andnodeid =2497 (accessed July 11, 2006).

Inoue, Hitoshi, Eisuke Naito, and Mika Koshizuka. "Mediacy: What Is It? Where to Go?" *International Information & Library Review* 29, nos. 3–4 (1997): 413–30.

International Association of School Librarianship. "School Libraries Make a Difference to Student Achievement." School Libraries Online. www.iasl-online.org/advocacy/ make-a-difference.html (accessed July 31, 2007).

International Federation of Library Associations. "Cooperation on Applications and Test-Beds." January 12, 1995. Document created in preparation for the G-7 Ministerial Conference on the Information Society, Brussels, February 25–26, 1995. www.ifla.org/documents/infopol/intl/g7/g7-113qa.txt (accessed July 22, 2006).

International Society for Technology in Education. *National Educational Technology Standards for Students.* Eugene, OR: International Society for Technology in Education, 2000.

International Telecommunication Union. *Tunis Agenda for the Information Society.* Tunis, Tunisia: World Summit on the Information Society, November 18, 2005.

Irving, Ann. *Study and Information Skills across the Curriculum.* London: Heinemann, 1985.

James, Leon. "Creating an Online Learning Environment That Fosters Information Literacy, Autonomous Learning and Leadership: The Hawaii Online Generational Community-Classroom." *Trends and Issues in Online Instruction* (Spring 1997). www .soc.hawaii.edu/leonj/leonj/leonpsy/instructor/kcc/kcc97.html (accessed July 31, 2007).

Janssen, Tanja. "Instruction in Self-Questioning as a Literary Reading Strategy: An Exploration of Empirical Research." *Educational Studies in Language and Literature* 2, no. 2 (2002): 95–120.

Jansson, Leena. "Fifty Decades Information Seeking Skills for Customers in Public Libraries." Paper presented at the Research in the Field of Public Libraries workshop, Riga, Latvia, September 16, 2004.

Johnson, David. *Cooperative Learning in the Classroom.* Alexandria, VA: Association for Supervision and Curriculum Development, 1994.

Johnson, David, and Gunther Kress. "Globalisation, Literacy and Society: Redesigning Pedagogy and Assessment." *Assessment in Education* 10, no. 1 (March 2003): 5–14.

Khoury, Raymond. "National ICT Priorities." Paper presented at ICT Lebanon 2004: The Arab Technology for Development Conference, Beirut, September 23, 2004. www.pca.org.lb/docs/dr.%20raymond%20khoury.ppt (accessed July 21, 2006).

Kirschner, Paul. "Using Integrated Electronic Environments for Collaborative Teaching/Learning." Keynote speech, 8th Annual Conference of the European Association for Research on Learning and Instruction, Gothenburg, Sweden, August 26, 1999.

Klaus, Helmut. "Information Literacy Education and Experiential Learning: Application of the Simulation Technique." *Education for Library and Information Services* 16, no. 2 (1999): 33–45.

Klinger, Don. *School Libraries and Student Achievement in Ontario.* Ontario, Canada: Ontario Library Association, 2006.

Kobelski, Pamela, and Mary Reichel. "Conceptual Frameworks for Bibliographic Instruction." *Journal of Academic Librarianship* 7 (May 1981): 73–77.

Kohlberg, Lawrence. *The Philosophy of Moral Development.* San Francisco: Harper & Row, 1981.

Kong, Siu, James Henri, Fong Lee, and Siu Li. "A Study on the Development of an Information Literacy Framework for Hong Kong Students." www.cite.hku.hk/people/jhenri/doc/IL-Report.pdf (accessed July 22, 2006).

Kuhlthau, Carol. *Seeking Meaning: A Process Approach to Library and Information Services.* 2nd ed. Westport, CT: Libraries Unlimited, 2004.

Larres, Patricia, Joan Ballantine, and Mark Whittington. "Evaluating the Validity of Self-Assessment: Measuring Computer Literacy among Entry-Level Undergraduates within Accounting Degree Programmes at Two UK Universities." *Accounting Education* 12, no. 2 (June 2003): 97–112.

Lashway, Larry. *Educational Indicators.* Eugene, OR: ERIC, 2001.

Lau, Jesus. "Information Literacy: An International State-of-the-Art Report." www.uv.mx/usbi_ver/unesco (accessed July 11, 2006).

Leder, Helmut, Benno Belke, Andries Oeberst, and Dorothee Augustin. "A Model of Aesthetic Appreciation and Aesthetic Judgments." *British Journal of Psychology* 95 (2004): 489–508.

Lee, Elizabeth. "Reading and the Information Literate Community." In *Leadership Issues in the Information Literate School Community*, edited by James Henri and Marlene Asselin, 65–78. Westport, CT: Libraries Unlimited, 2005.

Lee, Sandra, James Henri, and Eva Kandelaars. "Information Policy in Hong Kong and Beyond: A Review of the Literature with Implications for School Libraries." *New Review of Children's Literature and Librarianship* 11, no. 1 (2005): 63–72.

Limberg, Louise. "Information Seeking and Learning Outcomes: A Study of the Interaction between Two Phenomena." *Scandinavian Public Library Quarterly* 31, no. 3 (1998): 28–31.

Lorenzen, Michael. "A Brief History of Library Information in the United States of America." *Illinois Libraries* 83, no. 2 (2001): 8–18.

Louttit, Chauncey, and James Patrick. "Study of Students' Knowledge in the Use of the Library." *Journal of Applied Psychology* 16 (October 1932): 475–84.

Mackin, Alexius, and Michael Fosmire. "A Blueprint for Progress: Collaborating with Faculty to Integrate Information Literacy into the Curriculum at Purdue University." In *Libraries within Their Institutions: Creative Collaborations*, edited by William Miller and Rita Ella, 43–56. Binghamton, NY: Haworth Press, 2005.

MacKinnon, Dolly, and Catherine Manathunga. "Going Global with Assessment: What to Do When the Dominant Culture's Literacy Drives Assessment." *Higher Education Research and Development* 22, no. 2 (2003): 131–44.

MacLeod, W., Deborah Butler, and K. Syer. "Beyond Achievement Data: Assessing Changes in Metacognition and Strategic Learning." Paper presented at the American Educational Research Association conference, New York, April 1996.

Maki, Penny. "Developing an Assessment Plan to Learn about Student Learning." *The Journal of Academic Leadership* 28, no. 1 (2002): 8–13.

Marland, Michael. *Information Skills in the Secondary Curriculum*. New York: Metheun, 1981.

Maslow, Abraham. *Motivation and Personality*. New York: Harper, 1954.

McCormick, Mona. "Critical Thinking and Library Instruction." *Reference Quarterly* 22, no. 34 (1983): 31–36.

McNergney, Robert, and Joanne Herbert. *Foundations of Education: The Challenge of Professional Practice*. 3rd ed. Boston: Allyn and Bacon, 2000.

Merz, Lawrie, and Beth Mark. *Assessment in College Library Instruction Programs*. Chicago: American Library Association, 2002.

Mezirow, Jack, et al. *Learning as Transformation: Critical Perspectives on a Theory in Progress*. San Francisco: Jossey-Bass, 2000.

Microsoft Monitor Research Services. "Find Stuff, Start Something." *Microsoft Monitor Weblog* (May 15, 2005): 1. www.microsoftmonitor.com/archives/2005/05/find_stuff_star.html (accessed July 31, 2007).

Middle States Commission on Higher Education. *Developing Research and Communication Skills: Guidelines for Information Literacy in the Curriculum*. Philadelphia: Middle States Commission on Higher Education, 2003.

Ministry for Children and Families. *Cultural Competency Assessment Tool*. Victoria, British Columbia: Ministry for Children and Families, 2001. www.mcf.gov.bc.ca/publications/cultural_competency/assessment_tool/tool_4.htm (accessed May 8, 2007).

Moni, Karen, Christina Van Kraayenoord, and Carolyn Baker. "Students' Perceptions of Literacy Assessment." *Assessment in Education* 9, no. 3 (2002): 319–42.

Moore, Penny. "An Analysis of Information Literacy Education Worldwide." White paper prepared for UNESCO, the U.S. National Commission on Libraries and Information Science, and the National Forum on Information Literacy, for use at the Information Literacy Meeting of Experts, Prague, July 2002.

———. "Information Problem-Solving: A Wider View of Library Skills." *Journal of Contemporary Educational Psychology* 20 (1995): 1–31.

———. "Teaching Information Problem Solving in Primary Schools: An Information Literacy Survey." Paper presented at the International Federation of Library Association conference, Copenhagen, August 31–September 5, 1997.

Moore, Penny, and Nicki Page. "Teaching for Information Literacy: Online Professional Development Challenges." In *School Libraries for a Knowledge Society* (proceedings of the 31st Annual Conference of the International Association of School Librarianship, Seattle, 2002), edited by Diljit Singh, Abrizah Abdullah, Suscelah Foneska, and Brian de Rozario, 153–68. Zillmere, Australia: International Association of School Librarianship, 2002.

Mowl, Graham. *Innovative Assessment*. New Castle, UK: University of Northumbria, 1996.

Moyle, Kathryn. "Leadership and Learning with ICT: Voices from the Profession." Paper presented at the Ed-Media conference, Orlando, FL, June 2006.

Mueller, Richard. *Instructional Psychology: Principles and Practices*. Champaign, IL: Stipes Publishing, 1992.

Nabi, Robin. "Exploring the Framing Effects of Emotion: Do Discrete Emotions Differentially Influence Information Accessibility, Information Seeking, and Policy Preference?" *Communication Research* 30, no. 2 (2003): 224–47.

Nahl, Diane. "The User-Centered Revolution: 1970–1955." In *Encyclopedia of Microcomputers*, edited by Allen Kent and James G. Williams, vol. 19, 143–99. New York: Marcel Dekker, 1996.

National Center for Education Statistics. "Trends in International Mathematics and Science Study." nces.ed.gov/timss/ (accessed July 22, 2006).

Newell, Terrence. "Thinking beyond the Disjunctive Opposition of Information Literacy Assessment in Theory and Practice." *School Library Media Research* 7 (2004). www.ala.org/ala/aasl/aaslpubsandjournals/slmrb/slmrcontents/volume72004/beyond.cfm (accessed July 31, 2007).

Ng, Evelyn, and Carl Bereiter. "Three Levels of Goal Orientation in Learning." *Journal of the Learning Sciences* 1, nos. 3–4 (1991): 243–71.

Nissen, Laura, Daniel Merrigan, and M. Katherine Kraft. "Moving Mountains Together: Strategic Community Leadership and Systems Change." *Child Welfare* 84, no. 2 (2005): 12–140.

Nonaka, Ikujiro. "A Dynamic Theory of Organizational Knowledge Creation" *Organization Science* 5, no. 1 (1994): 14–37.

Nonaka, Ikujiro, and Hirotaka Takeuchi. *The Knowledge-Creating Company*. New York: Oxford University Press, 1995.

Oberg, Dianne. "Perspectives on Information Literacy." *School Libraries Worldwide* 7, no. 1 (January 2001): i–v.

———. "Principal Support: What Does It Mean to Teacher-Librarians?" Paper presented at the annual conference of the International Association of School Librarianship, Worcester, UK, August 1995.

OECD and Statistics Canada. *Literacy in the Information Age: Final Report of the International Adult Literacy Survey*. Paris: OECD and Statistics Canada, 2000.

Orlova, Natalia. "Helping Prospective EFL Teachers Learn How to Use Songs in Teaching Conversation Classes." *Internet TESL Journal* 9, no. 3 (2003). iteslj.org/Techniques/Orlova-Songs.html (accessed July 31, 2007).

Osborn, Marilyn, Ethel Thomas, and Dorothea Hartnack. "An Evolving Model of Knowledge Management in Education and the South African Reality: How Knowledge Management, Information Literacy and Reading Skills Are Information Learning at a High School and a Primary School in Gauteng, South Africa." In *Information Leadership in a Culture of Change: IASL Reports, 2005*, edited by Sandra Lee, Peter Warning, Diljit Singh, Eleanor Howe, Lesley Farmer, and Sandra Hughes, chap. 32, pp.1–15. Erie, PA.: International Association of School Librarianship, 2005.

Owen, Sue. "It Takes More Than Breadcrumbs to Learn Generic Skills: Collaborating to Improve Information Literacy." Paper presented at the HERDSA Annual Conference, Christchurch, New Zealand, July 7–9, 2003.

Pappas, Marjorie, and Ann Tepe. "Preparing the Information Educator for the Future." *School Library Media Annual* (1995): 37–44.

Parsons, Jeffrey. "Effects of Local versus Global Schema Diagrams on Verification and Communication in Conceptual Data Modeling." *Journal of Management Information Systems* 19, no. 3 (2002): 155–83.

Partnership for 21st-Century Skills. "Our Mission." www.21stcenturyskills.org/index .php? option=com_contentandtask=viewandid=188andItemid=110 (accessed July 22, 2006).

Paul, Richard. *Critical Thinking: What Every Person Needs to Survive in a Rapidly Changing World*. Rohnert Park, CA: Sonoma State University, 1990.

Pelligrini, Anthony, and Peter Smith, eds. *Major Writings in the Psychology of Education*. London: Routledge, 2000.

Picard, Rosalind, and Shaundra Daily. "Evaluating Affective Interactions: Alternatives to Asking What Users Feel." Paper presented at the CHI workshop on Evaluation Affective Interfaces, Portland, OR, April 2005.

Pillow, Bradford. "Children's and Adults' Evaluation of the Certainty of Deductive Inferences, Inductive Inferences, and Guesses." *Child Development* 73, no. 3 (2002): 779–92.

Polya, George. *How to Solve It*. Princeton, NJ: Princeton University Press, 1988.

Popper, Karl. *World of Propensities*. Bristol, England: Thoemmes, 1990.

Powell, John. *Why Am I Afraid to Tell You Who I Am?* Niles, IL: Argus Communications, 1969.

Raber, Douglas. *The Problem of Information*. Oxford: Scarecrow Press, 2003.

Rafste, Elisabeth, Tove Saetre, and Ellen Sundt. "Norwegian Policy: Empowering School Libraries." *School Libraries Worldwide* 12, no. 1 (January 2006): 50–59.

Reilly, Rob, Barry Kort, and Rosalind Picard. "External Representation of Learning Process and Domain Knowledge: Affective State as a Determinate of Its Structure and Function." Paper presented at the conference of the IEEE Artificial Intelligence in Education, San Antonio, TX, May 2001.

Robinson, Lyn, and David Bawden. "Libraries and Open Society; Popper, Soros and Digital Information." *Aslib Proceedings* 53, no. 5 (2001): 167–78.

Roe, Ernest. "$27 Million Dollars Worth of Better Education." *The Australian Library Journal* 18, no. 6 (1969): 194–99.

Rogers, Everett. *Diffusion of Innovations*. 4th ed. New York: Free Press, 1995.

Rosen, Robert, et al. *Global Literacies*. New York: Simon & Schuster, 2000.

Rosse, Joseph, and Herman Miller. "Toward a Comprehensive Model of the Employee Adaptation Decision Process." Paper delivered at the annual meeting of the Western Decision Sciences Institute, Portland, ME, April 18, 2000.

Rourke, Liam, Terry Anderson, D. Randy Garrison, and Walter Archer. "Assessing Social Presence in Asynchronous, Text-Based Computer Conferencing." *Journal of Distance Education* 14, no. 3 (1999): 51–70.

Ruble, Diane, and Gordon Flett. "Conflicting Goals in Self-Evaluative Information Seeking: Developmental and Ability Level Analyses." *Child Development* 59 (1988): 97–106.

Rudduck, Jean, Roland Chaplain, and Gwen Wallace, eds. *School Improvement: What Can Pupils Tell Us?* London: David Fulton, 1995.

Ryan, Sandra, and Vicki Hudson. "Evidence-Based Management, Transformational Leadership and Information Literacy at Santa Maria College." *Synergy* 1 (2003): 29–41.

Sanger, Jack. *The Teaching, Handling Information and Learning Project.* London: British Library, 1989.

Secretary's Commission on Achieving Necessary Skills. *What Work Requires of Schools: A SCANS Report of America 2000.* Washington, DC: Government Printing Office, 1991.

Seeds University Elementary School. *Managing Information in a Digital Age.* Los Angeles: University of California, 2002.

Senge, Peter. *The Fifth Discipline: The Art and Practice of the Learning Organization.* New York: Doubleday, 1990.

———. *Presence.* Waltham, MA: Pegasus, 2004.

Seufert, Sabine. "Cultural Perspectives." In *Handbook of Information Technologies for Education and Training,* edited by Haimo Adelsberger, Betty Collis, and Jan Powlowski, 411–24. Munich: Springer-Verlag, 2002.

Shapiro, Jeremy, and Shelley Hughes. "Information Technology as a Liberal Art." *Educom Review* (March 1996): 31–35.

Shenton, Andrew, and Pat Dixon. "The Development of Young People's Information-Seeking Behaviour." *Library and Information Research* 28, no. 90 (2004): 31–39.

Shores, Louis. "The Liberal Arts College: A Possibility in 1964?" *School and Society* 41 (January 26, 1935): 110–14.

Standing Conference of National and University Libraries. *Information Skills in Higher Education: A SCONUL Position Paper.* London: Standing Conference of National and University Libraries, 1999.

Stiggins, Richard. "Building a Productive Assessment Future." *NASSP Bulletin* 85, no. 621 (2001): 2–4.

Stigler, James, and James Hiebert. *The Teaching Gap.* New York: Free Press, 1999.

Sugrue, Brenda. "A Theory-Based Framework for Assessing Domain-Specific Problem Solving Ability." *Educational Measurement: Issues and Practice* 14, no. 3 (1995): 29–35.

Thompson, James. "Resource-Based Learning Can Be the Backbone of Reform Improvement." *Information Library. NASSP Bulletin* (May 1991): 24–28.

Todd, Ross. "Information Literacy in Electronic Environments: Fantasies, Facts, and Futures." Paper delivered at the Virtual Libraries: Virtual Communities IATUL Conference, Queensland University of Technology, Brisbane, Australia, 2000.

Toffler, Alvin. *Future Shock.* New York: Random House, 1970.

Tomlinson, Carol. *The Parallel Curriculum: A Design to Develop High Potential and Challenge High-Ability Learners.* Thousand Oaks, CA: Corwin Press, 2002.

Totolo, Angelina. "Information Technology Adoption in Botswana Secondary Schools and Its Implications on Leadership and School Libraries in the Digital Era." In *Information Leadership in a Culture of Change: IASL Reports, 2005,* edited by

Sandra Lee, Peter Warning, Diljit Singh, Eleanor Howe, Lesley Farmer, and Sandra Hughes, chap. 39, pp. 1–16. Erie, PA: International Association of School Librarianship, 2005.

Tripp, Steven, and Barbara Bichelmeyer. "Rapid Protoyping: An Alternative Instructional Design Strategy." *Educational Technology, Research and Development* 38, no. 1 (1990): 31–44.

Tuckett, Harold, and Carla Stoffle. "Learning Theory and the Self-Reliant Library User." *Reference Quarterly* 24 (Fall 1984): 58–66.

Turner, Philip, and Ann Riedling. *Helping Teachers Teach*. Westport, CT: Libraries Unlimited, 2003.

UNESCO Bangkok. "Communication and Information." www.unescobkk.org/index.php?id=1897 (accessed July 22, 2006).

United Nations. *Declaration of Principles. Building the Information Society: A Global Challenge in the New Millennium*. The Hague, Belgium: United Nations, 2003.

United Nations Educational, Scientific, and Cultural Organization (UNESCO). *Beacons of the Information Society: The Alexandria Proclamation on Information Literacy and Lifelong Learning*. Report from the High-Level Colloquium on Information Literacy and Lifelong Learning, Alexandria, November 6–9, 2005.

———. "Information Literacy." Information for All Programme (IFAP). portal.unesco.org/ci/en/ev.php/ URL_ID=21293&URL_DO=DO_TOPIC&URL_SECTION=201.html (accessed December 21, 2006).

———. *The Prague Declaration: Towards an Information Literate Society*. Washington, DC: U.S. National Commission on Libraries and Information Science, 2003. www.nclis.gov/libinter/infolitconf&meet/post-infolitconf&meet/PragueDeclaration.pdf (accessed July 22, 2006).

———. "Universal Declaration on Cultural Diversity." *Education*. www.unesco.org/education/imld_2002/unversal_decla.shtml (accessed July 22, 2006).

U.S. Department of Education. "Evidence Standards for Reviewing Studies." What Works Clearinghouse. http://ies.ed.gov/ncee/wwc/pdf/study_standards_final.pdf (accessed September 14, 2007).

Van Weering, Bram, and Tjeerd Plomp. "Information Literacy in Secondary Education in the Netherlands: The New Curriculum." *Computers and Education* 16, no. 1 (1991): 17–21.

Villegas, Jaime, Birger Rapp, and Bengt Saven. *Simulation Supported Industrial Training*. Linkoping, Sweden: Linkoping University, 2005.

Virkus, Sirge. "Information Literacy in Europe: A Literature Review." *Information Research* 8, no. 4 (July 2003): 1–64.

Webber, Sheila. "Getting the Knowledge." *Library and Information Update* 1, no. 7 (2002): 52–53.

Wells, Gordon. "Dialogue about Knowledge Building." In *Liberal Education in a Knowledge Society*, edited by Barry Smith, 111–38. Chicago: Open Court, 2002.

Wenger, Etienne. *Communities of Practice: Learning, Meaning, and Identity*. Cambridge: Cambridge University Press, 1998.

Wurman, Richard. *Information Anxiety*. New York: Doubleday, 1989.

Yip, Chee, Pui Cheung, and Cheng Sze. *Towards a Knowledge-Creating School*. Hong Kong: Pui Ching Middle School, 2004.

Zurkowski, Paul. *The Information Service Environment—Relationships and Priorities*. Washington, DC: National Commission on Libraries and Information Science, 1974.

Index

About the Authors

Lesley S. J. Farmer is professor at California State University, Long Beach, and coordinates the Library Media Teacher Program. She earned her MS in library science at the University of North Carolina, Chapel Hill, and received her doctorate in adult education from Temple University. Dr. Farmer has worked as a teacher librarian in K–12 school settings as well as in public, special, and academic libraries. She chairs the IASL Information Literacy SIG and serves in leadership roles within the American Library Association and other professional organizations. A frequent presenter and writer for the profession, Dr. Farmer has authored several books, most recently *The Human Side of Reference and Information Services in Academic Libraries* (2007) and *Collaborating with Administrators and Other Support Staff* (2006). In 2007 she received a Distinguished Scholarly and Academic Achievement Award from her campus. Her research interests include information literacy, collaboration, and educational technology.

James Henri was born in Tasmania and has been moving north ever since. In 1976 he was appointed teacher librarian in one of the first open plan secondary schools in Australia, and he has continued his attachment to that discipline ever since. He was employed at Charles Sturt University for twenty years and left there in 2001 to become associate professor in the Faculty of Education at the University of Hong Kong. His research interests span the fields of information literacy, information policy, social responsibility, reading and school library development in the third world, leadership, teacher librarian work practice, and education for information. He has over 250 published papers, chapters, and books.